UBIQUITOUS
LEARNING

UBIQUITOUS
LEARNING

Edited by Bill Cope & Mary Kalantzis

UNIVERSITY OF ILLINOIS PRESS
Urbana and Chicago

Manufactured in the United States of America
1 2 3 4 5 C P 5 4 3 2 1
This book is printed on acid-free paper.

Library of Congress Cataloging-in-Publication Data
Ubiquitous learning / edited by Bill Cope
and Mary Kalantzis.
p. cm.
Includes bibliographical references and index.
ISBN 978-0-252-03496-1 (cloth : alk. paper)
ISBN 978-0-252-07680-0 (pbk. : alk. paper)
1. Distance education—Computer-assisted instruction.
2. Individualized instruction. 3. Blended learning.
I. Cope, Bill. II. Kalantzis, Mary.
LC5803.C65U7 2010
371.33'4—dc22 2009034660

Contents

Introduction: The Beginnings of an Idea,
Mary Kalantzis and Bill Cope ix

Part A: Concepts

1 Ubiquitous Learning: An Agenda for Educational Transformation,
Bill Cope and Mary Kalantzis 3

2 Meanings of "Ubiquitous Learning," *Nicholas C. Burbules* 15

3 Ubiquitous Learning, Ubiquitous Computing,
and Lived Experience, *Bertram C. Bruce* 21

4 Participatory Transformations, *Caroline Haythornthwaite* 31

5 Ubiquitous Media and the Revival of Participatory Culture,
Jack Brighton 49

6 Notes toward a Political Economy of Ubiquitous Learning,
Michael A. Peters 62

7 From Ubiquitous Computing to Ubiquitous Learning,
Michael B. Twidale 72

Part B: Contexts

8 Ubiquitous Learning: Educating Generation I,
Evangeline S. Pianfetti 93

9 Ubiquitous Learning with Geospatial Technologies: Negotiating Youth and Adult Roles, *Lisa Bouillion Diaz* 100

10 Digital Divide and Higher Education in Sub-Saharan Africa, *Fazal Rizvi* 109

11 Cyberenvironments: Ubiquitous Research and Learning, *James D. Myers and Robert E. McGrath* 119

12 Immersive Environments for Massive, Multiperson, Online Learning, *Alan B. Craig, Steve Downey, Guy Garnett, Robert E. McGrath, and James D. Myers* 131

13 Let's Get Serious about E-games: A Design Research Approach toward an Emerging Perspective, *Wenhao David Huang and Tristan E. Johnson* 144

14 Access Grid Technology: An Exploration in Educators' Dialogue, *Sharon Tettegah, Cheryl McFadden, Edee Norman Wiziecki, Hanna Zhong, Joycelyn Landrum-Brown, Mei-Li Shih, Kona Taylor, and Timothy Cash* 156

15 Physical Embodiment of Virtual Presence, *Karrie G. Karahalios* 173

16 Administrative Implications of Ubiquitous Learning for Nonprofit Colleges and Universities, *Faye L. Lesht* 189

Part C: Practices

17 History: The Role of Technology in the Democratization of Learning, *Orville Vernon Burton, James Onderdonk, and Simon J. Appleford* 197

18 Computer Science: Pen-Enabled Computers for the "Ubiquitous Teacher," *Samuel Kamin* 206

19 Biology: Using a Ubiquitous Knowledge Environment to Integrate Teaching, Learning, and Research in Biology and Chemistry, *Eric Jakobsson* 216

20 Visual Arts: Technology Pedagogy as Cultural Citizenship, *Elizabeth M. Delacruz* 230

21 Writing (1): Writing with Video,
Maria Lovett and Joseph Squier 242

22 Writing (2): Ubiquitous Writing and Learning: Digital Media as Tools for Reflection and Research on Literate Activity,
Gail E. Hawisher, Paul Prior, Patrick Berry, Amber Buck, Steven E. Gump, Cory Holding, Hannah Lee, Christa Olson, and Janine Solberg 254

About the Contributors 265

Index 277

INTRODUCTION

The Beginnings of an Idea

MARY KALANTZIS AND BILL COPE

This book sets out to define an emerging field, a field that for the reasons we outline in the chapters that follow, we have chosen to call "ubiquitous learning." Ubiquitous learning is a new educational paradigm made possible in part by the affordances of digital media. Throughout this book, we will explain what we mean by this claim and marshal evidence in its support.

But first, who are we and how did we come to write this book? The starting point was a strategic initiative of the College of Education at the University of Illinois, the Ubiquitous Learning Institute, whose guiding ideas were developed in 2006 by a task force consisting of Chip Bruce, Nick Burbules, Cynthia Carter Ching, Michael Peters, Vanna Pianfetti, Sharon Tettegah, and Brendesha Tynes. This group set the agenda for the institute in the following terms:

> The world is changing rapidly from an industrial to an information- and media-driven economy. As the world around us becomes smaller, and communication and media become more global and more diffuse, the very nature of society and of who we are as human beings is quickly being defined by our ability to be both consumers and producers of knowledge. The nature of that knowledge, how and by whom it is created, and the spaces in which it is encountered are all rapidly evolving. Technology developments make it possible for information to be produced and disseminated by practically anyone, and learning can occur at any time and any place. This notion of "anytime/anywhere" has often been described as "ubiquitous" in the IT literature. Ubiquitous computing can mean using technology to bridge distance and time, the merging of physical and virtual, and bringing computing off the desk into social and public spaces through wearable and handheld devices. A focus on *learning,* and on the increasing prevalence of knowledge construction activi-

> ties being conducted in online environments by experts and novices alike, however, suggests that the definition of "ubiquitous" be expanded to include the idea that learners can engage with knowledge about "anything," and that this learning can be experienced by "anyone."

What we mean by learning, however, differs strongly from a common understanding. Traditionally, learning has been configured as a process whereby the learner encounters and soaks up knowledge or skill, much like a sponge, from some authoritative source. This definition is no longer sufficient to describe the convergence of knowledge conditions in the information society. Progressive theories of learning have long maintained that learners do not passively absorb, but rather actively create, personally meaningful knowledge out of their experiences in the world. Now, however, learning through knowledge creation is not just about designing the understandings in one's own head, so to speak. As we use Web technology to make sense of the world around us through blogs, wikis, mash-ups, podcasts, social software, online worlds, open-source and open-access media, and a whole host of other current and emergent online practices, the constructions of our own evolving understandings become information in the public sphere. In essence, the process of learning and the products of learning are rapidly merging into ubiquitous knowledge engagement. The implications of this profound transformation—for formal schooling, for online communities, for evolving definitions of public knowledge, and for global interconnectedness and economic development—cannot be underestimated.

This is a big agenda indeed, intellectually ambitious and with potentially enormous educational implications. From this initial statement of intent, we set a course to begin defining key concepts and exploring current practices. Although a College of Education initiative, we knew from the start that this would have to be a collaborative, cross-disciplinary endeavor. This book is the beginning of these next stages in the development of the Ubiquitous Learning Institute. It brings together some thirty different authors from across a broad variety of disciplines at the University of Illinois, Urbana-Champaign.

The ideas we present here are the product of an unique institution and an unusual cross-disciplinary partnership. At this university, two traditions of intellectual innovation stand out that are germane to the focus of the Ubiquitous Learning Institute and the themes of this book: a technological tradition and an educational tradition. On the technological side, this was the place where John Bardeen worked, who won a Nobel Prize for inventing the transistor, then a second one for discovering superconductivity. It is a place where the first readily available graphical Web browser, Mosaic, was created. It is also the birthplace of Eudora, Apache, PayPal, and YouTube. As we write, the university is building what will be the fastest, highest-capacity supercomputer available for open scientific research, Blue Waters. On the educational side, for half a century and more, the University of Illinois has been at the forefront of creating new approaches to pedagogy, from the "new" math and reading of the 1960s, to the invention of the idea of "special education," to the ideas of reciprocal teaching in communities of practice in the 1980s. And, at the intersection of these two foci of intellectual interest, there was PLATO, the world's first computer learning system. The University of Illinois is fertile ground indeed for discussion of the connections between technology and learning.

In this context, the aim of the contributors to this book is to take stock of current thinking and practices that use technology and learning, bringing together experts whose disciplinary perspectives were widely varied. The authors reflect a great depth of knowledge and represent remarkably diverse fields—from education (Nick Burbules, Bill Cope, Lisa Bouillion Diaz, Steve Gump, David Huang, Mary Kalantzis, Faye Lesht, Michael Peters, Vanna Pianfetti, Fazal Rizvi, and Sharon Tettegah); to computer science (Alan Craig, Steve Downey, Eric Jakobsson, Sam Kamin, Karrie Karahalios, Robert McGrath, James Myers, and Edee Wiziecki); to library sciences (Chip Bruce, Caroline Haythornthwaite, and Mike Twidale); to the humanities, media, and design (Patrick Berry, Jack Brighton, Amber Buck, Vernon Burton, Elizabeth Delacruz, Guy Garnett, Gail Hawisher, Cory Holding, Hannah Lee, Maria Lovett, Christa Olson, Paul Prior, Janine Solberg, and Joseph Squier).

The terrain these authors cover is broad indeed. To give shape to ideas that are at times expansive and challenging, the book has three parts. Part A explores key concepts of ubiquitous computing and ubiquitous learning. In the first chapter, we attempt to set the overall agenda for the book. Next, Nick Burbules examines the consequences of ubiquity: an "anywhere" spatial sense, portability, interconnectedness, blurring divisions between different spheres of life, an "anytime" temporal sense, and its globalized flows. Chip Bruce explores predigital attempts to create ubiquitous learning, from John Dewey's to those of a library science teacher at the University of Illinois in the 1940s. Caroline Haythornthwaite discusses the potential transformations, and the dangers, of the digital learning environment in the context of a broader opportunity to create a participatory culture. Jack Brighton discusses developments in digital radio as a touchstone for larger developments in the new, digital media—developments he calls "ubimedia," which have the potential to empower people and create a more participatory culture. Michael Peters speaks to the broader political economy of the new media, including legal questions of intellectual property and philosophical questions of disembodiment in an environment where human interaction is machine-mediated. And Mike Twidale writes of the connections between ubiquitous computing and informal and semiformal modes of learning, including what he calls "over the shoulder learning."

In part B, we examine contextual factors that influence the development of ubiquitous learning. Vanna Pianfetti describes "Generation I" and the kind of learning that will mesh with the skills and sensibilities of "digital natives." Lisa Bouillion Diaz discusses the dangers of disconnection of tech-savvy young people from formal learning and suggests ways in which learning that is more related to the real world and that uses ubiquitous computing devices can create a renewed sense of relevance. Fazal Rizvi, in his chapter, moves the contextual discussion to the international stage, where he explores the potentials for the African Virtual University, as well as the challenges it faces. Moving to an examination of the technological context, James Myers and Robert McGrath examine the potentials of cyberenvironments to provide a shared foundation for new forms of collaborative research, as well as, at the same time, access for learners to the same body of foundational research data—a phenomenon, they say, that will change the way science is done and the way science education works. In the next chapter, Alan Craig, Steve Downey, Guy Garnett, Robert McGrath, and James Myers explore the potential of virtual worlds for ubiquitous learning. Following from this, David Huang and Tristan Johnson investigate the nature and implications of gaming for ubiquitous learning. Sharon Tettegah and her colleagues examine the dynamics of access grid technology in virtual classrooms. Next, Karrie Karahalios describes her research into an environment that more closely links physical embodiment with virtual presence, in which a human-scale, anthropomorphic computer figure sits at a table. Finally in this section, Faye Lesht speaks of the administrative dynamics of e-learning programs.

Part C describes some ubiquitous learning practices. Vernon Burton, James Onderdonk, and Simon Appleford describe their "River Web" project, developing online history resources for the East Saint Louis area. Sam Kamin presents an experiment using notebook computers in a computer science class. Eric Jakobsson explains how the "Biology Workbench" is used as a tool for learning. Elizabeth Delacruz describes the place of technology in arts education. Finally, in two chapters, Maria Lovett and Joseph Squier and then Gail Hawisher, Paul Prior, Patrick Berry, Amber Buck, Steven Gump, Cory Holding, Hannah Lee, Christa Olson, and Janine Solberg describe approaches to multimodal composing that involve the use of digital video.

If we decide to make PLATO the starting point of a journey into computer-assisted learning, our travels so far have been slow—nearly half a century long. And it may well be that there is still a long way to go. It will be quite some time before the vision of ubiquitous learning is realized if we find progress blocked by forces of institutional inertia and heritage senses of what education should be like. However, the extraordinarily rapid spread of computing devices into every corner of our working, home, community, and learning lives may well make ubiquitous learning a practical possibility, or even a social imperative.

UBIQUITOUS
LEARNING

PART A

Concepts

1

Ubiquitous Learning

An Agenda for Educational Transformation

BILL COPE AND MARY KALANTZIS

Ubiquitous Computing

At first glance, it is the machines that make ubiquitous learning different from heritage classroom and book-oriented approaches to learning. These appearances, however, can deceive. Old learning can be done on new machines. Using new machines is not necessarily a sign that ubiquitous learning has arrived. And some features of ubiquitous learning are not new—as Chip Bruce highlights so clearly in his chapter, they have a proud place in the history of educational innovation, which stretches back well before the current wave of machines.

But to focus on the machines for the moment, there is an obvious link between ubiquitous learning and ubiquitous computing. The term "ubiquitous computing" describes the pervasive presence of computers in our lives. Personal computers and laptops have become an integral part of our learning, work, and community lives, to the point where, if you do not have access to a computer with reasonable bandwidth you can be regarded as disadvantaged, located as a "have not" on the wrong side of the digital divide. Meanwhile, many other devices are becoming more computerlike (in fact, more and more of them are computers or have computer power built in): mobile phones, televisions, global positioning systems, digital music players, personal digital assistants, video cameras, still cameras, and game consoles, to name a few. These devices are everywhere. They are getting cheaper. They are becoming smaller and more portable. They are increasingly networked. This is why we find them in many places in our lives and at many times in our days. The pervasive presence of these machines is the most tangible and practical way in which computing has become ubiquitous.

Does ubiquitous computing lay the groundwork for ubiquitous learning? Yes, it does. Does it require us to make a paradigm shift in our education paradigms? Certainly. However, our definition of ubiquitous learning in the first paragraph of our introduction was more conditional than this. We said: "Ubiquitous learning is a new educational paradigm made possible in part by the affordances of digital media." The qualifications in this statement are crucial. "Made possible" means that there is no directly deterministic relationship between technology and social change. Digital technologies arrive, and almost immediately, old pedagogical practices of didactic teaching, content delivery for student ingestion, and testing for the right answers are mapped onto them and called a "learning management system." Something changes when this happens, but disappointingly, it is not much. And another qualifier: "affordance" means you can do some things easily now, and you are more inclined to do these things than you were before simply because they are easier. You could previously have engaged in collaborative and inquiry learning in a traditional classroom and heritage institutional structures, but it was not easy. Computers make it easier. So, the new things that ubiquitous computing makes easier may not in themselves be completely new—modes of communication, forms of social relationship, or ways of learning. However, just because the new technology makes them easier to do, they become more obviously worth doing than they were in the past. Desirable social practices that at times went against the grain because of their idealistic impracticality become viable. The technology becomes an invitation to do things better, often in ways that some people have been saying for a long time they should be done.

However, to take the argument one step further, could we educators take the lead in the development of appropriate technologies rather than recycle hand-me-down technologies that were originally designed for another purpose? Here's an apocryphal technology story about the connections between technology and social relationships. PLATO, the world's first computer learning environment, was invented here at the University of Illinois in 1960 and went through extensive research and development processes that resulted in a number of iterations over the next two decades. PLATO can be credited as the beginnings, not just of e-learning, but the computing world we know today. It only took the form it did in order to meet specifically educational needs. In this sense, education, not technology, was the driver. Some remarkable inventions came out of this educational laboratory. In the 1960s, the plasma screen was invented because learners needed a visual interface, not computer punch cards, for ease of interaction in the learning context. The touch screen was also invented, so students could interact with the questions and information on the screen. In the 1970s, a pioneer messaging system was created so that teachers and learners could communicate with each other. This was perhaps the world's first online community, and the beginnings of communications technologies that soon became message boards, e-mail, online chat, and instant messaging. The first multiplayer online games were created for PLATO. The capacity to connect peripheral devices was also developed, and one of the first was an early music synthesizer used in music education and research, which also had the capacity to play computer-recorded music. Now that these technologies have become cheap and accessible, we find ourselves using their descendants every day of our lives. But it is salutary to know that they were invented in a moment of educational exploration, to support the endeavor of learning. Education led. The technology followed. To make progress with ubiquitous learning, this has to happen again.

Technologies are the product of social needs. When they work for us, their social benefits sometimes prove to be more revolutionary than their technical specifications. Before we get back to the educational story, consider the following social effects of what has, since the days of PLATO, become ubiquitous computing.

SITUATED COMPUTING

Ubiquitous computing situates information processing, communications, and recording and playback devices everywhere in our lives. We make meanings through these devices (to others as well as making sense of things for ourselves). We represent ourselves through digitized media, recording more and more of our lives, deliberately, impulsively, or incidentally. We do this in many media—image, text, and sound—because one of the key features of the world of computing is to reduce image, sound, and word to the same stuff, the stuff of zeros and ones.

INTERACTIVE COMPUTING

Ubiquitous computing is interactive. In one common combination, a person connects with the machine, and the machine answers on the basis of its programmed functions. The machine is "smart" only insofar as the programmer has supplied abstract variables and second-guessed in anticipation the range of user responses, but only in general terms. This is how, somewhat intelligently, the machine returns to the user whatever data it has been given the chance to record, sometimes in combinations that neither the person who entered the data nor the programmer quite anticipated. In an different interactive scenario, one person connects to another through the machine. Until recently, this happened through different, monomodal, and relatively separate analog media. Now the media are (literally, technically) converging around digitization—so we can connect synchronously or asynchronously via recording, using a remarkable range of permutations of text, sound, and image. Not only can we connect in more ways, we can do it more easily and more cheaply. Mike Twidale in his chapter highlights this inherently sociable character of ubiquitous computing.

PARTICIPATORY COMPUTING

Ubiquitous computing spawns ubiquitous media, which spawn participatory culture. Here are a few of the signs of our times: The centrally designed voice of experts, the print encyclopedia, is supplanted by the tens of thousands of unnamed authors, a "general public" that has contributed to Wikipedia and that updates and extends it daily. Competing with the traditional newspaper, blogs provide information and commentary on the events of the day—anyone can set one up; any reader can talk back. And competing with broadcast television, anyone can post a video to YouTube. In his chapter, Jack Brighton calls these new, digital media "ubimedia." Unlike the old media, they are cheap, accessible, and easy enough for anyone to master. This is the stuff of computer-enabled participatory culture, in which the distinctions between writer and readers, and creators and audiences, are rapidly becoming blurred (Jenkins 2006).

SPATIALLY AGNOSTIC COMPUTING

Ubiquitous computing creates new senses of space. Where you work, where you shop, where you learn, where you are entertained, and where you live—these all used to be defined spaces: built, institutionalized, impressively solid. Ubiquitous computing makes the boundaries between these spaces porous at least, but possibly even throws into question the long-term relevance of what were until recently regarded to be unshakable spatial, institutional, and life boundaries.

TEMPORALLY AGNOSTIC COMPUTING

Ubiquitous computing also creates new senses of time. To reframe the argument that Nick Burbules makes in his chapter, ubiquitous computing brings together the "now" and the "whenever." The start of the class, or the movie, or the working day does not need to begin at a specific time when the capacity to record easily and cheaply facilitates asynchronous communication. "Now" can be made sooner or later. Observing other people's timetables is increasingly replaced by scheduling for oneself.

COGNITIVELY INTEGRATED COMPUTING

Ubiquitous computing requires new ways of mental getting around, new logics of social navigation, new uses of the computer as an appendage to our thinking. We think by weaving our way through icons and hypertextual links. We search rather than follow instructions. We create our own reading paths rather than read things in the order in which the author thought would be good for us. New ways of thinking are emerging in which the mind uses the computer as a supplement to its own cognitive powers. Users work their way around the world of knowledge and imagination having mastered "semantic technologies" of ubiquitous computing: search algorithms, menus, formal schemas, user-generated tags, and folksonomies and ontologies. All of these allow you to work your way through the structured data of files and databases. In these activities, our thinking becomes computer-mediated.

INTUITIVE COMPUTING

As a matter of habit, ubiquitous computing becomes a deeply intuitive part of our life and world experience, a kind of second nature once we have mastered the devices. Adults have managed to learn their way into the world of ubiquitous computing, or at least those on the "have" side of the digital divide have done so. They have become fluent second-language speakers of the languages of ubiquitous computing. They speak it very well at times, but with an accent revealing traces of a predigital childhood. Like ducks to water, however, today's children have grown up as "digital natives." As Vanna Pianfetti says in her chapter, they speak ubiquitous computing as if it had always been a natural part of human affairs. So ubiquitous has this computing become that, for native and second-language speakers alike, it is at times hard to notice that it is even there. It's just what we do to live today.

Causes for Caution

For all the optimism about the social transformations that might be wrought as we explore the affordances of ubiquitous computing, we need to turn a cautious eye to its ever-present dangers. In a world where inequality is more common than equality, we need to build bridges across the digital divide to the "bandwidth disadvantaged," the dead zones, and the people who cannot afford to buy the latest and best devices, even though they are getting cheaper (Mitchell 1995; Virilio 1997). However, there are paradoxes in these new machines. They are often relatively cheap, with low-cost infrastructure, and thus more accessible than preceding media of knowledge, culture, representation, and communication. People who could never afford a landline are now getting mobile phones. People who did not have well-stocked libraries can now access a world of knowledge through a computer in a library or community center. And in education, the champions of ubiquitous computing are working on the problem of the digital divide in the form, for instance, of the One Laptop per Child initiative.

We also need to make sure we do more than mechanize and automate practices of the present out of conservative inertia when we have the opportunity to implement better ones or invent new ones. The machine-marked tests and the back-to-the-future learning management systems with their lockstep curriculum spring to mind. We need to do more than this, hence the notion of a transformed and transformative pedagogy in the environment of ubiquitous learning.

Moreover, we need to guard against "gray ecologies," in which we are tethered to machines, or, as Michael Peters says in his chapter, caught on one side or the other of the Cartesian dualism of mind and body. We might be able to make the machines more lifelike, better able to represent embodiment along the lines of the examples Karahalios and Tettegah describe in their chapters. However, just because the computing is ubiquitous, not all learning has to be machine-mediated and distanced from its natural and embodied sources. The machines need to be seen, not as ends in themselves, but as documentation devices for off-screen learner activity—for instance, digital photographs taken by learners engaged in nature study, video or audio recordings of oral or gestural performance, and the like. In other words, we need to guard against any reduction of the richness of person-to-person or hands-on activity. The solution for ubiquitous learning is "out there" documentation (take the documentation devices with you everywhere). In other words, the learner does not have to be confined to human-machine interaction or human-machine-human mediation, because the machine also serves as an ancillary documentary device for human-human, and human-activity learning.

And, as Caroline Haythornthwaite points out in her chapter, we need to watch out for networked individualism, outsourced learning-on-the-cheap that bypasses the teacher, and an anti-intellectual populism where the only thing that trumps the wisdom of the crowd is the wisdom of the sponsored link.

Ubiquitous Learning

We can use new technologies to learn old things in old ways. We can set up the ubiquitous computing devices in our contemporary world to do old-fashioned didactic teaching: the teacher or publisher puts content into a learning management system; the learners work through the content step by step; the learners take a test at the end and get a grade that indicates whether they have passed or failed. We can use computers to re-create traditional, transmission pedagogies that anticipate a mimetic relationship to knowledge: absorb the theories, the practice formulas, the facts, the greats, the canon, the sociomoral truths that others have deemed will be good for us. There are some differences, to be sure—the image of the solar system in the old science textbook stays still, but the planets move around the sun in the digital "learning object"—but the learners' relationships to knowledge and the processes of pedagogy have not changed in any significant way (Kalantzis 2006; Kalantzis and Cope 2008).

Following, we suggest seven changes in the educational milieu that are congruent with ubiquitous learning. Each of these proposed "moves" explores and exploits the potentials of ubiquitous computing. None, however, is a pedagogical idea or social agenda that is new to the era of ubiquitous computing. The difference today is that there is now no practical reason not to make any of these moves. The affordances are there, and if we can implement these strategies, perhaps we should. When we make more and more of these moves, we may discover a cumulative result, such that a new educational paradigm begins to emerge. As this paradigm takes shape, educators might also assume a leading role in technological innovation.

MOVE 1: BLUR THE TRADITIONAL INSTITUTIONAL, SPATIAL, AND TEMPORAL BOUNDARIES OF EDUCATION

In the heritage educational institutions of our recent past, learners needed to be in the same place at the same time, studying the same subject and staying on the same page. The classroom was an information architecture, transmitting content, one to many: one textbook writer to however many thousands of learners, one teacher to some thirty children, or one lecturer to one hundred or more university students. The spatial and temporal simultaneity of this information and knowledge system made practical sense. Today, in the era of cheap recording and transmission of any textual, visual, or audio content anywhere, such classrooms are less needed. Education can happen anywhere, anytime. Proud traditions of "distance education" and "correspondence schools" mean that these ideas are far from new. The difference now is that ubiquitous computing renders anachronistic and needlessly expensive, for many educational purposes, the old information architecture of the classroom, along with its characteristic forms of discourse and social relationships to knowledge. Even the problem of the duty to care for children is surmountable with mobile phones and global positioning devices. Knowing the location of a child in a classroom was never more accurate than the one-meter margin of error of GPS devices.

Another problem with traditional schooling was the idea that it could be preparation for life, sufficient for one's lifetime needs as a worker and a citizen, and anything new to be learned could be left to experience. But everything is now changing so rapidly that today's education easily becomes tomorrow's irrelevance. So, there have been calls to make ongoing training and formally accredited education "lifelong and lifewide." For people who work and have families, and are thus not able to commute to an institution or to schedule their time easily, ubiquitous computing can be a conduit for education beyond the traditional spatial and institutional boundaries. Coming together in specific times and places will, of course, remain important, but what we will choose to do when we meet may be different from what happens in classrooms today—these may be special times to focus on face-to-face planning, collaborative work, and community building. Then there's the new pervasiveness of pedagogy in spaces of informal and semiformal learning: help menus, "intuitive interfaces," gamelike staged learning, and what Mike Twidale calls in his chapter "over-the-shoulder-learning" from friends and colleagues. This kind of learning never needs to be more than just in time and just enough. It is now integral to our lifestyles, a survival skill in a world of constant change.

MOVE 2: SHIFT THE BALANCE OF AGENCY

In the traditional classroom, the teacher and blackboard were at the front of the room. The learners sat in straight rows, listened, answered questions one at a time, or quietly read their textbooks and did their work in their exercise books. Lateral student-student communication was not practicable—or even desirable, when it could be construed as cheating. Underlying this arrangement was a certain kind of discipline (listen to the teacher, read authority into the textbook), and a particular relationship to knowledge (here are the facts and theories you will need to know, the literature that will elevate, and the history that will inspire). This kind of education made a certain kind of sense for a certain kind of world, a world where supervisors at work shouted orders or passed down memos in the apparent productive interests of the workers, where the news media told the one main story we were meant to hear, and where we all consumed identical mass-produced goods because engineers and entrepreneurs had decided what would be good for us. Authors wrote and the masses read; television companies produced and audiences watched; political leaders led and the masses followed; bosses bossed and the workers did as they were told. We lived in a world of command and compliance.

Today, the balance of agency has shifted in many realms of our lives. Employers try to get workers to form self-managing teams, join the corporate "culture," and buy into the organization's vision and mission. Now the customer is always right, and products and services need to be customized to meet their particular practical needs and aesthetic proclivities. In the new media, ubiquitous computing has brought about enormous transformations. There's no need to listen to the top forty when you can make your own playlist on your iPod. There's no need to accept as authoritative the encyclopedia entry in Wikipedia when you, the reader, can talk back, or at least watch other people's arguments about the status of knowledge. There's no need to view only the sports TV producer's camera angles when you can choose your own on interactive television. There's no need to watch what the broadcast media has dished up to you, when you can choose among your own interests on YouTube, comment on what you are watching, and, for that matter, make and upload your own TV content. There's no need to relate vicariously to narratives when you can be a player in a video game (Gee 2003, 2005).

Haythornthwaite, in her chapter, calls this the "new relational order." This new order applies equally well to learning. There is no need to be a passive recipient of transmitted knowledge when learners and teachers can be collaborative co-designers of knowledge. The sources of knowledge are myriad, and sometimes problematically at variance with each other; we have to navigate our way around this. There are many sites and modalities of knowledge, and we need to get out there into these to be able to make sense of things for ourselves. Certain bodies of knowledge that we encounter may be widely accepted and thus authoritative, but these are always uniquely applied to specific and local circumstances—and only we can do this, in our own place and at our own time. Myers and his co-authors in their chapter note that this is a phenomenon of blurring distinctions between teachers and learners, knowledge makers and knowledge users. In this environment, teachers will be required to be more knowledgeable, not less. Their power will be in their expertise and not in their control or command routines.

MOVE 3: USE DIFFERENCES AMONG LEARNERS AS A PRODUCTIVE RESOURCE

Modern societies used to value uniformity: we all read the same handful of newspapers and watched the same television channels; we all consumed the same products; and if we were immigrant, or indigenous, or of an ethnic minority, we needed to assimilate so we could all comfortably march to the same national beat. And so it was in schools: all the pupils had to listen to the teacher at the same time, stay on the same message on the same page, and take the same test at the end to see whether they had learned what the curriculum expected of them. Today there are hundreds of television channels, countless Web sites, infinite product variations to suit one's own style, and if you are immigrant, or indigenous, or a minority, your difference is an aspect of our newfound cosmopolitanism. This is all part of a profound shift in the balance of agency. Give people a chance to be themselves, and you will find they are different in a myriad of ways: material (class, locale), corporeal (age, race, sex and sexuality, and physical and mental characteristics), and symbolic (culture, language, gender, family, affinity, and persona).

In schools today, these differences are more visible and insistent than ever. And what do we do about them? Ubiquitous learning offers a number of possibilities. Not all learners must be on the same page; they can be on different pages according to their needs. Every learner can connect the general and the authoritative with the specifics and particulars of his or her own life experiences and interests. All learners can be knowledge makers and cultural creators, and in every moment of that making and creating they remake the world in the timbre of their own voices and in a way that connects with their experiences. Learners can also work in groups, as collaborative knowledge makers, where the strength of the group's knowledge arises from their ability to turn to productive use the complementarities that arise from their differences. In this context, teachers will need to be engaged members of cosmopolitan learning communities and co-designers, with learners, of their learning pathways.

MOVE 4: BROADEN THE RANGE AND MIX OF REPRESENTATIONAL MODES

Ubiquitous computing records and transmits meanings multimodally—the oral, the written, the visual, and the audio. Unlike previous recording technologies, these representational modes are reduced to the same stuff in the manufacturing process, the stuff of zeros and ones (Cope and Kalantzis 2004). Also, as never before, there is next to no cost in production and transmission of this stuff. Now, anyone can be a filmmaker, a writer who can reach any audience, an electronic music maker, a radio producer. Traditional educational institutions have not managed to keep up with this proliferation of media, although, as Chip Bruce says in his chapter, educators have known for a long time the value of "learning through the senses." But, if educators have not yet made as much as they could of the easy affordances of the new media, the students have. When educators do catch up, the learning seems more relevant, and powerful, and poignant (Cope and Kalantzis 2000, 2007; Kress 2003). Educators will need to understand the various grammars of the multiple modes of meaning making that the digital has made possible, in the same depth as traditional alphabetic and symbolic forms.

MOVE 5: DEVELOP CONCEPTUALIZING CAPACITIES

The world of ubiquitous computing is full of complex technical and social architectures that we need to be able to read in order to be a user or a player. There are the ersatz identifications in the form of file names and thumbnails, and the navigational architectures of menus and directories. There is the semantic tagging of homemade folksonomies, the formal taxonomies that define content domains, and the standards that are used to build Web sites, drive Web feeds, define database fields, and identify document content. These new media need a peculiar conceptualizing sensibility, sophisticated forms of pattern recognition, and schematization. For these reasons (and for other, much older, good educational reasons as well), ubiquitous learning requires higher-order abstraction and metacognitive strategies. This is the only way to make one's way through what would otherwise be the impossibilities of information quantity. Teachers then need to become masterful users of these new meaning-making tools, applying the metalanguage they and their learners need alike in order to understand their affordances.

MOVE 6: CONNECT ONE'S OWN THINKING TO DISTRIBUTED COGNITION

In the era of ubiquitous computing, you are not what you know but what you can know, the knowledge that is at hand because you have a device in hand. Before these devices, of course, we had libraries available, or experts we could consult, and we still do. Cognition has always been distributed, and intelligence, collective. The most remarkable technology of distributed cognition is language itself (Gee 1992). However, today there is an immediacy, vastness, and navigability of the knowledge that is at hand and accessible to the devices that have become more directly an extension of our minds. Those who used to remember telephone numbers will notice that something happens to their minds when the numbers they need are stored on the mobile phone—the phone remembers for you. It becomes an indispensable extension of your mind. This should spell doom for the closed-book exam. Educators will need to create new measures to evaluate learners' capacities to know how to know in this new environment.

MOVE 7: BUILD COLLABORATIVE KNOWLEDGE CULTURES

Ubiquitous computing invites forms of social reflexivity that can create "communities of practice" to support learning. Lisa Bouillion Diaz, in her chapter, calls this "facilitating mutuality." In the ubiquitous learning context, teachers harness the enormous lateral energies of peer-to-peer knowledge making and the power of collective intelligence. This builds on the complementarity of learners' differences—experience, knowledge, ways of thinking, and ways of seeing. Learners also engage with people who would formerly have been regarded as outsiders or even out-of-bounds in the learning process: parents and other family members, interested friends, or experts. The digital workspaces of "social networking" technologies are ideal places for this kind of work, at once simple and highly transparent when it comes to auditing differential contributions. Teachers need higher-order skills to build learning communities that are genuinely inclusive, such that all learners reach their potential.

Clearly, the emergence of ubiquitous computing creates new conditions for all those who are working as education professionals or learning as students. The key is not the logic or technical specifications of the machines. Rather it is the new ways in which meaning is created, stored, delivered, and accessed. This, we believe, will change the educational world in some fundamental ways—and also allow some older but good and disappointingly neglected educational ideas to work at last, and to work widely. The journey of ubiquitous learning is only just beginning. As we take that journey, we need to develop breakthrough practices and technologies that allow us to reconceive and rebuild the content, processes, and human relationships of teaching and learning.

Readings and References

For a broader discussion of newly emerging educational paradigms, see our book, *New Learning*, referenced below. Henry Jenkins is a key thinker in the development of the idea of participatory culture, exploring its implications for education. James Paul Gee and Gunther Kress have produced seminal work on the interactions between new, multimodal media and learning.

Cope, Bill, and Mary Kalantzis, eds. 2000. *Multiliteracies: Literacy Learning and the Design of Social Futures*. London: Routledge.
———. 2004. "Text-Made Text." *E-Learning* 1:198–282.
———. 2007. "New Media, New Learning." *International Journal of Learning* 14:75–79.
Gee, James Paul. 1992. *The Social Mind: Language, Ideology, and Social Practice*. New York: Bergin and Garvey.
———. 2003. *What Video Games Have to Teach Us about Learning and Literacy*. New York: Palgrave Macmillan.
———. 2005. *Why Video Games Are Good for Your Soul: Pleasure and Learning*. Melbourne: Common Ground.
Jenkins, Henry. 2006. *Confronting the Challenges of Participatory Culture: Media Education for the 21st Century*. Chicago: John D. and Catherine T. MacArthur Foundation. Available at http://newmedialiteracies.org/files/working/NMLWhitePaper.pdf.
Kalantzis, Mary. 2006. "Elements of a Science of Education." *Australian Educational Researcher* 33:15–42.
Kalantzis, Mary, and Bill Cope. 2008. *New Learning: Elements of a Science of Education*. Cambridge: Cambridge University Press.
Kress, Gunther. 2003. *Literacy in the New Media Age*. London: Routledge.
Mitchell, William J. 1995. *City of Bits: Space, Place, and the Infobahn*. Cambridge, Mass.: MIT Press.
Virilio, Paul. 1997. *Open Sky*. London: Verso.

2

Meanings of "Ubiquitous Learning"

NICHOLAS C. BURBULES

This collection invokes the term "ubiquitous learning." Here I would like to examine the different meanings this expression might have—different kinds of ubiquity, and in relation to that, different ways in which we ought to rethink teaching and learning. The most ordinary meaning is captured in the expression "anytime, anywhere" learning. In contemporary markets, the instantaneous and highly customizable availability of services and information is becoming a standard branding device. This ranges from 24/7 customer service hotlines to being able to send and receive text messages from your cell phone. In education, online programs are frequently marketed around the convenience of asynchronous and flexible class schedules, allowing people to study and complete assignments on their own timetables. This has led to a broader shift in attitudes toward such courses and programs, in which students-as-customers expect an even higher degree of customization and accommodation to their preferences, not only in terms of scheduling. As customers, they know they can take their business elsewhere.

In this essay, I want to press the idea of ubiquitous learning beyond an "anytime, anywhere" marketing slogan and to suggest six interrelated dimensions along which its meaning can be fruitfully extended.

First, there is a spatial sense of ubiquity (the "anywhere" half of the previous slogan). In developed societies, digital technologies are always around: not only in computers and other overt computing devices, but in cars, in public kiosks, and so on. Regional wi-fi means that Internet access is only a click away, wherever you are. Constant access to information, however, also entails that others have constant access to *you*. Citizens and workers, in developed urban areas particularly, are situated in networks that make them available to others—whether they choose to be or not. The dystopic implications of these trends have been played out in popular films like *The Net* or *Enemy of the State,* but at the same time these trends reflect an increased public tolerance, if not even expectation, of perpetual digital presence. A colleague of mine had his computer bag stolen in a hotel in London, and within hours he held in his hands video printouts of the act taking place—while other surveillance cameras recorded the thief as he got on a public bus, rifled through the contents of the bag, and got off a few stops later. In a post-9/11 society, more and more people interpret this state of surveillance as increased security.

From a learning standpoint, spatial ubiquity means continual access to information to an extent that we have never witnessed before. The traditional distinction between formal and informal education is blurred once we recognize that physical location is no longer a constraint on where and how people learn; the processes of learning and memory themselves may be changing as people are less required to carry around in their heads all that they need to know to get through a day effectively—if you need something, you can always look it up. I will return to this theme later.

Second, there is a portability aspect to ubiquity: handheld computing devices, even "wearable" devices, are becoming more commonplace. Portable devices *can* be always with you—which tends to establish and reinforce a social expectation that they *should* always be with you. The portability of these devices, in turn, creates new kinds of social practices—young people who no longer wear watches but use their phones to keep track of time; the many uses and conventions of text messaging that are created simply by virtue of the expectation that others will be constantly online and available. A program in Ireland, intended to help young people learn and preserve the Celtic language, gave them free phones that were loaded with grammar and vocabulary software. The instructors wanted to be sure that wherever the students were, they could immediately access linguistic information, and it made more sense to use a device that young people would always have with them, knew how to use, and that was already seamlessly integrated into their daily social and linguistic practices. (Of course, they were constantly using the phones as phones too.) I cannot think of a better, simpler encapsulation of the principles of ubiquitous learning—in this case, learning reinforced by portability and practical integration into the activities of daily life.

Third, there is ubiquity in the sense of interconnectedness. Automobiles now come equipped with GPS units and dashboard devices that can tell you where the next gas station or hospital is. Driving on the highway, you can find a hotel, estimate your arrival time, and book your reservation while you are still five hundred miles away. "Smart homes" connect relevant devices together to share information; or, you can turn off your coffeemaker with your phone without returning home.

For the learner, this interconnectedness creates an "extensible intelligence," extensible in two related senses. Technologically, one's knowledge, memory, and processing power are enhanced by constantly available devices that can supplement and support what we are able to do in our own heads. Socially, one is perpetually in contact with others who may know things or be able to do things that we cannot do ourselves. In a real sense, people can be smarter because they have access to networked intelligence, whether it is technologically or socially distributed, or both. Educational agencies, for all age levels, have yet to come to grips with the question of what knowledge, skills, and capacities people *do* still need to carry around in their heads, and which ones may be less necessary than they used to be. What is necessary knowledge for the future, and what does this portend for the standard views of curriculum?

Fourth, there is ubiquity in a practical sense: how new technologies blur sharp divisions between activities or spheres of life that we have traditionally viewed as separate. Work/play, learning/entertainment, accessing/creating information, public/private are distinctions that conceptually might never have been as clear-cut as our usage suggested them to be, but for a host of social and cultural reasons they are becoming increasingly untenable as sharp distinctions today. These changes are not all technological in nature, at least not directly so: changes in popular culture, in the nature of work, in the structure and activities of home or family life, and so on, have brought with them a host of different expectations and ways of thinking about where, how, when, and why learning takes place. It is not just that the traditional monopoly of those places we call schools, and those times we call "class periods" as the sole or even primary sources of learning, are being challenged. More substantively, the entire economy of attention, engagement, and motivation to learn needs to be rethought. Learning as a practical human activity, which is always embedded in a wider network of social and institutional contexts, needs to be seen in relation to a new set of genres and practices.

"Virtual" learning environments need to be understood not primarily in relation to technologically based "virtual reality" experiences, but as immersive learning places in which creativity, problem solving, communication, collaboration, experimentation, and inquiry support a fully engaged experience. These "places" are virtual not by virtue of any kind of "synthesized" reality, as that is normally understood, but in relation to dynamics of interest, involvement, imagination, and interaction that support an active engagement between a learner and a learning environment. "Ubiquity" is a different issue from "virtuality," but they intersect at the point where immersive learning activities are fully integrated into a flow of practical tasks, where there is no separation between action, reflection, and inquiry. New digital technologies, as I have tried to show, can play a crucial role here; yet the larger shift I am describing is not itself dependent on any technology, but rather a shift in thinking about how structured learning opportunities can be made meaningful and relevant to learners.

Fifth, there is ubiquity in a temporal sense; the "anytime" dimension of anytime, anywhere (which is of course closely linked with spatial ubiquity and constant interconnectedness). But this temporal shift goes beyond the simple language of 24/7 availability; it reflects a *changed* sense of time. The use of recording devices to "time-shift" television shows and the growing prevalence of asynchronous modes of communication (for example, in online education programs) reflect a certain customization of scheduling. This yields different expectations and practices that change one's subjective relation to time—of trying to conform the timing of events to one's habits and preferences, and not only vice versa. These new and varied rhythms suggest a different relation, in turn, to learning opportunities—easy availability and convenience, but also a pacing and flow that are more continuous, that allow "stopping in" and "stopping out" at different moments. Every moment is potentially a learning moment, not only in the quotidian way in which that was always true—but in the sense of structured, intentional learning opportunities, more seamlessly integrated into the routine practices of home, work, and entertainment.

Another, related, sense of temporal ubiquity involves the idea of "lifelong learning," but now instantiated in a new way. Generally this term refers to principles of adult and continuing education, but in the present context it expands to mean the truly perpetual availability of learning opportunities and a changed set of expectations about *continual* growth and development of skills and knowledge. It is almost a cliché now to talk about frequent career changes, the need to upgrade skills and knowledge even within an ongoing career, and the shifting demands of a knowledge economy. But "lifelong learning" here means something more: it means that learning is not relegated to a certain age or time, a certain institutional setting, and a certain set of externally oriented motivational structures. Rather, in this changed world view, *to be is to learn.*

Sixth, there is ubiquity in the sense of globalized, transnational networks and "flows" (in Arjun Appadurai's sense): flows of people, information, ideas, and so on. One is never simply where one happens to be; one is also situated within a set of relations and contingencies that affect, and are affected by, these increasingly global processes. Learning for a global future, therefore, involves more than having e-mail pen-pals in another country, going on tours or exchange programs, or learning about the customs and exports of exotic, faraway places. It is coming to recognize the fundamental interconnections among disparate people, places, and processes, and the ways in which these influence and constrain even apparently local and individual choices.

In the picture of education I am sketching here, the nature and activities of schooling will have to change. It means that traditional boundaries need to be broken down in both directions: not only sending out new and different kinds of projects and "homework" to students, but bringing *in* to the classroom activities involving other learning tools and resources that have not typically been seen as part of schools. Schools, and teachers in schools, need to think of themselves not as the sole (and perhaps not even the primary) source of learning for many of their students—especially students above a certain age—but as *brokers* of a certain sort.

The school, in this model, is a kind of hub: a place that brings together, coordinates, and synthesizes disparate learning resources. The spokes radiating out from this hub are the connections to other learning places and activities; many of them largely if not entirely separate from the control or influence of educators. But where educators do still have influence is in helping young people evaluate and integrate the varied learning experiences they have in these other, less-planned environments. Educators also have an important role to play as equalizers between those students who have a tremendous range and number of such opportunities outside school, because of their family situation or location, and those who have far fewer opportunities. In a system of mandatory education, the school is still the one common learning place that students share; and this gives it a unique and important responsibility, compared with other learning places. But starting from this premise yields a different basis for planning about what needs to take place there, one that links school aims and activities much more fundamentally to learning that is taking place elsewhere.

Readings and References

For further reading on ubiquitous technologies and some of their implications for learning, see Abowd and Mynatt 2000. For more on the notion of "anytime/anywhere" learning, see Bruce 1999. For more on rethinking the "virtual" as a learning space, see Burbules 2005.

Abowd, Gregory D., and Elizabeth D. Mynatt. 2000. "Charting Past, Present, and Future Research in Ubiquitous Computing." *ACM Transactions on Computer-Human Interaction* 7(1): 29–58.

Andrews, Richard, and Caroline Haythornthwaite, eds. 2007. *Handbook of E-learning Research*. London: Sage.

Appadurai, Arjun. 1996. *Modernity at Large: Cultural Dimensions of Globalization*. Minneapolis: University of Minnesota Press.

Bruce, Bertram C. 1999. "Education Online: Learning Anywhere, Any Time." *Journal of Adolescent and Adult Literacy* 42(8): 662–66.

Burbules, Nicholas C. 2005. "Rethinking the Virtual." In *The International Handbook of*

Virtual Learning Environments, ed. Joel Weiss, Jason Nolan, and Peter Trifonas, 3–24. Dordrecht: Kluwer.

Csikszentmihaly, Mihalyi. 1991. *Flow: The Psychology of Optimal Experience.* New York: Harper Collins.

Dewey, John. 1956. *The Child and the Curriculum and the School and Society.* Chicago: University of Chicago Press.

3

Ubiquitous Learning, Ubiquitous Computing, and Lived Experience

BERTRAM C. BRUCE

Ubiquitous learning is more than just the latest educational idea or method. At its core the term conveys a vision of learning that is connected across all the stages on which we play out our lives. Learning occurs not just in classrooms, but in the home, workplace, playground, library, museum, nature center, and in our daily interactions with others. Moreover, learning becomes part of doing; we do not learn in order to live more fully but rather learn as we live to the fullest. Learning happens through active engagement, and significantly, it is no longer identified with reading a text or listening to lectures but rather occurs through all the senses—sight, hearing, touch, smell, and taste.

It is understandable to think that ubiquitous computing is necessary for this kind of ubiquitous learning and sufficient to make it possible. Education would certainly be easier to promote if we could simply identify some new technologies that would make ubiquitous learning occur. But in the sense presented above, the new technologies are neither necessary nor sufficient for this to happen. This chapter develops these ideas further, arguing that it is our vision for ubiquitous learning that matters most, not just the technical affordances. We need to define ubiquitous learning in a historically legitimate way, one that recognizes the possibilities presented by the new technologies without reducing the argument to a technocentric position.

Why Do We Need Ubiquitous Learning?

Writing in 1939, Harold Benjamin imagined a "saber-tooth curriculum." It is based on teaching students skills that were useful in the Stone Age but are no longer needed in the modern world. Even though the skills are irrelevant to present-day life, they are still taught, and then justified on the grounds that they foster the development of skills that *might* carry over to life. For example, "wise old men" say "we don't teach tiger-scaring to scare tigers; we teach it for the purpose of giving that noble courage which carries over into all the affairs of life" (Benjamin 1939, x).

Instead of seeking learning environments that would help students develop courage in relation to their current experiences, the saber-tooth curriculum presents essentially artificial activities, disconnected from those lived experiences. Benjamin believed that in a similar way, much of the curricula of his own day was outmoded and irrelevant to the world he and the students inhabited. One might describe that curriculum as the antithesis of ubiquitous learning. Benjamin argues that the curriculum should instead respond dynamically to a changing world and connect to the lived experiences within that world. He would have celebrated ubiquitous learning as the alternative curriculum for today.

Benjamin was undoubtedly influenced by John Dewey and others of the progressive education era. In the revised edition of *The School and Society* (1915), Dewey articulates a similar vision. He starts by identifying a problem in the separation of academic knowledge from daily life. He might have responded to this separation by relegating schooling to one or the other of these pursuits. In the former case, schooling would be focused on classroom-based study through books and lectures; in the latter, it would be apprenticeship in contemporary work. But Dewey rejects this dichotomy. Instead he envisions connecting the school to life. Activities in the school would occur in spaces lying between the academic realm represented by disciplines, libraries, and museums on the one hand, and the everyday realm of work and family life. Figure 3.1 shows how this school might be laid out, with a library at the center and rooms at each corner that are linked to activities in life beyond the school. In fact, the activities would serve to integrate these realms, thus making everyday life richer and more reflective, and making academic work more relevant to lived experience. Within the full development of this idea lies Dewey's belief that education is key to social reform.

Dewey's vision rests on the idea of three sets of technologies:

technologies of the workplace, farm, and home—the technologies of the living society;
technologies of the academy, such as curricula, books, and libraries; and, sitting between these,
technologies of learning, which exist in the kitchen or shop of the school.

Dewey judged that the technologies of the first two spheres of activity had grown far apart.

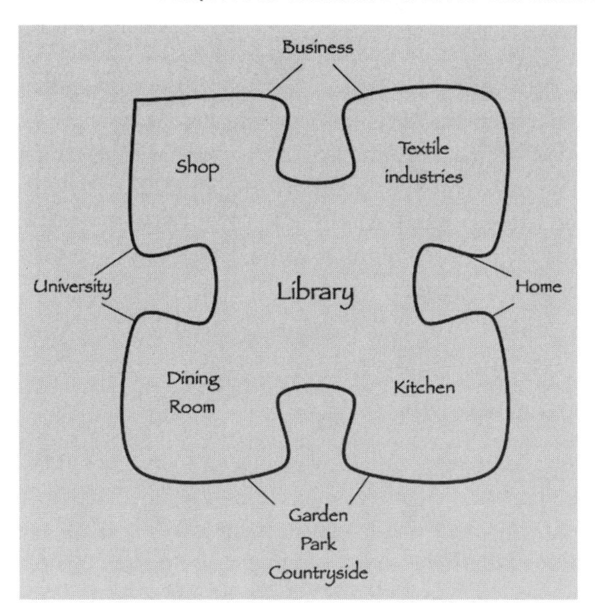

Figure 3.1. Part of Dewey's vision of schooling connected to life, adapted from *The School and Society,* chart 3.

Just as Benjamin saw the irrelevance of the saber-tooth curriculum, Dewey criticized the formal learning of his day as irrelevant to a changing world. An elaborate apparatus was then needed to connect students' experiences with those of the school, including procedures to ensure compliance, increase motivation, or simply to explain what was going on. Dewey felt that the distance between the technologies of learning and those of life made them difficult to relate to one another, and as a result, they could not be used to respond effectively to the dramatic social and technological changes under way in the world at large.

Dewey's school would instead give students the opportunity to combine theory and action in a way that would enrich both, make learning more exciting and meaningful, and thereby establish a model for progress in the larger society. The school that became the actual Laboratory School is important for what it showed about the possibilities for learning, as well as for its failures (Tanner 1997). Dewey's vision and the photos of engaged learners from the early days of the Laboratory School are inspiring. And yet, because the activities of the factory, the school, and the university were dissimilar; the school had to be radically transformed to mesh them together.

In contrast today, we find that ubiquitous computing has become part of home, community, work, and the academy. We connect with a friend, shop for a toaster, build a business, study medieval history, write a memoir, or arrange travel online, often using the same tools regardless of the sphere of activity. Dewey's dream of schooling that links the mind and the body, theory and action, or disciplines and ordinary experience seems more realizable than ever. It seems clear that ubiquitous computing is both necessary for this and sufficient to make it happen. But is it either necessary or sufficient? Do we have to have the new technologies to promote ubiquitous learning? If we have them, will ubiquitous learning automatically occur?

Is Ubiquitous Computing Necessary for Ubiquitous Learning?

For Dewey, the consequence of radical change in social life was that the school required a similar transformation. This led him to imagine new technologies for learning. Are there more seamless alternatives to his way of addressing this problem? Do we need to leap all the way to nanotechnology or implanted computers in order to enact more dynamic and robust learning?

Nearly a half century after the first edition of *The School and Society* (1900) and a half century before the Deep Blue (a computer) defeated Garry Kasparov in two chess matches, Gwladys Spencer was an instructor at the University of Illinois Library School. This was during what most people would consider the prehistory of the information age (see more in Bruce 2003). I found a list of "Audio-Visual Materials and Equipment to Be Utilized by Libraries in the Educational Program" from a course she taught in 1946.

This is a remarkable list, including expected items such as "blackboards and bulletin boards," but many unexpected ones as well. She included television (in 1946!), showing that she had foresight about its eventual prominence as a communications medium. She also included tools for investigation, such as microscopes and "models, objects, specimens." She clearly saw that audiovisual materials were more than simply devices for transmitting information. But more striking still is the inclusion of "pantomimes, playlets, pageants, puppet shows, shadow plays" and "trips, journeys, tours, visits." The presence of these items says that she saw all of the elements of her list as opportunities for enriching experiences rather than simply as media for transmitting information.

TYPES OF AUDIO-VISUAL MATERIALS AND EQUIPMENT TO BE UTILIZED BY LIBRARIES IN THE EDUCATIONAL PROGRAM

1. Blackboards and bulletin boards
2. Posters, cartoons, clippings
3. Dramatics: pantomimes, playlets, pageants, puppet shows, shadow plays

4. Trips, journeys, tours, visits
5. Models, objects, specimens
6. Charts: organization or flow, table, tree or stream
7. Graphs: area, bar, diagram, line, pictorial statistics
8. Maps: flat, relief, projected, electric, globe (celestial or terrestrial)
9. Microscopes
10. Microprojectors, reading machines; microfilms, microphotographs, microprint
11. Stereoscopes; hand, binocular, televiewers; stereographs, disc for televiewers
12. Flat pictures; photographs, prints, postcards, positive transparencies
13. Still pictures projectors and projected-opaque, filmslides, slides (glass, cellophane, ceramic, etc.)
14. Sound filmslides projectors; sound filmslides
15. Motion pictures projectors and projected: silent films, sound films
16. Sound recorders: transcriptions
17. Phonographs; disc, wire; recordings
18. Talking books
19. Radios, loudspeakers, public address systems, intercommunicating systems
20. Television

Taking our cue from Dewey's diagram, we might represent some of Gwladys Spencer's vision as in figure 3.2. Here, the activity spaces include dramatics, investigations, trips, and working with objects, just some of the activities implied by her list. Just as Dewey proposes, she emphasizes opportunities for learners to act in and on the world. Even the presentational media on her list seem to be conceived in a manner quite different from today's emphasis on using PowerPoint presentations to convey course content. The posters, charts, and pictures are there because they are important media in the world and much can be learned by investigating them, not because they are a convenient way for instructors to organize their notes in easily digestible chunks.

Aside from the details of which tools she had available, the list shows that Spencer had a broad view of how libraries could support learning and, more important, a vision of what learning could be. Today, we are excited about multimedia in education. But what we often mean is simply that a computer display can show students moving pictures with sound. Interactivity is an important additional component. But our vision of what that multimedia really means for learning needs to go beyond the technical features of the display to consider what students can do and how they can extract meaning from their own experiences. Spencer saw that there were many tools and media that could enhance learning. She drew from traditional as well as emerging technologies to lay out a spectrum of pos-

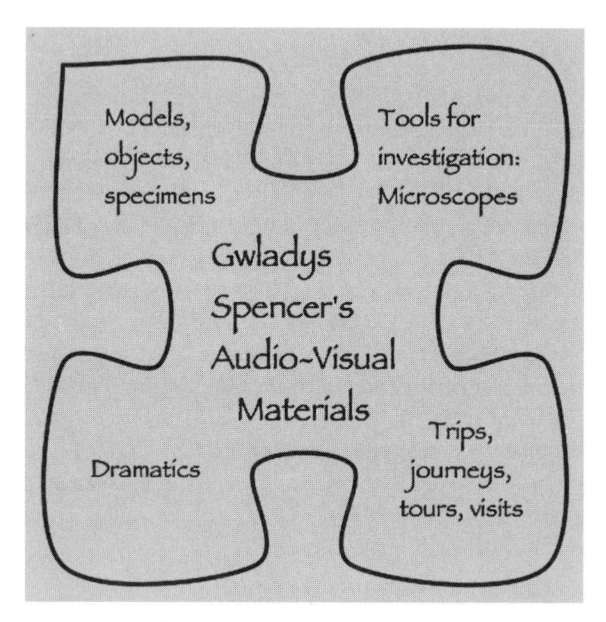

Figure 3.2. Gwladys Spencer's view of audiovisual materials.

sibilities for teaching and learning. Her list suggests an openness to diverse ways of learning and, moreover, a view of learners as active constructors of meaning. In so doing, she shows that ubiquitous learning depends more on our pedagogy than on our technology.

Is Ubiquitous Computing Sufficient for Ubiquitous Learning?

In recent work, the vision of ubiquitous learning has been linked closely to an array of new information and communication technologies. No longer confined within large metal boxes or even tied to the wall with wires, these technologies have become portable, wearable, and distributed. They are embedded in dishwashers, cameras, and medical monitors, and make possible "smart" cars, roads, houses, and offices. As ubiquitous computing has become more and more part of our everyday reality, ideas related to ubiquitous learning have likewise become more prevalent.

If you walk across a college campus today you will see students plugged into their iPods and cell phones, with laptops in their backpacks and maybe personal digital assistants as well. They appear oblivious to the natural world around them, to the point of endangering their lives crossing the street. Always multitasking, they connect with friends through social network sites, live through online games and immersive environments, capture events with digital cameras, and write about their most intimate experiences and thoughts in their blogs. Watching them learn through Google and YouTube, finding their way with GPS, and maintaining social relations through constant electronic connections, it is difficult to escape the thought that new forms of living and learning have already arrived.

Even if we do not embrace all that is new here, it seems imperative to engage with it to some extent if we are to understand literacy in the information age (Bruce 2003; Coiro et al. 2008). It also appears that a kind of ubiquitous learning has arrived without any intention or forethought; the technologies alone have made it happen. There is no doubt that new forms of learning are already happening through social networking, online video sites, and environmental sensors.

Are these technologies sufficient, or do we still need the vision of a Gwladys Spencer? A recent study addresses this question in the context of a university course, Plants, Pathogens, People, that uses a rich array of both new and old information and communication technologies (D'Arcy, Eastburn, and Bruce, 2009) (see figure 3.3). The authors began with an attempt to identify which of these technologies were most effective at promoting engaged and connected learning. They were especially interested in fostering connections between the university

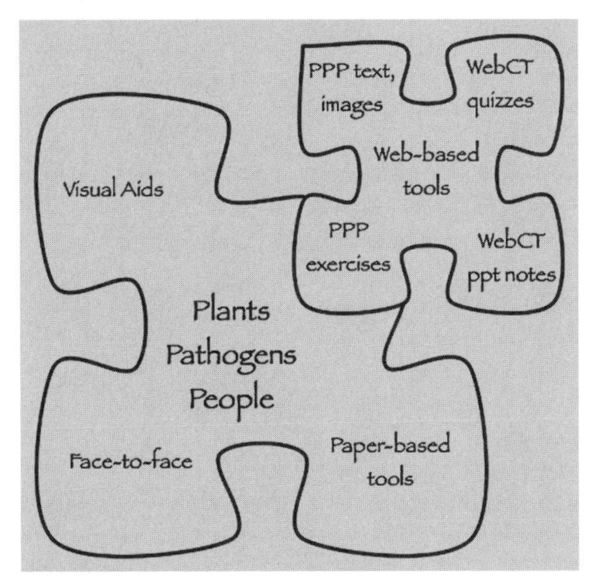

Figure 3.3. Some of the nineteen media used in the Plants, Pathogens, People course, with the Web-based tools expanded.

classroom and life outside, as well as learning that integrates laboratory work, scientific theories, history, and public policy. They introduced new media, such as podcasts, which seemed to be salient in the students' lives. In short, they sought to make the college classroom more conducive to ubiquitous learning.

The major result of the study was that across diverse learning styles, majors, and genders, many of these media were deemed to be useful for all learners. Moreover, the usefulness of a particular medium depended much more on how it fit with others, how it related to course content, how the instructors used it, and other contextual factors than it did to any intrinsic media properties. Overall, the findings suggest there is no ideal instructional medium, nor even specific media that are best for particular students. It is true that there are differences according to student learning style or instructor teaching style, but the overriding message is the need to consider the entire learning ecology (Bruce 2008; Bruce and Hogan 1998; Cross 2007; Nardi and O'Day 1999).

A similar message comes through the work of Barbara Ganley (EdTechTalk 2006; Ganley 2007). Building on her students' experiences with new media and social software, she works with them to create a blog community, which connects within the classroom and reaches beyond it to people and experiences around the world. It is noteworthy that Ganley devotes two weeks at the beginning of each class to develop a shared vision of learning, community, and technologies. Just as in the study described above, the technologies alone are far from sufficient. Instead, we need to think about the histories of learners, how technologies serve in relation to changing learning needs, and how diverse resources can be used in a concerted way. Technologies need to be re-created in line with a vision of ubiquitous learning if they are to achieve that goal (Bruce and Rubin 1993).

Conclusion

As with many of the modified names for particular kinds of learning—active learning, engaged learning, situated learning—it is tempting to strip away the modifier, in this case, "ubiquitous." Learning is an aspect of living, not of place. We have always been able to learn in diverse settings other than the formal classroom, and often in a more pleasant, memorable, and useful way. Nevertheless, ubiquitous learning serves to remind us of the need to continually reexamine how learning occurs and to attend to the affordances of new technologies.

The examples here reinforce the value of ubiquitous learning and suggest ways that various technologies may support it. They also remind us to situate technologies in a larger context and to see them organically (Bruce 2008; Haythornthwaite et al. 2007). Arguing that it is time to move from the teaching machine metaphor to Dewey's idea of tools, Karin Wiburg writes: "An expanded concept of instructional design that includes the purpose of education, the need to teach the person as well as the content, and the importance of the social context of learning is required before we can implement computer-based collaborative learning for the children in our schools" (Wiburg 1995).

The array of technologies that we might group under ubiquitous computing can help implement an expanded concept of not just instructional design but of learning in all its contexts and forms. Yet we must maintain a critical stance. Speaking in 1984, but with an enlarged relevance today, Ursula Franklin said: "In the powerful trends of the new industrial revolution, people have to adapt to the work, habits, and values of the machines. People are generally regarded as the sources of problems, while devices are considered as means to solutions. . . . The elimination of some of these social settings [a consequence of redesigning activities of production] also eliminates the opportunities of developing those human skills that are fundamentally different from the skills of machines: abilities such as listening, interpreting, instructing, and working out to mutually acceptable accommodations. But it is the skills, more than anything else, that the global village needs" (Franklin 2006, 214).

Our vision of ubiquitous learning must maintain at its core a concept of those fundamental human skills. We feel that ubiquitous computing technologies help us solve problems, create and access knowledge, and build community. We feel that they do it in a way that links work, family and friends, learning, and life. But the very seamlessness of these technologies is seductive. Jacques Ellul's concept of the technological milieu is still a propos: "Every technique makes a fundamental appeal to the unconscious" (Ellul 1964, 403). We need to ensure that employing new technologies enhances rather than diminishes our capacity to develop as whole human beings.

Readings and References

Benjamin, Harold R. W. [J. Abner Peddiwell, pseud.]. 1939. *The Saber-Tooth Curriculum, Including Other Lectures in the History of Paleolithic Education.* New York: McGraw-Hill.

Bruce, Bertram C., ed. 2003. *Literacy in the Information Age: Inquiries into Meaning Making with New Technologies.* Newark, Del.: International Reading Association.

———. 2008. "Coffee Cups, Frogs, and Lived Experience." *International Journal of Progressive Education* 4(2): 22–39. Also available at http://www.inased.org/v4n2/bruce.html.

Bruce, Bertram C., Heather Dowd, Darin M. Eastburn, and Cleo J. D'Arcy. 2005. "Plants, Pathogens, and People: Extending the Classroom to the Web." *Teachers College Record* 107:1,730–53.

Bruce, Bertram C., and Maureen C. Hogan. 1998. "The Disappearance of Technology: Toward an Ecological Model of Literacy." In *Handbook of Literacy and Technology: Transformations in a Post-typographic World,* ed. David Reinking, Michael C. McKenna, Linda D. Labbo, and Ronald D. Kieffer, 269–81. Hillsdale, N.J.: Lawrence Erlbaum.

Bruce, Bertram C., and Andee Rubin. 1993. *Electronic Quills: A Situated Evaluation of Using Computers for Writing in Classrooms.* Hillsdale, N.J.: Lawrence Erlbaum.

Clapp, Elsie R. 1952. *The Use of Resources in Education.* New York: Harper and Bros.

Coiro, Julie, Michele Knobel, Colin Lankshear, and Donald Leu, eds. 2008. *The Handbook of Research in New Literacies.* Hillsdale, N.J.: Lawrence Erlbaum.

Computer Science Unplugged. University of Canterbury in Christchurch, New Zealand. Web site with articles, video, and learning activities. http://csunplugged.com.

Cross, Jay. 2007. "Designing a Web-Based Learning Ecology." Learning Circuits, http://www.learningcircuits.org/unworkshop2.htm (accessed May 22, 2007).

D'Arcy, Cleo J., Darin M. Eastburn, and Bertram C. Bruce. 2009. "How Media Ecologies Can Address Diverse Student Needs." *College Teaching* 57(1): 56–63.

Dewey, John. 1915. *The School and Society.* Rev. ed. Chicago: University of Chicago Press.

———. 1956. *The Child and the Curriculum and the School and Society.* Chicago: University of Chicago Press.

EdTechTalk. 2006 (August 5). "EdTechTalk#24 with Barbara Ganley." EdTechTalk, http://edtechtalk.com/EdTech_Talk_24_with_Barbara_Ganley (accessed May 29, 2007).

Ellul, Jacques. 1964. *The Technological Society.* American ed., trans. John Wilkinson. New York: Vintage. Original French ed., 1954.

Franklin, Ursula M. 2006. *The Ursula Franklin Reader: Pacifism as a Map.* Toronto: Between the Lines.

Ganley, Barbara G. 2007. "Bgblogging." bgblogging, http://mt.middlebury.edu/middblogs/ganley/bgblogging (accessed May 22, 2007).

Haythornthwaite, Caroline, Bertram C. Bruce, Richard Andrews, Michelle M. Kazmer, Rae-Ann Montague, and Christina Preston. 2007. "New Theories and Models of and for Online Learning." *First Monday* 12(8)(August): available at http://www.uic.edu/htbin/cgiwrap/bin/ojs/Index.php/fm/index.

Lansdown, Brenda, Paul E. Blackwood, and Paul F. Brandwein. 1971. *Teaching Elementary Science through Investigation and Colloquium.* New York: Harcourt Brace Jovanovich.

Nardi, Bonnie A., and Vicky L. O'Day. 1999. *Information Ecologies: Using Technology with Heart.* Cambridge, Mass.: MIT Press.

Research Center for Educational Technology. 2006. *Ubiquitous Computing: How Anytime, Anywhere, Anyone Technology Is Changing Education.* DVD-ROM. Kent, Ohio: Kent State University.

Tanner, Laurel N. 1997. *Dewey's Laboratory School: Lessons for Today.* New York: Teachers College Press.

van't Hooft, Mark, and Karen Swan. 2007. *Ubiquitous Computing in Education: Invisible Technology, Visible Impact.* Mahwah, N.J.: Erlbaum Associates.

Wiburg, Karin M. 1995. "An Historical Perspective on Instructional Design: Is It Time to Exchange Skinner's Teaching Machine for Dewey's Toolbox?" 385–91. In New Mexico State University, *Proceedings of CSCL '95.* Mahwah, N.J.: Lawrence Erlbaum Associates.

4

Participatory Transformations

CAROLINE HAYTHORNTHWAITE

Learning, in its many forms, from the classroom to independent study, is being transformed by new practices emerging around Internet use. "Conversation," "participation," and "community" have become watchwords for the processes of learning promised by the Internet and accomplished via technologies such as bulletin boards; wikis; blogs; social software; shared Internet-based repositories; devices such as laptops, PDAs, cell phones, and digital cameras; and infrastructures of Internet connection—telephone, wireless, and broadband. Early discussion of the Internet extolled its transformative potential for democracy, perhaps best demonstrated by the U.S. presidential nomination campaign that developed around Howard Dean in 2000 and contemporary political blogging. This kind of inclusive, participatory action has now spread to many other aspects of daily life, demonstrated by e-mail lists and discussion groups; recommender systems (Resnick and Varian 1997); cooperative classification systems (folksonomies) (Mathes 2004); collaboratively built, wiki-based encyclopedias (Wikipedia), dictionaries (Wiktionary), and local resources; and citizen journalism in blogs and photoblogs. These emergent, participatory trends are often brought together under the rubrics of research and ideas about social software, collective intelligence, distributed cognition, and collaboration. They are also brought together in the commercial sector under the label Web 2.0 (O'Reilly 2005), in the economic sphere under discussion of peer production (Benkler 2002, 2004, 2005), and most recently in education under the idea of participatory culture (H. Jenkins et al. 2006).

In education—in learning and teaching—participatory trends herald a radical transformation in who learns from whom, where, under what circumstances, and for what and whose purpose. They bring changes in where we find information, who we learn from, how learning progresses, and how we contribute to our learning and the learning of others. These transformations are captured in ideas such as computer-supported collaborative learning (CSCL) (Koschmann 1996), community-embedded learners (Kazmer 2007), braided learning (C. Jenkins 2004; Preston 2008), online learning communities (Jorbring and Kommers 2008), and wherever terms such as "e-learning" and "networked learning" signify a transformation in learning rather than simply a transition from offline to online (Andrews and Haythornthwaite 2007; Steeples and Jones 2002). In their impact on learning inside and outside the classroom, these trends indicate a transformation to *ubiquitous learning*—a continuous anytime, anywhere, anyone contribution and retrieval of learning materials and advice on and through the Internet and its technologies, communities, niches, and social spaces.

While there are great benefits to be obtained from online action and interaction, it is also important to consider what is being overlooked in this process, as these unexpected outcomes may become barriers to successful learning experiences. Many transformations act at the periphery of the general movement to ubiquitous learning. Trends that accompany distributed practices include outsourcing, offshoring, disintermediation, networked individualism (Wellman 2001), and the downstreaming of processes and responsibilities to individuals. Autonomous learners become responsible for, and are often alone in creating, their own learning context and content as they search the Internet for materials to support their needs. Although writers such as Jenkins extol the virtues of students learning to engage in "collective intelligence" in a "community that knows everything and individuals who know how to tap the community to acquire knowledge on a just-in-time basis" (H. Jenkins et al. 2006, 42), such an ideal can overstate the knowledge that may be present in such communities, the imbalance in who does the work and who benefits, and the actualities of altruistic contribution necessary to maintain critical mass and to support working knowledge communities. It understates the work needed to sustain useful and usable resources and ignores the efforts and techniques embodied in certain roles and practices, now swept away as every individual is his or her own teacher, journalist, librarian, writer, and publisher.

There are two sides to participatory transformations that need attention: retrieval and contribution. On the *retrieval* side, there are issues of user responsibilities for critical evaluation of retrieved information, online authors, online sites, and search engine algorithms. While passing reference is made to the use of traditional information gatekeepers—professional editors and librarians—little is mentioned of the work that devolves to the user when such gatekeepers are absent. Without these roles, individuals are left on their own to vet sources, sort fact from fiction, and distinguish commentary from original data. These are skills that can be addressed through education in critical media literacy for those still in the educational system, but it is unclear how the ubiquitous learner outside this system will gain such skills. While academics lament students' reluctance to examine print resources, how many among us turn around to pull a dictionary from the shelf when our hands are on the keyboard? The Pew Internet and American Life Project (Horrigan 2006) reports that convenience heavily outweighs accuracy as a reason for using the Internet for obtaining information. Specifically for science information, it reports that 71 percent of the adult population surveyed turns to the Internet because of its convenience, and only 13 percent because they feel it is more accurate (another 12 percent feel the information they want is only available online). The report also confirms that the work of verifying resources has fallen to the user; 80 percent of these adults do some sort of "fact-checking" of this science information. They consult at least another online source (62 percent), an offline source (54 percent), or the original report (54 percent).

Another retrieval literacy issue exists in our routes to information. Figures indicate that one search engine—Google—dominates as our retrieval mechanism for information on the Web. While we encourage critical attention to the information retrieved, we give over our source selection to one or at most two hidden algorithms owned by search engine companies. In July 2007, Google was used for 50–65 percent of all searches in the United States, followed by Yahoo (20–27 percent), MSN (8–10 percent), and Ask (3–5 percent)(sources are comSource and Hitwise, as cited on the ClickZ site in Burn 2007). In February 2007, Google dominated globally as the search engine most used (77 percent) (source is Hitwise, as cited on the ClickZ site in Jarboe 2007). Although Nielsen ratings also note that users are expanding beyond a single search engine, with about two-thirds using at least two search engines (Jarboe 2007), how many of us choose to search for a particular item using more than one search engine? What are we missing by searching using only one or two algorithms for retrieval?

Google's dominance implies that our information practices are becoming fixed not just around what information is or is not online, but also around the common source(s) we use to locate such material. This is also brought home in the statistics about the use of Wikipedia. A Pew report for March 2007 shows that of the Internet traffic classified as relating to an education and reference cluster of Web sites, Wikipedia nets 24 percent of the traffic, followed far behind by 3–5 percent for Yahoo! Answers, Dictionary.com, and Answers.com, and 1–2 percent for SparkNotes, Google Scholar, Google Book Search, Find Articles and U.S. National Library of Medicine (source is Hitwise data for the week ending March 17, 2007, as quoted in Rainie and Trancer 2007). Verifying facts, using more than one search engine, and going beyond one source are all aspects of a new information literacy. Critical media literacy now entails more than just whether the information is credible or not, but also whether the search has been inclusive and diverse enough to provide more than one resource on a topic, or one entry to the information on a topic.

Beyond retrieval, we also need to consider the dynamics and importance of *contribution.* Who is contributing what kinds of information? What is the meaning of participation in an age of wiki wars, information saboteurs, and information vandals (Kleeman 2007)? How do we teach, encourage, and model participatory practices in a way that promotes useful and usable online information? New social skills, or perhaps older ones now transformed online, become essential for a workable online future. Individual retrieval becomes collaborative participation. As Henry Jenkins and his collaborators state: "The new media literacies should be seen as social skills, as ways of interacting within a larger community, and not simply an individualized skill to be used for personal expression" (2006, 20).

However, in this ideal of training all to participate online in an equal, democratic manner, little attention has been given to likely changes in distribution of activity and access. Discussions that extol the open Web as a limitless source of information ignore the potential and reality of knowledge enclaves. These may be seen positively as think tank retreats (e.g., in password protected sites), with entry by invitation only, permitting the selected few to work unharassed by novices and random visitors. Or they may be seen negatively as gated communities, segregated from outside influence or input, carrying on in private, creating internally constructed views of reality. Given that many of us joined e-mail lists and academic discussions at their inception and have accumulated a ten- to twenty-year growth in our common community, what are our tolerance limits for newbie questions, yet more requests for literature on an well-worn subject, and the discoveries and social practices of the next generation? What will be the profile of these sites in a few years—their demographics, interaction norms, and content levels?

Such trends and concerns, both pro and con, deserve considerable attention from educators and professionals, since one potential outcome is an outsourcing and bypassing of professional roles, resulting in further burdens on individuals to create and enact their own learning. However, an alternative is the rejuggling of roles to address the needs of learning in a participatory culture. This remainder of this paper explores the participatory trends affecting Internet use and learning, with a view to understanding the transformations that are happening and poised to happen in learning roles, locations, and practices.

Participation

Participation connotes contribution to a community and, in particular, contribution that furthers the goals and agenda of the community. It signals engagement and identity with the whole, demonstrated through attention and, in most cases, conformance to community norms and practices. Nonconformist contributions have their place but entail participation only where eventually accepted as furthering the group agenda rather than that of the individual. "Trolls" in online forums and "griefers" in online games do not participate but instead exercise personal dominance by commanding attention to themselves and away from the group. By contrast, participants are notable for their attention to others and to ongoing community interaction, as well as a reflexivity about their visibility—whether in text, through video, or by physical presence. As Benkler notes, contributors exhibit a "self-conscious use of open discourse" (2005, 15)—for example, in Wikipedia, which models a "self-conscious social-norms-based dedication to objective writing" (2005, 14).

To participate requires knowing how to provide a contribution, which is predicated on knowledge about the reach, content, and extent of community membership, behaviors, and concerns. It shares commonalities with ideas of collaboration (see Haythornthwaite 2006a, 2006b; Haythornthwaite et al. 2006; Swan 2006), and in many senses a "collaborative culture" may be synonymous with a "participatory culture." If there is a distinction to be made, it is that the former tends to be used in referring to smaller working groups, particularly in the sciences; in interdisciplinary collaborations; and in the more general conception of "communities of practice" (Lave and Wenger 1991; Wenger 1998). Collaborative culture tends to refer to groups that do the (often hard) work of learning to work with each other toward common goals and outcomes. By contrast, participatory culture signals a trend to societal practice, used more widely to encompass youth as well as adult practice, arts and humanities as well as sciences, and low barriers to entry (e.g., the simplicity of wiki syntax or participation without membership). Indeed, low technological barriers to participation appear as a key defining feature of participatory culture, as Henry Jenkins and his coauthors (2006, 3) describe: "A participatory culture is a culture with relatively low barriers to artistic expression and civic engagement, strong support for creating and sharing one's creations, and some type of informal mentorship whereby what is known by the most experienced is passed along to novices. A participatory culture is also one in which members believe their contributions matter, and feel some degree of social connection with one another (at the least they care what other people think about what they have created)."

Low barriers do not, however, mean no barriers. Because participation requires awareness of others—or at least that there is an audience of some known or unknown size and range—apprehensions about visibility and the persistence of postings remain as social barriers (Bregman and Haythornthwaite 2003; Sproull and Kiesler 1986, 1991). The continuous appearance of new technologies, even as these become simpler to use, represents another barrier, as norms and practices are constantly learned and relearned.

Moreover, in the rush to get people involved in posting, the invisible work related to posting and the role and place of invisible participants in participatory cultures remains—well—invisible. The work of learning to post, which is often learned as part of peripheral participation, is forgotten as irrelevant to a participatory culture. The hidden work of gaining access to the technology, learning the ins and outs of the applications, and learning the social norms of participation are overlooked in favor of attention to postings. Yet, watching at the periphery as a way of apprenticing with the expert is indeed legitimate participation, as so identified by Lave and Wenger (1991). As more and more effort goes into considering how to encourage participation, an equal effort must go into considering the work of becoming a poster, as well as the place of lurkers, observers, apprentices, and nonusers in the practice of participatory culture. Susan Leigh Star's writings on invisible work and infrastructure are relevant in this context (Star 1999; Star and Bowker 2002; Star and Strauss 1999), as is a report on nonusers and the Internet (Lenhart et al. 2003).

Another aspect of participatory culture that requires attention is its directionality: both giving, posting, and conversing, *and* retrieving, reading, and absorbing. Onto this directionality we impose reflexivity. As described above, participation requires knowledge of the culture into which one posts, and, in the action of posting, it also involves reflection on the post in the context of its posting, including its form and purpose (genre), audience, and conformity or defiance of norms (see also Bakhtin 1986; Miller 1984, 1994; Swales 1990). An equal amount of reflection should be given to retrieval of such posts. As Henry Jenkins et al. (2006) and many others contend, education about critical literacy and critical media skills come to the fore in such a free-for-all posting and participatory culture. Skills need to be inculcated to recognize wheat from chaff—skills that have, until now, largely been embodied in publishers' selection criteria, library collection development policies, and educators' curriculum and course development practices.

Reflexive participatory practice also implies mobility, as we enter into and out of "affinity spaces," enjoying fluid and dynamic membership in different communities (H. Jenkins et al. 2006, 9). While Jenkins describes these affinity spaces as "highly generative environments from which new aesthetic experiments and innovations emerge," this may again be a somewhat overstated, utopian view of online engagement, and one that ignores the very benefits of lightweight participation, picking and choosing not only what space one will engage in, but also the extent of that engagement. Indeed one of the very purposes of such spaces is to learn and enjoy the status quo and, at most, to participate in evolution rather than revolution. Imitation may be the highest form of flattery, but it is also an important part of language and community building. Copying others' behaviors, language, visualizations, narrative style, and genres has long been recognized as signaling membership in a community (Miller 1984, 1994). It is practice to be embraced, and taught.

In embracing participation, both light- and heavyweight engagement need to be considered, in parallel to ideas of weak- and strong-tie social network formation (Haythornthwaite 2007). Each kind of participation has its own merits. Mobility affords the opportunity to engage in information tourism, visiting sites, treading lightly in the online venue, viewing without making a mark, and retreiving without making a contribution. Mobility also allows finding the site where you want to settle, put down roots, and engage with community values and directions. Each has its own informational, social, and communal merits—weak ties for wider exposure to opinions and ideas; strong ties for personal commitment and motivated contribution. They exist in parallel, and the spectrum of engagement is a constituent part of what is participation. Thus, each space depends on some heavyweight users and the many more lightweight users who connect this space to other venues. As in other areas of technology development, emphasis on the strong-tie only connection has largely ignored lightweight participation, and emphasis on in-depth communal relations has ignored the benefits to diversity of multisite, multitask engagement (for more on strong and weak ties in online communities, see Haythornthwaite 2002).

The New Relational Order

New technologies forge new relations and new roles for participants. This is highly evident in the way online spaces are transforming educational and authoritative practice. The following discussion lists, in brief, some emergent trends evident in current practice that affect and are affected by the development of participatory culture, with particular attention to learning contexts.

CHANGE IN RELATIONSHIPS WITH LEADERS

What is expertise in the age of participatory learning, and whose definition is it anyway?

Perhaps the greatest fear among those who have spent years earning doctorates and then tenure is that they will become obsolete or unimportant in the classroom. Similarly, information professionals, who have done the work of collecting, classifying, and establishing retrieval mechanisms for information feel bypassed as students and readers move to unvetted online sources and search engines. What value does expertise have if learners are only learning from each other, if everyone can get the information on the Web? The latter concern is another overstated one: textbooks have been available for less than the cost of a personal computer for a long time, so why the worry about online resources? A greater worry should be that learners will think the experts unnecessary, turning to online forums, blogs, and communally defined encyclopedias for what they need. For example, why grapple with library collections when user-generated tagging in social bookmarking systems such as CiteULike, Connotea, or del.icio.us produces folk taxonomies (folksonomies) that are at our fingertips and may better reflect contemporary organization of information (Mathes 2004)? So, too, why grapple with university degrees and diplomas if learning can be achieved through online communities? To some extent the major job of the twenty-first century may be selling a university education in the age of digital competition—and not just competition from online universities, but also from user-generated learning communities. True, the certification conferred by a degree from a particular university may still matter, but we have to ask, "to whom will it matter?" (see also A. Levine 2003; Pittinsky 2003).

CHANGE IN RELATIONSHIPS WITH CONCURRENT LEARNERS

In an age of participatory culture and participatory learning, what are the roles of learners and teachers? What are the practices required of each?

A result of the past ten or more years of online learning has been the evolution and renegotiation of what is required of teachers and learners. For example, where bulletin board contributions replace classroom participation, as they do in online learning courses, equal and sustained student participation becomes vital to a successful class. The role of students changes; they become more responsive to each others' questions and needs, thus changing the role of the teacher. The teacher's position as the "sage on the stage" is being altered into that of the facilitating "guide on the side." Furthermore, the idea of the students as "empty vessels" is being replaced by the conception of "learner-leaders" (Montague 2006), who lead and contribute both to their own learning and to learning by others in the community.

Participatory learning entails instructors' ceding leadership and control of learning, giving it over to participants, and encouraging a new form of co-learning pedagogy. Learning practices change from models of transfer of knowledge from one to many (e.g., instructor to students) to exchange of knowledge among many (students to students), and from transfer from expert(s) to novice(s) to collaborative, peer-to-peer learning and discovery. In this new paradigm, novices help each other make sense of the information they are receiving. They create explanations of phenomena that fit their local setting, resupplying context that is often lost in decontexualized learning and then feeding that information back into the learning environment (Kazmer 2005; Montague 2006). Where appropriate, participants come to shared definition of meanings through collaborative, conversational interaction. Such emergent learning practices reinforce ideas posited by collaborative learning theories. For more on new models, see Haythornthwaite et al. 2007 and the models described there, including Kazmer's (2005, 2007) "embedded learners," Preston's (2002, 2008) "braided learning," and Montague's (2006) "learner-leader" model.

Changes also occur with the entry of computerized personal space into the public space. While some view laptops in the classroom as threats to engagement because students can continue to participate in out-of-room communities (via social software or e-mail), others adopt strategies for co-opting and integrating the use of laptops into daily practice (disseminating lecture materials to laptops for enhanced note-taking or involving students in class in searching or other online exercises).

Of course, one of the questions arising from all this participation from newbies and nonexperts is whether it is creating a nation of citizens or a "nation of ankle-biters." Steven Levy (2004) writes: "I celebrate the liberating tools that let people post their thoughts unfiltered. But as with many other utopian predictions about how the open nature of the Net will create arenas that transcend foibles of the physical world, our faults have followed us to cyberspace. We were promised a society of philosophers. But the Blogosphere is looking more and more like a nation of ankle-biters." His frustration with bloggers is easily mirrored in experiences of e-mail list and online class participation. Murphy and Collins (1997) noted early on the need to manage online discussion in classes so that students engaged appropriately. However, this early attention focused on inhibiting inappropriate and off-topic behavior. Now, the focus is on how to increase participation in online classes, trying to compensate for the reduced cues of the online environment on the way to creating online learning communities (Barab, Kling, and Gray 2004; Jorbring and Kommers 2008; Renninger and Shumar 2002; Swan 2006).

But generalized participation has its limits. In forums open to anyone, current learners may abide questions about the basics, but when novices mix in forums for experts, such questions are likely to be answered by being told to read the FAQ, search the archive, or search the Web. The mix of levels of expertise in a forum, e-mail list, or participatory space requires tolerance of continuous reinvention of the wheel. Such multilevel interaction suggests a limit to the utility of a single forum, leading to factions and splinter groups (for a negative connotation), or to specialty groups (for a positive connotation). Prime movers may themselves move out as their spaces become inhabited by newcomers or by intolerably disruptive behaviors. Unbridled participation without attention to group and space norms will have fallout. We can expect to see more gated communities and moderated lists arising as the tragedy of the commons strikes repeatedly in cyberspace.

CHANGE IN RELATIONSHIPS WITH PREVIOUS LEARNERS

What will become of the persistent record left by so much participation? Will its historical record be used? How will it be mined for learning?

Online conversations and postings in e-mail lists, bulletin boards, Web pages, blogs, and wikis, leave an accessible record that can be reviewed and revisited. Such persistent records can leave earlier learners still present in an online conversation long after they have left the community. Although written accounts have persisted in the past, the easy search and retrieval of online records makes their impact all the greater. Searching now often turns up essays written for classes, syllabi of courses, or discussions on e-mail lists. Although not generally made public, whole course conduct is saved in iterations of online classes. What use will be made of these various persistent records?

As noted above, in open forums many levels of expertise may mingle. Already the FAQs represent some conversation with earlier participants, as does examining the archive of a list for previous discussion. Multilevel interaction can be expected in some learning communities, along with the coexistence of different trajectories and continuities of participation and narrative.

Persistence in the data record also allows for near-term use. How will transaction records be used to enhance, monitor, and/or assess online interaction in learning settings? Hyperlink analyses already examine interconnections among ideas (e.g., in the areas of Webometrics, Thelwall and Vaughn 2004; and hyperlink network analysis, Park 2003). Efforts in data mining are just now beginning to enter the learning area; although not yet used extensively, it can easily be imagined that it will not be long before at least some basic statistics from such applications will be integrated with learning management systems (Haythornthwaite and Gruzd 2007; Minaei-Bidgoli, Kortemeyer, and Punch 2004).

CHANGE IN RELATIONSHIPS WITH DOCUMENTS

What's in a name? What is the worth of a publisher's or journal's name in the age of Wikipedia?

As more and more information goes online, as noted above, the effort to establish what is correct, truthful, balanced, and worth paying attention to is increasingly falling to users. Although this may seem to have been the case in choosing what to read in the past, the number of books on a topic, or journals of good repute are far more limited than the potential of postings to the Web. Yet, the Web is at our fingertips, and at the fingertips of learners. Hence, the relationship with documents changes in subtle ways that need to be examined in more depth than is possible in this short chapter. Suffice it to say for now, that some of the key issues involve trustworthiness of sources; mutability of online resources (e.g., in wikis); authorship (e.g., have all the postings signed "R. Smith" been written by the same person?); conversation as textual sources (e.g., taking one's evidence from blog postings); disappearance of sources (e.g., when Web sites are no longer maintained or when sites move); text as conversation (wikis) and conversation as text (bulletin boards, e-mail lists, blogs); and nontext documents as texts (video, multimedia texts). Again, there is an increased role for media literacy, that is, critical evaluation and (de)construction of meaning for online contexts—and this applies to adults as much, if not more so, than to school-age youth.

CHANGE IN RELATIONSHIPS WITH LOCAL COMMUNITIES AND NETWORKS

What does "local" mean when you are learning online? Who is in your community?

The meaning of the term "local" changes in the context of learning and participating online. We still live in a local, geographically based community with its own culture, where we meet face-to-face with friends, family, and coworkers. But there is also the online community, perhaps several, where we engage with others about work or personal interests. Our online community may be highly local in the personal sense, as we engage with friends and family online, or local in the regional sense, as we engage with others about critical events in our locale. For example, during the foot-and-mouth disease crisis in the United Kingdom, the Internet became a lifeline for exchanging information and support about dealing locally with the disease and its impact on the lives and livelihoods of farm neighbors (Hagar and Haythornthwaite 2005). Finally, we may find that our personal postings are no longer local, but instead have taken on global character as the entire Web-reading community gains access to our texts. In posting to the open Web, what is personal becomes global, and in collaboration with others may also be multicommunal and multinational.

As many have noted already about the Internet, virtual communities may spread widely across geographical areas while remaining glued together by common interest. For example, BurdaStyle provides a Web site (http://www.burdastyle.com) for sewing enthusiasts from around the world (Abousteit 2007). Building on the company's offline reputation for sewing patterns and fashion,

BurdaStyle provides patterns in an open-source manner, that is, they may be modified, used, sold, and uploaded again to the site. A growing community of BurdaStyle members contribute not only patterns but also instructional videos and photo sequences for teaching sewing techniques, definitions for a sewing terms dictionary, and discussion of techniques. The features of the site and the efforts of the organizers lay the foundations for a learning community, one that is rapidly gaining critical mass toward self-maintenance. It demonstrates many ways in which enthusiastic amateurs (and some aiming for professional careers) distributed across geographical regions, can come together to create and sustain a learning community.

As the Web reaches worldwide, education via the Web is increasingly becoming globalized. Different skills are emerging for teaching and for learning on a global scale for a global practice, including how to teach and learn in multi–time zone, multi-institutional, and multicultural settings. Asynchronous learning networks (ALN) help with crossing time zones (see the *Journal of Asynchronous Learning Networks,* http://www.sloan-c.org/publications/jaln), but local social practices are enacted to deal with time-distributed conversations and learning communities. Multi-institutional alliances are developing that provide opportunity for thinly distributed specialists to share expertise and learn from each other. For example, the World Universities Network (http://www.wun.ac.uk) supports distributed seminars facilitated through high-end videoconferencing that is supported through grid technology. Another example is the Web-based Information Science Education (WISE) program that shares seats in online classes across participating institutions (http://www.wiseeducation.org).

Through such programs, online skills, knowledge, and practices spread along geographies different from those of offline learning. Kazmer (2005, 2007) describes how online learners form important learning relationships with both their local-online fellow students *and* their local-offline workmates and community members. Online learning is simultaneously embedded in the geographically based community, providing an opportunity for learners to engage locally and to share experiences globally.

With all the emphasis on participation and engagement online, and with taking classes anywhere, anytime, the simultaneous demands of the local context and multiple social worlds continue to be overlooked; they remain an invisible part of learning contexts. Discussion of online learning overwhelmingly concentrates on the world of the class, but online learners are simultaneously juggling commitments in their home and work worlds, often adding learning as a "third shift" (Kramarae 2001). Locally, accommodations are made in the physical and social arrangement of home and work to partition learning from these other worlds. For example, parents report carving out at-home space and time for their online education, requiring others to care for children at that time (Haythornthwaite and Kazmer 2002). Overall, this raises the question of what kinds of boundaries we will need to re-create in our local worlds to reinvent those borders that were formerly defined physically but that now must be enacted socially. And, as e-mail, cell phones, and mobile computing increasingly engage us in anywhere-anytime-anyone communication, how will we partition time and attention in our cyberworlds as messages about work, home, or learning reach us at any time of day or night in any one of those local physical settings? (For more on the juggling of worlds and accommodations made in home settings, see Haythornthwaite and Kazmer 2002; Kazmer 2005, 2007; Kramarae 2001; and Salaff 2002.)

Toward an Agenda for Ubiquitous Learning

This chapter has briefly addressed some transformations affecting learning that are emerging from social and technical practices around participation, and which are creating a culture of ubiquitous learning that occurs anywhere, anytime, and with contributions by anyone. These transformations include less regulated information content and retrieval, changing roles in who leads and who follows as authorities and consumers or learners, and a greater role for the individual in information management, information contribution, and participatory citizenship. Transformations are also occurring in the who and where of how we learn and engage with others. Traditional university instruction changes from the classroom to online or blended (on- and offline) classes, from single institutional offerings to classes chosen from regional or global offerings. Learning leaves the classroom and local geographical area to engage regionally and worldwide in online learning communities, sustained by participation and contributions by and for learners. These are trends to follow, important for understanding local, in-class, on-campus learning practices, as well as the wider, global, open Web, ubiquitous learning happening everywhere and every day.

As this phenomenon unfolds, an agenda to both promote and monitor the progress of ubiquitous learning may take many directions. The main point made in this chapter is to consider both the visible and invisible aspects and consequences of these participatory transformations. An agenda for ubiquitous learning involves understanding its full ecology—from individual contribution to communal practice, from submission to retrieval, from lurker to community leader, and from the local to the global. A movement is already under way that gives enhanced attention to participation—for example, in discussions of peer production, participatory culture, virtual communities, and learning communities. Critical media literacy already lays the groundwork for assessment and evaluation of resources retrieved from online sources. But there is still work to be done in understanding participatory transformations and how to prepare individuals to teach and learn in this new culture.

First, a critical retrieval literacy is needed that includes not just notions of whether a source is credible but also whether contributions are being made equally across societal sectors (e.g., considering current manifestations of the digital divide) and whether retrieval via available search engines is creating exclusive and exclusionary paths to information (e.g., whether popularity should be the top criterion for relevance).

As individuals increasingly become contributors to the wealth of information and knowledge on the Web, it is important that contributions be representative of different histories, experiences, and worldviews. This involves examining the range and breadth of contributions to see how the digital representation of cultures is unfolding online, and encouraging and making possible online representation of a wide range of cultures as well as making room for new cultural expressions. This involves issues of access to contemporary technology, education in the use of technologies, creation of culture-friendly sites and resources, and representation in multiple languages.

Education is essential for assessing content and materials online. As noted, new forms of contribution, participation, and organization shift the work of information assessment and evaluation to the individual user. Moreover, education in the underlying information and technology structures can aid in understanding both how to put information online and how it is likely to be found by others. Critical technology evaluation—from the basics of classification systems to the hidden work of search engines—is important, if not essential, for the educated poster and retriever of the future.

An agenda for ubiquitous learning also needs to engage with understanding the community networks being created and sustained via the Web, as well as the ecologies of on- and offline life and information. Each contribution to a central server also affects locals at each retrieval site and influences who then finds a common home in that online space. It is of great interest to see how this unfolds as participatory culture takes hold, providing an understanding of participatory communities as well as cultures.

Readings and References

For further reading on participatory culture and education, see the white paper by Henry Jenkins, prepared for the MacArthur Foundation. For more on peer production, see Eric Raymond on the "cathedral and the bazaar" models of contribution, Yochai Benkler's *The Wealth of Networks,* and the work by Lawrence Lessig (http://www.lessig.org) on Creative Commons licensing (http://creativecommons.org). For recent papers on participation, transformation, and leading trends in education and e-learning, see the *Handbook of E-learning Research* (Andrews and Haythornthwaite 2007), and literature reviews on the Futurelab site (http://www.futurelab.org.uk).

Abousteit, Nora. 2007. "Sewing 2.0: BurdaStyle.com." Paper presented at the annual conference for Print, Internet, and Community, Tel Aviv, Israel.

Andrews, Richard, and Caroline Haythornthwaite, eds. 2007. *Handbook of E-learning Research.* London: Sage.

Bakhtin, Mikhail M. 1986. "The Problem of Speech Genres." In *Speech Genres and Other Late Essays,* ed. Caryl Emerson and Michael Holquist, trans. Vern W. McGee, 60–102. Austin: University of Texas Press. (Orig. pub. 1953.)

Barab, Sasha A., Rob Kling, and James H. Gray, eds. 2004. *Designing for Virtual Communities in the Service of Learning.* New York: Cambridge University Press.

Benkler, Yochai. 2002. "Coase's Penguin, or, Linux and the Nature of the Firm." *Yale Law Journal* 112:369–446.

———. 2004. "Sharing Nicely: On Sharable Goods and the Emergence of Sharing as a Modality of Economic Production." *Yale Law Journal* 114:273–358.

———. 2005. *Common Wisdom: Peer Production of Educational Materials.* Logan: COSL Press (Center for Open and Sustainable Learning at Utah State University). Available at the author's Web site, http://www.benkler.org/Common_Wisdom.pdf (accessed May 7, 2007).

———. 2006. *The Wealth of Networks: How Social Production Transforms Markets and Freedom.* New Haven, Conn.: Yale University Press.

Bregman, Alvan, and Caroline Haythornthwaite. 2003. "Radicals of Presentation: Visibility, Relation, and Co-presence in Persistent Conversation." *New Media and Society* 5(1): 117–40.

Burn, Enid. 2007. "U.S. Search Engine Rankings, April 2007." ClickZ, http://www.clickz.com/showPage.html?page=3626020 (accessed July 5, 2007).

Futurelab: Innovation in Education. Literature reviews. Available at http://www.futurelab.org.uk/resources/publications_reports_articles/literature_reviews.

Hagar, Chris, and Caroline Haythornthwaite. 2005. "Crisis, Farming and Community." *Journal of Community Informatics* 1(3). Available at http://ci-journal.net/viewarticle.php?id=89&layout=html.

Haythornthwaite, Caroline. 2002. "Building Social Networks via Computer Networks: Creating and Sustaining Distributed Learning Communities." In *Building Virtual Communities: Learning and Change in Cyberspace,* ed. K. Ann Renninger and Wes Shumar, 159–90. Cambridge: Cambridge University Press.

———. 2006a. "Articulating Divides in Distributed Knowledge Practice." *Information, Communication and Society* 9(6): 761–80.

———. 2006b. "Facilitating Collaboration in Online Learning." *Journal of Asynchronous Learning* 10(1). Available at http://www.sloan-c.org/publications/jaln/index.asp.

———. 2007. "Peer Production and Virtual Communities: Light and Heavy-weight Models for Collaborative Publishing." Paper presented at the Annual Conference for Print, Internet, and Community, Tel Aviv, Israel.

Haythornthwaite, Caroline, Bertram C. Bruce, Richard Andrews, Michelle M. Kazmer, Rae-Anne Montague, and Christina J. Preston. 2007. "New Theories and Models of and for Online Learning." *First Monday* 12(8). Available at http://firstmonday.org/issues/issue12_8/haythorn/index.html.

Haythornthwaite, Caroline, and Anatoliy Gruzd. 2007. "A Noun Phrase Analysis Tool for Mining Online Community." In *Communities and Technologies 2007: Proceedings of the Third Communities and Technologies Conference, Michigan State University,* ed. Charles Steinfield, B. T. Pentland, M. Ackerman, and N. Contractor, 67–86. London: Springer.

Haythornthwaite, Caroline, and Michelle M. Kazmer. 2002. "Bringing the Internet Home: Adult Distance Learners and Their Internet, Home and Work Worlds." In *The Internet in Everyday Life,* ed. Barry Wellman and Caroline Haythornthwaite, 431–63. Oxford: Blackwell.

Haythornthwaite, Caroline, Karen J. Lunsford, Geoffrey C. Bowker, and Bertram C. Bruce. 2006. "Challenges for Research and Practice in Distributed, Interdisciplinary Collaboration." In *New Infrastructures for Science Knowledge Production,* ed. Christine Hine, 143–66. Hershey, Penn.: Idea Group.

Horrigan, John B. 2006. "The Internet as a Resource for News and Information about Science." Pew Internet and American Life Project, http://www.pewinternet.org/pdfs/PIP_Exploratorium_Science.pdf (accessed July 5, 2007).

Jarboe, Greg. 2007. "Stats Show Google Dominates the International Search Landscape." ClickZ, http://searchenginewatch.com/showPage.html?page=3625072 (accessed July 5, 2007).

Jenkins, Christine. 2004. "The Virtual Classroom as Ludic Space." In *Learning, Culture, and Community in Online Education: Research and Practice,* ed. Caroline Haythornthwaite and Michelle M. Kazmer, 229–42. New York: Peter Lang.

Jenkins, Henry, with Katie Clinton, Ravi Purushotma, Alice J. Robison, and Margaret Weigel. 2006. *Confronting the Challenges of Participatory Culture: Media Education for the 21st Century.* Chicago: MacArthur Foundation. Available at http://www.digitallearning.macfound.org/atf/cf/ percent7B7E45C7E0-A3E0-4B89-AC9C-E807E1B0AE4E percent7D/JENKINS_WHITE_PAPER.PDF (accessed May 1, 2007).

Jorbring, Ove, and Piet Kommers. 2008. "Online Learning Communities in Context." *International Journal of Web-Based Communities* 4(2): whole issue.

Kazmer, Michelle M. 2005. "Community-Embedded Learning." *Library Quarterly* 75(2): 190–212.

———. 2007. "Community-Embedded Learning." In *Handbook of E-learning Research,* ed. Richard Andrews and Caroline Haythornthwaite, 311–27. London: Sage.

Kleeman, Jenny. 2007. "Wiki Wars." *The Observer,* March 25. Available at http://technology.guardian.co.uk/news/story/0,,2042368,00.html (accessed July 5, 2007).

Koschmann, Timothy, ed. 1996. *CSCL: Theory and Practice of an Emerging Paradigm.* Mahwah, N.J.: Lawrence Erlbaum.

Kramarae, Cheris. 2001. *The Third Shift: Women Learning Online.* Washington, D.C.: American Association of University Women.

Lave, Jean, and Etienne Wenger. 1991. *Situated Learning: Legitimate Peripheral Participation.* Cambridge: Cambridge University Press.

Lenhart, Amanda, John Horrigan, Lee Rainie, Katherine Allen, Angie Boyce, Mary Madden, and Erin O'Grady. 2003. *The Ever-Shifting Internet Population: A New Look at Internet Access and the Digital Divide.* Pew Internet and American Life Project, http://

www.pewInternet.org/pdfs/PIP_Shifting_Net_Pop_Report.pdf (accessed December 23, 2005).

Levine, Arthur. 2003. "Higher Education: A Revolution Externally, Evolution Internally." In *Wired Tower: Perspectives on the Impact of the Internet on Higher Education,* ed. Matthew S. Pittinsky, 13–39. Upper Saddle River, N.J.: Prentice Hall.

Levy, Steven. 2004. "Memo to Bloggers: Heal Thyselves." *Newsweek,* October 4. Available at http://www.msnbc.msn.com/id/6098633/site/newsweek (accessed May 17, 2007).

Mathes, Adam. 2004. "Folksonomies—Cooperative Classification and Communication through Shared Metadata." Available at the author's Web site, http://www.adammathes.com/academic/computer-mediated-communication/folksonomies.html (accessed July 9, 2007).

Miller, Carolyn R. 1984. "Genre as Social Action." *Quarterly Journal of Speech* 70:151–67.

———. 1994. "Rhetorical Community: The Cultural Basis of Genre." In *Genre and the New Rhetoric,* ed. Aviva Freedman and P. Medway, 67–78. Basingstoke, U.K.: Taylor and Francis.

Minaei-Bidgoli, Behrouz, Gerd Kortemeyer, and William F. Punch. 2004. "Enhancing Online Learning Performance: An Application of Data Mining Methods." Paper presented at the 7th IASTED International Conference on Computers and Advanced Technology in Education (CATE), Kauai, Hawaii. Available at http://www.lon-capa.org/papers/Behrouz_CATE2004.pdf (accessed May 21, 2007).

Montague, Rae-Anne. 2006. "Riding the Waves: A Case Study of Learners and Leaders in Library and Information Science Education." Ph.D. diss., University of Illinois at Urbana-Champaign.

Murphy, Karen L., and Mauri P. Collins. 1997. "Communication Conventions in Instructional Electronic Chats." *First Monday* 2(1). Available at http://www.firstmonday.dk/issues/issue2_11/murphy/index.html.

O'Reilly, Tim. 2005. "What Is Web 2.0 Design? Patterns and Business Models for the Next Generation of Software." O'Reilly, http://www.oreillynet.com/pub/a/oreilly/tim/news/2005/09/30/what-is-web-20.html (accessed February 18, 2009).

Park, Han Woo. 2003. "What Is Hyperlink Network Analysis? A New Method for the Study of Social Structure on the Web." *Connections* 25(1): 49–61.

Pittinsky, Matthew S., ed. 2003. *Wired Tower: Perspectives on the Impact of the Internet on Higher Education.* Upper Saddle River, N.J.: Prentice Hall.

Preston, Christina J. 2002. "Braided Learning: Teachers Learning with and for Each Other." Paper presented at the National Interactive Media Association, Tokyo.

———. 2008. "Braided Learning: An Emerging Practice Observed in E-communities of Practice." *International Journal of Web-Based Communities* 4(2): 220–43.

Rainie, Lee, and Bill Trancer. 2007. "Wikipedia Users, Data Memo." Pew Internet and American Life Project, http://www.pewinternet.org/pdfs/PIP_Wikipedia07.pdf (accessed July 5, 2007).

Raymond, Eric S. 1999. *The Cathedral and the Bazaar: Musings on Linux and Open Source by an Accidental Revolutionary.* Cambridge, Mass.: O'Reilly.

Renninger, K. Ann, and Wes Shumar, eds. 2002. *Building Virtual Communities: Learning and Change in Cyberspace.* Cambridge: Cambridge University Press.

Resnick, Paul, and Hal Varian. 1997. "Recommender Systems." *Communications of the ACM* 40(3): 56–58.

Salaff, Janet. 2002. "Where Home Is the Office: The New Form of Flexible Work." In *The*

Internet in Everyday Life, ed. Barry Wellman and Caroline Haythornthwaite, 464–95. Oxford: Blackwell.

Sproull, Lee, and Sara Kiesler. 1986. "Reducing Social Context Cues: Electronic Mail in Organizational Computing." *Management Science* 32(11): 1,492–512.

———. 1991. *Connections: New Ways of Working in the Networked Organization.* Cambridge, Mass.: MIT Press.

Star, Susan Leigh. 1999. "The Ethnography of Infrastructure." *American Behavioral Scientist* 43(3): 377–91.

Star, Susan Leigh, and Geoffrey C. Bowker. 2002. "How to Infrastructure." In *Handbook of New Media,* ed. Leah Lievrouw and S. Livingstone, 151–62. Thousand Oaks, Calif.: Sage.

Star, Susan Leigh, and Anselm Strauss. 1999. "Layers of Silence, Arenas of Voice: The Ecology of Visible and Invisible Work." *Computer Supported Cooperative Work* 8(1–2): 9–30.

Steeples, Christine, and Chris Jones. 2002. *Networked Learning: Perspectives and Issues.* London: Springer.

Swales, John M. 1990. *Genre Analysis: English in Academic and Research Settings.* Cambridge: Cambridge University Press.

Swan, Karen. 2006. "Collaboration Online." *Journal of Asynchronous Learning Networks* 10(1): whole issue. Available at http://www.sloan-c.org/publications/jaln/v10n1/index.asp.

Thelwall, Mike, and Liwen Vaughn. 2004. "Webometrics." *Journal of the American Society for Information Science and Technology* 55(14): whole issue.

Wellman, Barry. 2001. "Physical Place and Cyber-place: The Rise of Networked Individualism." *International Journal for Urban and Regional Research* 25:227–52.

Wenger, Etienne. 1998. *Communities of Practice: Learning, Meaning, and Identity.* Cambridge: Cambridge University Press.

5

Ubiquitous Media and the Revival of Participatory Culture

JACK BRIGHTON

Mass media technologies historically have been controlled by elite minorities. Not surprisingly, the products, authorship, and distribution patterns of media have largely served the interests of their masters. To be sure, many efforts have been made to establish models of public service media in pursuit of the "public interest, convenience, or necessity" (McChesney 1993, 18). But domination of media control by political and corporate elites, made possible by the demands of existing media technologies and economies, has largely tipped the balance in favor of private, commercial, and political interests.

The emergence of broadcasting brought consolidation of media control to a new peak, by entrenching a literal "one-to-many" relationship between authors and audience. This model encodes an equation of authorship with authority, and audience with passivity. The technical and economic demands of broadcasting and of "professional journalism" have effectively discouraged participation in media-making by individuals and nonprofessional groups.

What happens if this is no longer the case? What would it mean if anyone could create, publish, and share media on a global scale? We are not quite there yet, but the concept of a ubiquitous open media system, for the first time in the history of media, no longer seems farfetched. Several large barriers and contested areas of interest remain unresolved: intellectual property law, proprietary systems and formats, and resistance from established media models and entities, to name a few. But for those of us interested in public service media, we now have enough examples of "participatory ubimedia" to move forward with some confidence, perhaps even hope.

Digital Depression

In early 2003, I found myself in a state of despair over the direction of news media on the Internet. I had just attended the first annual conference of the Integrated Media Association, a sort of think tank for public broadcasting on the Web. The keynote speaker was Merrill Brown, senior vice president at RealNetworks, who unveiled the company's new (and short-lived) marketing slogan "All You Need Is One." That would be the RealOne player, which in Brown's RealSpeak is a "consumer appliance, not the piece of software." Actually the RealOne player was more than that. It was an all-purpose digital rights management system, the core of a new media business model. And Brown brought the announcement of a major new media business breakthrough: an exclusive deal with CNN to stream online news video only through the RealOne paid subscription service.

Many of my colleagues were nodding their heads. We were all scrambling for ways to cover costs for streaming our public radio and TV content. Those costs include expensive servers and lots of bandwidth, which for most public stations could total between one thousand and ten thousand dollars per month, depending on the scale. The "streaming conundrum" held that the more successful you become at developing an audience for online media, the less you could afford it. If you succeed, you fail. Unless you find ways to make users pay for the service, said Merrill Brown, and suddenly we were talking about subscription models and charging people for public TV and radio content on the Web. We were advised by resident gurus and industry consultants to adopt a "shopping mall" model for online media, serving boutique content to affluent customers and low-quality bits for the freeloaders.

I came up in journalism during a time when we considered our work vital to the health of community, democracy, and culture, when our product was in essence not media but informed and engaged citizens. In public broadcasting we are supposed to be shining a light on the world, exploring histories and cultures, and helping people understand other peoples' stories. You can have that for a monthly charge of $29.95? I could not imagine hustling that. Some of us thought the promise of the Internet was to make information accessible, not lock it behind firewalls and logins. We believed public media should be truly public, on the air and on the Internet. So we declared ourselves "open content radicals," and began plotting ways to steer the public broadcasting system toward an open media philosophy. We launched a Web site focused on methods of sharing content as "open source media" (Brighton and Tynan 2004). We got busy developing a metadata standard and technical infrastructure for publishing and aggregating media collections throughout the public broadcasting system in order to make content findable and more useful for audiences everywhere. And we vowed an ongoing conspiracy to undermine the shopping mall metaphor in favor of a public library model for public media on the Web.

Flash forward to 2007. Broadband penetration in U.S. homes reached over 80 percent (King 2007). In January 2007 alone, 123 million people in the United States viewed 7.2 billion videos online. For ages eighteen to twenty-six, Internet use has surpassed television (Boland 2007). And at the Integrated Media Association annual conference in Boston in February 2007, no one was still talking about charging users for access to online news. Almost everyone in the public broadcasting system has become focused on how to make content freely available, how to better catalog it and expose its metadata. The BBC plans to put its entire archive online for free (Robinson 2007), and we are taking this as our own mandate in the United States. We are now talking about open source Web applications, social networking, Creative Commons licensing, and user-generated content. By now even most commercial news organizations can read the writing on the blog. The *Chicago Tribune* launched a community journalism Web site with the majority of its content written by readers. TV news cannot cover breaking events with its own reduced news staff, but it can broadcast cell phone video e-mailed in by viewers. Multimedia is exploding on the Internet, mostly created by nonprofessionals. "With today's technology," says filmmaker Michael Wiese, "there is absolutely nothing to stop anyone from having a good idea and expressing it visually" (*News-Gazette* 2007, F-4). Adds *Wall Street Journal* technology columnist Lee Gomes, "Anyone who wants to create a TV channel just needs a computer and a Web address" (Gomes 2007, B1). With a growing number of free hosting providers, you do not even need your own server. Anyone with a valid e-mail address can now publish media. Four years after Merrill Brown's "breakthrough," CNN is no longer charging for access to its online archives.

We might call it the YouTube effect. It certainly had nothing to do with our little open content conspiracy in public broadcasting. The truth is that Merrill Brown and company got it wrong by almost 180 degrees: The online media business model is not about serving content to passive consumers through a rights-controlled bottleneck. It's about people freely creating and sharing stories, passions, and ideas. We are not "users" or "consumers" of online media so much as we are members of a global media community made possible by amazing, inexpensive media tools and the interconnection of everything. Put another way, what we used to call The Media has lost control of the media. And if you care about community and democracy, this is a very hopeful turn of events.

But is this dawning of ubiquitous open media for all just another passing moment? Is the very idea of universal and free public media simply the fantasy of a few open content radicals? We still have some work to do, but we can hardly do worse than the era we hope is now passing.

A Short History of Broadcasting, in Which Media Become Unfree

The phrase "new media" could be applied in many times and places during our experiments with literacy and communications technology. Once upon a time, a new technology called wireless telegraphy was developed by scientists and inventors, credited primarily to Nikola Tesla, Guglielmo Marconi, and Alexander Popov (Hong 2001). What we now call radio was understood in the early twentieth century as a point-to-point medium, that is, an improvement on wired telegraphy. By the time Marconi received a patent for the invention of radio in 1904, the United States had already been well wired for telegraphy, and the corporation that controlled most of those wires, Western Union, saw no profit in making them obsolete. But one place where wires could not reach was a ship at sea, so on April 14, 1912, when the RMS *Titanic* struck an iceberg, the world learned of the unfolding tragedy by way of a "point-to-point" radio transmission from the ship. The message was received by a Marconi employee named David Sarnoff, operating the wireless telegraph in New York's Wanamaker Department Store. Over the next two days Sarnoff relayed the names of survivors to a public eager for news, serving as one of the very few "points" of reception from the news source at sea. The experience for Sarnoff was a revelation: If one could expand the number of receivers, wireless telegraphy would no longer be merely point-to-point, but one-to-many. In that instant, the idea of radio as a mass medium was born.

Sadly for open content radicals, the story of radio soon took a proprietary turn. Sarnoff pursued his vision of "broadcasting" at the helm of the Radio Corporation of America, a creation of General Electric after its purchase of the American Marconi Company. RCA began marketing a "radio music box" for home use, and by 1922 a growing number of "broadcasters" were driving mass demand for the new media device. "A significant percentage of the stations were operated by nonprofit organizations like religious groups, civic organizations, labor unions, and in particular, colleges and universities," writes Robert McChesney (1993, 14) in his classic history of broadcasting in the United States. While Chicago had commercial station WLS (for World's Largest Store, owned by Sears Roebuck and Company), it also had WCFL (run by the Chicago Federation of Labor). But the proliferation of radio transmitters run by "amateurs," schools, and community organizations lead to a conflict over rights to the electromagnetic spectrum on which broadcasting depends. The drafting of the Federal Radio Act of 1927 became a high-stakes contest between a few increasingly powerful commercial radio corporations and a larger but fragmented group of nonprofit radio operators and enthusiasts. A quick scan through the radio dial today will reveal all you need to know about who won.

But before we jettison radio as a medium for community, education, and democracy, let's consider what it would take to start your own station today. You must first conduct a frequency search over a thirty-mile radius from your intended transmitter site, after which you may (if you find an available frequency) file a Petition for Rulemaking with the FCC with a fee of $1,795. Within ninety days, the FCC will issue a public notice called the Notice of Proposed Rulemaking. After a period of public comment, the FCC has nine months to issue a Report and Order declaring an acceptance or rejection of your petition. If your petition is accepted, the FCC will open a thirty-day auction for the frequency you selected, during which you and anyone else may file a bid (with filing fee) to operate a station using that frequency. You may now file FCC Form 175 (along with engineering work from FCC Form 301 and another fee) to inform the commission about your technical plans. The FCC has thirty days to accept this form and another thirty days for public comment before designating your form as "Accepted for Filing." If you win the frequency auction, you must then submit a complete FCC Form 301, along with another filing fee. If approved by the FCC, you will be awarded a Construction Permit within ninety days. You are now about ninety-two weeks into the process and have paid more than nine thousand dollars in engineering and application fees. But good news! You now have thirty-six months to build your radio station, including studios and production facilities, tower, antenna, and transmitter. If your ambitions are meager, you might accomplish this for a million dollars or less, but more likely much more. The costs for maintaining and staffing your station will be in the tens to hundreds of thousands of dollars per year.

You could replace the word "radio" with "television" in the above paragraph and multiply the cost factors by at least ten. Except you would not find an available frequency in any area that is actually populated, and if by some miracle you did, you would be outbid by one of the dwindling number of large broadcast corporations. That, for the most part, is broadcasting in America, and it is why radio and television have become increasingly irrelevant to the communities they ostensibly serve.

Which leads me to my first bullet-point worthy dictum:

> Media technologies and economies that require a corporate structure for functionality and viability will tend to empower the corporate structure.

In general, TV and radio broadcasting does not work for people and communities. The requirements of organization and capital raise the entrance barrier too high for all but a wealthy few. The few owners then must monetize the attention of their audience by selling your eyes and ears to advertisers. The flow of broadcast media is from them to you, and your job is to receive the message they send. Your only choice is to change the channel or turn off the receiver, thus disengaging from the medium. In essence, while you remain engaged, you work for them.

The Revolution Will Not Be Televised

Just a century ago most Americans celebrated their arts and cultural heritage by actively participating in them. Before we had access to mass-produced news and entertainment, we made our own. People told family stories and shared what news they had, made more dear by its scarcity. Families made music together, and the influx of musical traditions and instruments fueled an American folk music culture that lead to jazz, blues, and their offspring. "Everyone was encouraged to take part, both men and women, from practiced musicians to visitors and children, and in the nineteenth-century home the quality might at times be excellent," writes music historian Tim Brookes. "Yet in a sense that was not the point. . . . It was an active, participatory tradition as opposed to the passive listening to radio and recordings" (Brookes 2005, 45–46).

Henry Jenkins denotes a moment in time when the new mass media made possible by broadcasting quite naturally tapped the deep roots of American folk culture:

> Initially, the emerging entertainment industry made its peace with folk practices, seeing the availability of grassroots singers and musicians as a potential talent pool, incorporating community sing-a-longs into film exhibition practices, and broadcasting amateur-hour talent competitions. The new industrialized arts required huge investments and thus demanded a mass audience. The commercial entertainment industry set standards of technical perfection and professional accomplishment few grassroots performers could match. The commercial industries developed powerful infrastructures that ensured that their messages reached everyone in America who wasn't living under a rock. Increasingly, the commercial culture generated the stories, images, and sounds that mattered most to the public. (Jenkins 2006, 135)

We are now in a moment when grassroots production of cultural products reemerges as a realistic possibility for individuals and communities. The cost of producing high-quality media (text, image, audio, video) has dropped to about the price of a laptop. The cost of distributing that media content online, for those with access to an Internet connection, is close to zero. The rapid growth in the numbers of people producing digital media for online distribution, and the numbers of people looking to experience it, testifies to the value we derive in producing media for purely personal reasons. There may be no profit in this activity. It is true that one person's blog may never reach more than a few dozen other people. But in the long tradition of folk culture, profit and reaching a mass audience were never the point. We have seen examples of "one person's blog" having a profound impact on other people, communities, and perhaps the outcome of a presidential election (Eberhart 2005). But regardless of the reach of today's "new media," its impact and value can never be measured by Neilson or Arbitron ratings. If we want to make media more useful for human and community purposes, we must not deceive ourselves into thinking the mass media model developed in the twentieth century is the only valid model.

We find ourselves, then, in a moment of transition between a "culture of mass media," where the technologies and cultural products are controlled by a handful of powerful corporate elites, to a time when almost anything goes. "The story of American arts in the twenty-first century might be told in terms of the public reemergence of grassroots creativity," says Jenkins, "as everyday people take advantage of new technologies that enable them to archive, annotate, appropriate, and recirculate media content" (Jenkins 2006, 136). Predictably, this scares the bejesus out of corporate media elites, who jealously guard their assets under the guise of copyright and intellectual property law. Never mind that almost all mass media assets are drawn from the same well as our centuries-old folk traditions. The act of borrowing from the songs and stories of other cultures is as old as culture itself. But in the current phase-transition, storytelling itself is a contested act. Which leads to my second big bullet point:

> Participatory culture is not new; it's just that we are no longer used to it.

Is it any great surprise that in a moment when folk practices are in a digital renaissance, many of the same "commercial" mass media stories, images, and sounds are being reclaimed and remade on YouTube, Boing Boing, Ourmedia, and blogs everywhere? The content currency of the emerging online media commons highlights the power and cultural resonance of twentieth-century mass media industries, but there is a fundamental difference: we are reclaiming our own voices and making the stories our own.

From the perspective of an elite mass media corporation, this is bad enough. Add to this the rapid shift from "watching television" in the linear sense to the increasing consumption of media "on demand," which undermines just about everything sacred about mass media economics. Market leaders can no longer rely on their traditional methods of reaching targeted demographics. Especially in the coveted eighteen-to-twenty-six age bracket, "consumers are increasingly relying on search, recommendations from friends, and blogs to surface content," says PBS's John Boland. "To an increasing degree, consumers control the creation, distribution, and marketing of content" (Boland 2007).

But it this enough to satisfy those of us who self-identify as open content radicals? In my view, technologies do not determine how they are inevitably used (Nardi and O'Day 1999, 40). The emergence of ubiquitous media does not guarantee equal access to authorship and distribution. But the "network of networks" structure of the Internet provides the first realistic opportunity to disrupt the "one-to-many" media model that has so thoroughly consolidated control of media in the interests of political and economic elites in the twentieth century.

So, another bullet-point:

> Media that can be mastered and managed by the individual will tend to empower the individual.

To the extent that we once bought into the idea of "Media with a capital M" as master of the market, ultimately what I am suggesting is a redefinition of media. It's personal now. It no longer does what it did in the fading broadcast era, and we have a chance to make it what it used to be: a communications channel between people for any purpose they imagine.

The Rise of Ubiquitous Folk Media

My station runs a community project called the Youth Media Workshop. We train kids aged twelve to eighteen about how to capture and edit digital audio and video, how to do interviews and research, and how to tell stories. In many cases they have amazing stories of their own, but they thought they did not have permission to tell them. We try to disabuse them of that notion. The results are often startling: kids headed for trouble turn into honor roll students, discover they have a voice, and begin dreaming about lives and careers they never thought they could imagine. Storytelling has always held great power to stir the souls of listeners and tellers alike. To see the transformations in these young students is to lose one's cherished cynicism.

From this we have learned much about how participation in media can be promoted and facilitated. It will take great effort to overcome the habits of thought ingrained by the dynamics of the previous mass media era. We must deliberately train and encourage our students (and ourselves) to be participants and creators of "folk media with a global reach." As media creators, we are no longer beaming knowledge (or commercial messages) down from on high, but acting as participants in a continuing conversation about knowledge and community.

As professionals matriculated in the pre-ubimedia age, we must also acknowledge that much of our hard-earned technical expertise may no longer be unique or even relevant. This presents a special challenge to media educators: as immigrants, we speak digital with an analog accent. Given our background and pedagogical traditions, we may come to our knowledge of digital technologies with justifiable skepticism. But to the ears of our students, our warnings about technology's perils sound quaint. Most of us above the age of forty do not even text-message, so what do we know about its value in the lives of today's young digital natives? While a Pulitzer Prize–winning journalism professor must be taught how to use a digital recorder, just about every teenager with a cell phone knows how to upload video to YouTube. We speak knowingly about the dangers of the digital divide, but in important ways we are the ones on the other side.

Maria Lovett and Joseph Squier address this tension in the third part of this book, noting that "students have . . . to confront a growing disconnection between their lived experience and the norms of the academy." In the digital media world, composition is more than writing text; literacy now requires facility with text, images, and sound in combination. This is not just about YouTube; it is increasingly about citizenship and employability. For many of us born in the predigital media age, claims like "video is the new literacy" sound almost heretical. But learning to teach new forms of literacy is not the biggest transition facing the academy.

In the preceding chapter, Caroline Haythornthwaite alludes to a mode of participatory learning that "entails instructors' ceding leadership and control of learning, giving it over to participants, and encouraging a new form of co-learning pedagogy." This is precisely the challenge for both education and media in the digital age: how to cede control and foster co-learning. Or rather, how to gracefully acknowledge that control has already largely been ceded for us and to find a useful new role in the emerging ubiquitous learning environment. With increasing access to the affordances of digital media, we are increasingly all co-learners and co-creators of the products of learning. As educators we are no longer simply imparting some measure of knowledge onto our students but helping them engage with the emerging ubiquitous knowledge environment.

We are entering an era when the power to tell stories, create knowledge, and make art is augmented by ubiquitous digital media, networked globally by the Internet. This is not a trivial observation. In his treatise on the innovators of personal computing, Howard Rheingold observes: "Less than a century after the invention of moveable type, the literate community in Europe had grown from a privileged minority to a substantial portion of the population. People's lives changed radically and rapidly, not because of printing machinery, but because of what that invention made it possible for people to know" (Rheingold 1985, 14). Networked digital media, connected by the Internet and fueled by a resurgence of personal creativity with great production tools, can do more than make it "possible for people to know." It can make it possible for them to speak, sing, draw, paint, capture, and share their stories and vision with other people anywhere. This is what I mean now by the word "media," and it's quickly becoming ubiquitous.

What Does Ubiquitous Media Have to Do with Ubiquitous Knowledge?

Many people in academia are familiar with software such as EndNote, which allows the user to store references to books, journals, and other media objects. You can use the software to record metadata about these media objects (title, year, author, publisher, URL, etc.) in a variety of standard formats, along with nonstandard information, such as your own keywords and abstracts. You can then easily search your collection based on any of this metadata and filter the results. EndNote also facilitates the expression of your metadata in a growing number of standardized formats, such as the APA style of chapter notes. It can also export XML documents, which can then be transformed into any other text format and manipulated by other software for whatever purpose. It can even create Web pages to display a set of records or your entire reference library if you choose. So what you have with EndNote is a tool for adding meaning to media and for retrieving, expressing, and sharing that meaning with whomever you choose. As a bonus, it also makes creating chapter notes a snap.

Libraries, journals, and collections managers are working furiously to facilitate ingestion of information about their content into EndNote. There is also an EndNote Web service, where users can store individual collections online and access them from anywhere. All this allows the user to cultivate a personal information ecology drawing from global information resources to create a private reference library . . . or more precisely, a private library of references.

At another point on the ubiquitous knowledge spectrum are social bookmark tools like del.icio.us that enable users to store URLs with annotations and keywords. Since the annotations and keywords are part of the "public record" in relation to that URL, they help other people find online content relevant to any particular interest or search. Because user-generated keywords ("folksonomies") are not participants in any kind of controlled vocabulary, they may at times add noise to the signal. But it seems that the relevance curve increases with the number of people tagging a particular resource, and folksonomies are becoming very well accepted among respectable information architects (Morville and Rosenfeld 2006, 184).

Many other information environments likewise "harness collective intelligence" (O'Reilly 2005): Flickr, JotSpot, Google Video, Backpack, Digg, Ourmedia, and the poster child for the Web 2.0, Wikipedia. Some of these sites are more or less commercial and proprietary (which could be a problem down the road if they are firewalled or go dark). In large part, search engines and social bookmark tools index them all continuously. Increasingly, rich media and knowledge resources are findable via the meanings and perspectives contributed by the people who use them (Morville 2005, 139). These are examples of drawing from personal information ecologies and practices to create a global library of references.

When personal and global reference systems become fully interoperational, things could get interesting. In *Rainbows End,* computer scientist and novelist Vernor Vinge envisions a world in which access to all online knowledge is continuously available via wearable devices and ubiquitous computing (Vinge 2006). In the story, new medical technology has also enabled Alzheimer's patients to fully recover their mental facilities, but with twentieth-century minds they cannot quite get the hang of the new interfaces to the ubiquitous twenty-first-century network. Their personal memories are clear as ever before, but they are not comfortable integrating with continuously available external knowledge resources. In chapter 1 of this volume, Cope and Kalantzis refer to these new mental facilities as "intuitive computing," through which, "as a matter of habit, ubiquitous computing becomes a deeply intuitive part of our life and world experience." It is precisely these facilities that we must now cultivate as educators/students. And so, a call to action:

A MODEST NEW MEDIA MANIFESTO

Learn about and participate in new media
Teach how to participate, including technical, analytical, and narrative skills
Use the emerging global information commons to research, write, create, tell stories, publish, share, archive, and preserve content and metadata
Develop useful personal information ecologies, and connect them with the global ones
Use, teach about, and advocate for open standards and nonproprietary tools
Keep access to the Internet as open and public as possible

Much more needs to be said about challenges to open access: intellectual property law, government and corporate censorship, and proprietary systems and formats. But we will not muster the determination to address these challenges unless we can imagine and articulate a vision of what ubiquitous media could mean for human knowledge, culture, and commerce.

Those of us who grew up immersed in the broadcasting era are cynical about changes in media. We've seen changes: from AM radio to FM radio to television to AM stereo to HD and now to digital broadcasting, such as it is. This makes us inclined to be slightly too skeptical to fully appreciate the opportunities before us.

But despite all that, we have to stop looking in the rearview mirror and get busy. To be in media is to be engaged. So here is perhaps the most radical proposition of all: To access ubiquitous knowledge, share your own.

Readings and References

Two scholarly books stand in stark contrast as regards the state of media, yet somehow encapsulate my argument: Robert W. McChesney's outstanding history of U.S. broadcasting, *Telecommunications, Mass Media, and Democracy* (McChesney 1993), and Henry Jenkins's *Convergence Culture: Where Old Media and New Media Collide* (Jenkins 2006). Whereas McChesney's view is that corporate dominance dooms media for purposes of community and democracy unless and until it is overthrown, Jenkins argues that corporate media is increasingly irrelevant and is being expropriated by the peasants regardless of what the tsar wants. Jenkins gives a nod to McChesney in his book while not backing down in the slightest, and they are both all the more dear for the dialectic. Other authors weighing in on the subject include Don Tapscott and Anthony Williams in *Wikinomics: How Mass Collaboration Changes Everything* (Tapscott and Williams 2006), the title of which is mostly self-explanatory but still a worthy read; Howard Rheingold in *Smart Mobs: The Next Social Revolution* (Rheingold 2002), which waxes (perhaps a bit too) enthusiastic about spontaneous social organization via instant-access technology; Howard Rheingold again with *Tools for Thought: The History and Future of Mind-Expanding Technology* (Rheingold 1985), a brilliant read about some brilliant people who somehow invented personal computers and network technology; David Weinberger in *Small Pieces Loosely Joined: A Unified Theory of the Web* (Weinberger 2002) and in the marvelous—well—manifesto titled *The Cluetrain Manifesto: The End of Business as Usual* (Weinberger et al. 2000); and, speaking of manifestos, McKenzie Wark's *A Hacker Manifesto* (Wark 2004), which cries out to be hacked by more of us; Stewart Brand, a writer who saw lots of this new media stuff coming even before the Web, in *The Media Lab: Inventing the Future at MIT* (Brand 1987); Bonnie Nardi and Vicki O'Day, who remind us in *Information Ecologies: Using Technology with Heart* (Nardi and O'Day 1999) that nothing is inevitable about how we choose to use things, so why not make choices that serve our interests (and oh, by the way, what are they?); Richard Adler with a deep look at how the "media industry" is shaking in its boots about new media in *Next-Generation Media: The Global Shift* (Adler 2007); and for a practical look at what to actually understand and do to make knowledge "findable," Peter Morville's plucky little book *Ambient Findability* (Morville 2005), which we should all find, along with *Information Architecture for the World Wide Web* (Morville and Rosenfeld 2006) for those who want to get totally geeked. When it comes to structuring ubiquitous knowledge, searchability is good, but findability is even better.

Adler, Richard P. 2007. *Next-Generation Media: The Global Shift.* Washington, D.C.: Aspen Institute.

Boland, John. 2007. "Opportunities and Threats in the Changing Media Landscape." Paper presented at the PBS Tech Conference, April 12, Las Vegas, Nev.

Brand, Stewart. 1987. *The Media Lab: Inventing the Future at MIT.* New York: Viking.

Brighton, Jack, and J. Tynan. 2004. "IMA Discussion Notes from Jack." Open Source

Broadcasting, http://opensourcebroadcasting.org/2004/05/ima-discussion-notes-from-jack_11.html.
Brookes, Tim. 2005. *Guitar: An American Life.* New York: Grove Press.
Eberhart, Dave. 2005. "How the Blogs Torpedoed Dan Rather." Newsmax.com, http://www.newsmax.com/archives/articles/2005/1/28/172943.shtml.
Gomes, Lee. 2007. "Suddenly, the Web Is Giving Eggheads Something to Watch." *Wall Street Journal,* April 18.
Hong, Sungook. 2001. *Wireless: From Marconi's Black-Box to the Audion.* Cambridge, Mass.: MIT Press.
Jenkins, Henry. 2006. *Convergence Culture: Where Old and New Media Collide.* New York: New York University Press.
King, Andy. 2007. "US Broadband Penetration Breaks 80% among Active Internet Users." WebSiteOptimizaton.com, http://www.websiteoptimization.com/bw/0703.
McChesney, Robert W. 1993. *Telecommunications, Mass Media, and Democracy: The Battle for the Control of U.S. Broadcasting.* New York: Oxford University Press.
Morville, Peter. 2005. *Ambient Findability.* Sebastopol: O'Reilly Media.
Morville, Peter, and L. Rosenfeld. 2006. *Information Architecture for the World Wide Web.* 3rd ed. Sebastopol: O'Reilly Media.
Nardi, Bonnie A., and Vicki L. O'Day. 1999. *Information Ecologies: Using Technology with Heart.* Cambridge, Mass.: MIT Press.
News-Gazette. 2007. "Filmmaker Coming Home for Screening." *Champaign-Urbana News-Gazette,* April 22.
O'Reilly, Tim. 2005. "What Is Web 2.0? Design Patterns and Business Models for the Next Generation of Software." O'Reilly, http://www.oreillynet.com/pub/a/oreilly/tim/news/2005/09/30/what-is-web-20.html.
Rheingold, Howard. 1985. *Tools for Thought: The History and Future of Mind-Expanding Technology.* Cambridge, Mass.: MIT Press.
———. 2002. *Smart Mobs: The Next Social Revolution.* New York: Perseus.
Robinson, James. 2007. "BBC to Put One Million Hours of Its Past Online." *The Observer,* April 15. Available at http://observer.guardian.co.uk/uk_news/story/0,,2057465,00.html.
Scott-Heron, Gil. 1970. "The Revolution Will Not Be Televised." Hard to Find CDs, http://www.gilscottheron.com/lyrevol.html.
Tapscott, Don, and Anthony D. Williams. 2006. *Wikinomics: How Mass Collaboration Changes Everything.* New York: Penguin.
Vinge, Vernor. 2006. *Rainbows End: A Novel with One Foot in the Future.* New York: Tor Books.
Wark, McKenzie. 2004. *A Hacker Manifesto.* Cambridge, Mass.: Harvard University Press.
Weinberger, David. 2002. *Small Pieces Loosely Joined: A Unified Theory of the Web.* New York: Perseus.
Weinberger, David, Rick Levine, Christopher Locke, and Doc Searls. 2000. *The Cluetrain Manifesto: The End of Business as Usual.* New York: Perseus.

6

Notes toward a Political Economy of Ubiquitous Learning

MICHAEL A. PETERS

Substantial claims are currently being made for ubiquitous learning (UL). It is seen as an emergent new set of revolutionary learning technologies that is to be distinguished from conventional IT-aided learning, e-learning, and distance learning, through its utilization of new mobile technologies for the construction of collaborative, distributed, often peer-to-peer learning platforms. Thus, for instance, Ellen D. Wagner (2005, 40) in *EDUCAUSE Review* claims: "The mobile revolution is finally here. Wherever one looks, the evidence of mobile penetration and adoption is irrefutable. PDAs (personal digital assistants), MP3 players, portable game devices, handhelds, tablets, and laptops abound. No demographic is immune from this phenomenon." The strengths of UL follow from its pervasive utility. It is said to possess a family of distinguishing features that emphasize *accessibility*, access from anywhere at any time; *interactivity*, including interaction with experts or peers in synchronous or asynchronous communication; *immediacy*, with potential for quick information retrieval and storage; *permanency*, with an accent on continuous and instant recording; and everyday situatedness, where learning is embedded in everyday life (Chen et al. 2002; Curtis et al. 2002; Ogata and Yano 2004). It is claimed that on the basis of the new mobile technologies, learners will be able to select the best means for learning from the available alternatives (including conventional means) depending on time, place, and other critical factors and that they will therefore "be able to learn at any time, any place, as and if they wish" (Ogata and Yano 2004, 27). These understandings are usefully developed by Bill Cope and Mary Kalantzis in chapter 1 of this work, emphasizing the link to ubiquitous computing and its situated, interactive, and participatory nature. They also acknowledge the need for caution, which is understandable in view of the failures of educational technology, especially instructional radio and television.

These developments of ubiquitous technology are seen as part of a set of wider trends in which, as Judy Brown (2007) puts it, "Everything is connected; Everything is aware; Everything is digital; and, Everything talks to everything." These trends will be enhanced as the size, battery life, and cost diminish, while power, connectivity, and capabilities increase. Mobile learning technologies are not limited simply to handhelds but encompass a range of different devices and technologies. Naismith et al. (2004) provide a useful classification of mobile technologies in figure 6.1.

The general ethos of the emerging core of UL is alleged to make full use of Web 2.0 as platform and to exhibit the following characteristics: rich learner-user experiences, learner-user as contributor, learner-user self-service, learner controls own data, and radical trust. It is sometimes defined by a series of contrasts with Web 1.0—tagging not taxonomy, participation not publishing, Wikipedia not Britannica Online, DoubleClick not Google AdSense, mp3.com not Napster, search engine optimization not domain name speculation, syndication not stickiness (O'Reilly 2005). Doubts have been raised about whether Web 2.0 is a coherent concept, although blogs, wikis, podcasts, RSS feeds, social software,

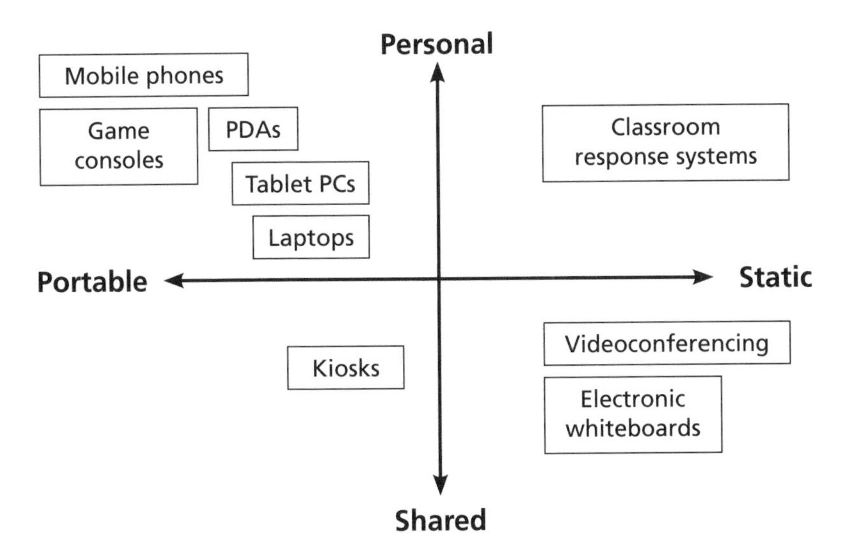

Figure 6.1. Classification of mobile technologies. Based on figure 1 in Laura Naismith et al., *Literature Review in Mobile Technologies and Learning,* report 11 (Bristol, U.K.: NESTA Futurelab Series, 2004).

and online Web services do seem to indicate a change in Web usage. These developments, if their promise is realized, do really constitute a new paradigm in education, as Cope and Kalantzis claim and which they ably detail in a set of seven "moves" in the game, including that of building "collaborative knowledge cultures," a strategy that I think goes to the heart of a new political economy of peer-to-peer production and collaboration (M. Peters and Besley 2006).

Major claims have been made concerning the *distinctiveness* of this set of new learning technologies. They are claimed to be part of a worldwide proliferation of wireless handheld devices (WHDs) that in turn help to support the trend toward ubiquitous computing through "the potential of WHDs to enable sophisticated types of instructional designs" and "WHD's fostering of new, media-based learning styles" (Dieterle et al. 2007, 35). New learning styles propagated by WHDs promote "fluency in multiple media" where "each medium, moreover, is valued for the types of communication, activities, experiences, and expressions it empowers, evading functional fixedness and over-reliance on one preferred medium." Further, these new learning styles "capture learning based on collectively seeking, sieving, and synthesizing experiences rather than individually locating and absorbing information from a single best source" and "value active learning based on experience (real and simulated) that includes frequent opportunities for reflection" (Dieterle et al. 2007, 53).

As an additional reason for taking ubiquitous learning seriously, apart from its situated ubiquity, flexibility, and contexuality, is the fact that "informal learning using mobile technologies is already embedded in our daily lives," as the author of a report to the Australian government suggests (K. Peters 2005, 1), thus promoting a strong relationship of education to the workplace. She goes on to observe: "Millions of web-enabled phones are being used by learners (who may not be enrolled in formal courses) to seek information to build their own knowledge base. Use of mobile phones, PDAs and laptops in organisations is well-established and interviews with employers indicate that m-learning is integrated with the use of these mobile technologies at the workplace" (ibid.). And she concludes: "With consumers driving the global uptake of mobile telephony, and the growing functionality of these devices, it appears that m-learning is here to stay. Managing m-learning as a part of a suite of services that offer greater choice to learners will have benefits for providers as it frees teachers from delivery to focus on the management of learning, and will help learners to gain the skills needed by knowledge workers in the new economy" (ibid.).

In this chapter, I accept both this broad description and the promise of new mobile learning technologies (UL) but inquire into their technological *enframing* and their underlying philosophical, political, and economic framework, suggesting some reasons for caution as well as recognizing their promise for new and open forms of education. The criticisms of ubiquitous learning thus raised should be regarded as ongoing lines of investigation as the new paradigm unfolds and develops.

Locating Ubiquitous Learning in the History of the Emergence of New Media

We now live in a socially networked universe in which the material conditions for the formation, circulation, and utilization of knowledge and learning are rapidly changing from an industrial to an information- and media-based economy. Increasingly the emphasis has fallen on the "learning economy," on improving learning systems and networks, and the acquisition of new literacies as a central aspect of development considered in personal, community, regional, national, and global contexts. These megatrends signal both changes in the production and consumption of symbolic goods and also associated changes in their contexts of use. They accent the learner's coproduction and active production of meaning in a variety of networked public and private spaces, where knowledge and learning emerge as new principles of social stratification, social mobility, and identity formation.

Communication and information technologies not only diminish the effect of distance; they also thereby conflate the local and the global, the private and the public, work and home. Digitalization of learning systems increases the speed, circulation, and exchange of knowledge, highlighting the importance of the digital archive, digital representations of all symbolic and cultural resources, and new literacies and models of text management. At the same time the radical concordance of image, text, and sound, and development of new information/knowledge infrastructures have created new learning opportunities while encouraging the emergence of a global media network linked with a global communications network together with the growth a global Euro-American consumer culture and the rise of global edutainment media conglomerates. The question, therefore, of who owns and designs mobile learning systems is of paramount political and philosophical importance, for "how a system is designed will affect the freedoms and control the system enables" (Lessig 2001, 35).

Ubiquitous learning and the new mobile technologies are part of the larger framework of e-learning, which itself can be located within the model of flexible learning (K. Peters 2005). Further, these nesting technologies can be seen as part of wider historical emerging technology systems that promote greater interconnectivity and encompass all of its different modes that characterize communication: the telegraph (city-to-city); the media (one-to-many); the telephone (one-to-one); the Internet (one-to-one, one-to-all, all-to-one, all-to-all, many-to-many, etc.); the World Wide Web (collective by content but connective by access); and the mobile/cell phone (all the interconnectivity modes afforded by the Web and Internet, plus a body-to-body connection).

One of the elements of the long-term appraisal of ubiquitous learning implicitly depends on philosophy of technology and a set of starting assumptions concerning its nonneutrality and the way in which it is rooted in social relations and social contexts of use.

Questioning the Value of Ubiquity

There are many accounts of ubiquitous learning that extol its virtues and few that raise possible questions and mention the dangers that it might also represent. In talk after talk, I have witnessed what might be called "technical presentations" that enumerate the capacity and properties of various devices and applications, without a moment's contemplation of the context of use or wider questions of philosophy and political economy. Nearly everyone agrees and takes for granted that the *value* of ubiquity is primary and also significant. There are very few accounts that seem to want to question its primary value or what we might call the "metaphysics of ubiquity." Yet to quote a line from a popular song, "you're everywhere and nowhere baby!"; ubiquity has no home, no place, no belonging. From the Latin *ubique* the word carries the meaning "existence or apparent existence everywhere at the same time." Yet to be everywhere and nowhere raises questions about our rootedness, our physical presence, our precise temporal-spatial location—in short, our embodied identities—that figure greatly in learning and are the basis of our phenomenal experiences of the world.

This critique of the value of ubiquity is perhaps best articulated by Hubert Dreyfus, whose analysis of the Internet is not yet another contribution to the hyperinstrumentalist discourse typified by a "gee-wiz" ethos touting efficiency gains and the lasting technical transformation of education. Dreyfus lines up with Nietzsche, Kierkegaard, Heidegger, and Merleau-Ponty, a group of philosophers who were dedicated to overcoming the dualisms ruling Cartesian thought and who argued for a phenomenology of the body and its central importance in human learning. He succinctly sums up his thesis in the final paragraph of *On the Internet:*

> As long as we continue to affirm our bodies, the Net can be useful to us in spite of its tendency to offer the worst of a series of asymmetric trade-offs: economy over efficiency in education, the virtual over the real in our relation

> to things and people, and anonymity over commitment in our lives. But, in using it, we have to remember that our culture has already fallen twice for the Platonic/Christian temptation to try to get rid of our vulnerable bodies, and has ended in nihilism. This time around we must resist this temptation and affirm our bodies, not in spite of their finitude and vulnerability, but because, without our bodies, as Nietzsche saw, we would be literally nothing. (Dreyfus 2001, 106–7)

It is a thesis as powerful as it is frightening, as simple and elegant as it is prophetic. We stand at the threshold of the Net as a kind of technological *enframing* of being. It contains both the danger and the saving power. If we allow it to transcend the limits of the body, we will also allow it to ignore our moods, our cultural location and belongingness, our finitude and vulnerability, our animality that helps comprise our linguistic and cultural identities, and also the meaning we give our lives. By leaving the body behind we will succumb to the same nihilistic impulses in our culture that began with Platonism and was repeated by Christianity. Dreyfus is a long-standing critic of computer ideologies and, in particular, the cognitive science modeling of the brain on the computer in books like *What Computers Can't Do* and *What Computers Still Can't Do* (Dreyfus 1972, 1992).

Dreyfus thus lines up behind Nietzsche, Kierkegaard, Heidegger, and Merleau-Ponty's phenomenology of the body. He quotes Merleau-Ponty thus: "The body is our general medium for having a world." Of course, Dreyfus is no stranger to Merleau-Ponty or to Heidegger or Kierkegaard, for that matter. His account of the acquisition of skill is indebted to Merleau-Ponty, and his commentary on Heidegger has now become a standard. In *Mind over Machine* (Dreyfus and Dreyfus 1986) he argues that where human beings begin learning a new skill by understanding and carrying out its rules as a novice, only to leave rules behind as they become expert, the best that a computer can attain is a sort of "competence" that consists in carrying out the rules it has been taught, albeit very quickly and reliably. A version of this argument appears in *On the Internet.* Indeed, Dreyfus outlines the stages by which a student learns—novice, advanced beginner, competence, proficiency, expertise, practical wisdom.

If there are some philosophical problems that I would want at least to mention concerning ubiquitous learning, some metaphysical anxieties about the technical emphasis on the speed, efficiency, and compression of communication considered as a pedagogical problem, then there are also arguments from liberal political economy that deserve mention, if only to highlight potential problems and pitfalls and in order to overcome them as obstacles to the pedagogical realization of ubiquitous learning.

Proprietary and Nonproprietary Forms of Ubiquitous Learning

An argument from critical political economy suggests in essence that ubiquitous learning is the quickest way of handing public education over to the new, technoscientific, global information conglomerates whose profit margins dictate planned obsolescence and an endless product cycle of innovation and fashion. This criticism raises a question concerning the way in which ubiquitous learning is handed over to the corporation as a marketable product capable of endless development and how learning becomes a matter of possessing the latest product. Ubiquitous learning cannot be considered outside its relationship to informational or digital capitalism. The clearest example here is the potential of educational television, the promise of which has been eclipsed partly because broadcasting in the United States developed as a commercial entity. The failure of the project of education television (as with radio a generation earlier) is well known. As the Web site of the Museum of Broadcast Communications explains, "Within this system efforts to use the medium for educational purposes always struggled to survive, nearly overwhelmed by the flood of entertainment programming designed to attract audiences to the commercials that educated them in another way—to become active consumers. Despite its clear potential and the aspirations of pioneer broadcasters, educational television has never realized its fullest potential as an instructional medium" (http://www.museum.tv/archives/etv/E/htmlE/educationalt/educationalt.htm).

The very pervasiveness of the new learning technologies that constitute ubiquitous learning collapses the distinctions between home and work, school and leisure, public and private, school and work, formal and informal education and delivers the school into the hands of endless commodity cycles that have little to do with the aims and purposes of education. And yet at the same time ubiquitous learning seems also to promise a new kind of "social production" that heralds the promise of a utopian moment. In a study of how social production transforms markets and freedom, Yochai Benkler begins his authoritative work, *The Wealth of Networks,* with the following words:

> Information, knowledge, and culture are central to human freedom and human development. How they are produced and exchanged in our society critically affects the way we see the state of the world as it is and might be; who decides these questions; and how we, as societies and polities, come to understand what can and ought to be done. For more than 150 years, modern complex democracies have depended in large measure on an industrial information economy for these basic functions. In the past decade and a

> half, we have begun to see a radical change in the organization of information production. Enabled by technological change, we are beginning to see a series of economic, social, and cultural adaptations that make possible a radical transformation of how we make the information environment we occupy as autonomous individuals, citizens, and members of cultural and social groups. . . . The change brought about by the networked information environment is deep. It is structural. It goes to the very foundations of how liberal markets and liberal democracies have coevolved for almost two centuries. (Benkler 2006, 1)

Benkler is not alone in making what seem like extravagant claims. His work rests on, and is in turn reinforced by, a range of scholars mostly working in the related areas of informatics, international law, and political economy, including James Boyle, Hal Abelson, and Lawrence Lessig. They concur that the role of nonmarket and nonproprietary production promotes the emergence of a new information environment and networked economy that both depends on and encourages greater individual freedom, democratic participation, collaboration, and interactivity. This "promises to enable social production and exchange to play a much larger role, alongside property- and market-based production, than they ever have in modern democracies" (Benkler 2006, 3). Peer production of information, knowledge, and culture enabled by the emergence of free and open source software permits the expansion of the social model production beyond the software platform into every domain of information and cultural production. The model of social production identified and analyzed by Benkler has its important counterpart and infrastructure in the increasing ubiquity of Linux, which "has progressed from marginal status as a platform for intelligent devices to a position of ubiquity, even dominance, in embedded design" (Weinberg 2006).

Lawrence Lessig in *The Future of Ideas* provides a useful model arguing that digital technologies have dramatically changed the conditions of creativity, essential to both new learning and the knowledge economy. For Lessig, the future of ideas and "the fate of the commons in a connected world" (the subtitle of his book) is a question of freedom or control in relation to the development of the Internet. Applying the notion of "the commons" to the Internet, Lessig defines the Internet as a communication system composed of three discrete layers: first, the "physical" layer made up of computers and wires linking computers to the Internet; second, a "logical" or "code" layer that makes the hardware operational, including the protocols that define the Internet and the software on which they run; third, the "content" layer, that is, the material that gets transmitted across the Internet, including the digital images, texts, and sounds. As he observes, in principle each of these layers could be either controlled or free: "Each, that is, could be owned or each could be organized in a commons" (Lessig 2001, 23).

The question of freedom versus control is of central importance to understanding the precarious nature of various emerging open knowledge production regimes such as open source, open access, and the free science movements and their applications in open learning systems (Peters and Besley 2006). Open knowledge production is based on an incremental, decentralized, asynchronous, and collaborative development process that transcends the traditional proprietary market model. Commons-based peer production is based on free cooperation, not on the selling of one's labor in exchange for a wage, nor motivated primarily by profit or for the exchange value of the resulting product. It is managed through new modes of peer governance rather than traditional organizational hierarchies, and it is an innovative application of copyright that creates an information commons and transcends the limitations attached to both the private (for-profit) and public (state-based) property forms. (I based this formulation on Michel Bauwens's P2P Foundation work at the P2P Foundation Web site, http://p2pfoundation.net/3. P2P_in_the_Economic_Sphere.)

Ubiquitous learning offers great possibilities but also presents uncharted educational dangers; its technological forms and corporate development must also be subjected to wider philosophical scrutiny and its emergence, development, and adoption in public education must proceed with an understanding of wider questions developed from philosophy and political economy.

Readings and References

For further readings on philosophy of technology, see Andrew Feenberg's (1999) *Questioning Technology*; for philosophy of educational technology, see Peters (2006a, 2006b). For informational on digital capitalism, see Castells (2000) and Schiller (2000). For liberal political economy of networks, see Benkler (2006) and his Web page (http://www.benkler.org).

Benkler, Yochai. 2006. *The Wealth of Networks: How Social Production Transforms Markets and Freedom.* New Haven, Conn.: Yale University Press.

Brown, Judy. 2007. "Mobile Learning: Where We Are and Where Are We Going?" Available at http://www.judybrown.com/docs/20070711SOF.pdf.

Castells, Manuel. 2000. *The Rise of the Network Society.* Vol. 1 of *The Information Age: Economy, Society and Culture.* Oxford: Blackwell.

Chen, Y. S., T. C. Kao, J. P. Sheu, and C. Y. Chiang. 2002. "A Mobile Scaffolding-Aid-Based Bird-Watching Learning System." In *Proceedings of IEEE International Workshop on Wireless and Mobile Technologies in Education,* 15–22. Washington, D.C.: IEEE Computer Society Press.

Curtis, Michael, Kathleen Luchini, William Bobrowsky, Chris Quintana, and Elliot Soloway. 2002. "Handheld Use in K-12: A Descriptive Account." In *Proceedings of IEEE International Workshop on Wireless and Mobile Technologies in Education,* 23–30. Washington, D.C.: IEEE Computer Society Press.

Dieterle, Edward, Chris Dede, and Karen Schrier. 2007. "'Neomillennial' Learning Styles Propagated by Wireless Handheld Devices." In *Ubiquitous and Pervasive Knowledge and Learning Management: Semantics, Social Networking and New Media to Their Full Potential,* ed. M. Lytras and A. Naeve, 35–66. Hershey, Penn.: Idea Group.

Dreyfus, Hubert 1972. *What Computers Can't Do: A Critique of Artificial Reason.* New York: Harper and Row.

———. 1992. *What Computers Still Can't Do: A Critique of Artificial Reason.* Cambridge, Mass.: MIT Press.

———. 2001. *On the Internet.* London: Routledge.

Dreyfus, Hubert, and Stuart Dreyfus. 1986. *Mind over Machine.* New York: Free Press.

Feenberg, Andrew. 1999. *Questioning Technology.* London: Routledge.

Lessig, Lawrence. 2001. *The Future of Ideas: The Fate of the Commons in a Connected World.* New York: Vintage.

Naismith, Laura, Peter Lonsdale, Giasemi Vavoula, and Mike Sharples. 2004. *Literature Review in Mobile Technologies and Learning.* Available at http://www.futurelab.org.uk/resources/documents/lit_reviews/Mobile_Review.pdf.

Ogata, Hiroaki, and Yoneo Yano. 2004. "Context-Aware Support for Computer-Supported Ubiquitous Learning." In *Proceedings of the 2nd IEEE International Workshop on Wireless and Mobile Technologies in Education.* IEEE Computer Society, http://csdl2.computer.org/persagen/DLAbsToc.jsp?resourcePath=/dl/proceedings/&toc=comp/proceedings/wmte/2004/1989/00/1989toc.xml&DOI=10.1109/WMTE.2004.1281330.

O'Reilly, Tim. 2005. "What Is Web 2.0? Design Patterns and Business Models for the Next Generation of Software." O'Reilly, http://www.oreillynet.com/pub/a/oreilly/tim/news/2005/09/30/what-is-web-20.html.

Peters, Kristine. 2005. *Learning on the Move: Mobile Technologies in Business and Education.* Canberra: Australian Government, Department of Education, Science and Training. Available at http://pre2005.flexiblelearning.net.au/projects/resources/2005/Learning%20on%20the%20move_final.pdf.

Peters, Michael A. 2006a. "Towards Philosophy of Technology in Education: Mapping the Field." In *The International Handbook of Virtual Learning Environment,* ed. J. Weiss, J. Nolan, J. Hunsinger, and P. Trifinoas, 95–116. Dordrecht: Springer.

———. 2006b. "From Knowledge to Information: Virtual Classrooms or Automated Diploma Mills?" In *Defining Technological Literacy: Towards an Epistemological Framework,* ed. J. Dakers, 297–314. New York: Palgrave.

Peters, Michael A., and Tina Besley. 2006. *Building Knowledge Cultures: Education and Development in the Age of Knowledge Capitalism.* Lanham, Md.: Rowman and Littlefield.

Schiller, Dan. 2000. *Digital Capitalism.* Cambridge, Mass.: MIT Press.

Wagner, Ellen. 2005. "Enabling Mobile Learning." *EDUCAUSE Review* 40(3): 40–53.

Weinberg, Bill. 2006. "The New Era of Mobile Linux Ubiquity: Access Industries." Access, http://www.access-company.com/PDF/Mobile%20Linux%20Ubiquity.pdf.

Yang, Stephen J. H. 2006. "Context Aware Ubiquitous Learning Environments for Peer-to-Peer Collaborative Learning." *Educational Technology and Society* 9(1): 188–201.

7

From Ubiquitous Computing to Ubiquitous Learning

MICHAEL B. TWIDALE

Introduction: The Origins of Ubiquitous Computing

This chapter examines the research area of ubiquitous computing for indications of productive lines of analysis and synthesis in ubiquitous learning. As such it views the rich set of issues related to ubiquitous learning through a single lens, albeit one that allows me to focus on a certain set of key concerns. In taking this approach, the aim is to complement the work of other chapters that address the concept of ubiquitous learning from other very different and frequently richer perspectives. The main argument is that ubiquitous computing has generated a set of concepts about ubiquity, inherent learning issues, and challenges that should be borne in mind as we consider the potential directions of ubiquitous learning, its potentials and problems.

As computing hardware became ever smaller and cheaper, a number of computer science researchers began to consider the potential implications of this for how we might use computers in the future. The term "ubiquitous computing" (often shortened to "ubicomp") is used to describe research in applications, resultant activities, and the social consequences of having many computational resources per person always at hand wherever you are. In essence, the argument is an extrapolation from the history of computer applications and use.

Early computers were very big and very expensive. People were expected to configure themselves to the convenience of these devices. The typical piece of hardware was the mainframe, and the typical application was payroll processing for a large corporation. Many people shared the use of a single computer and had to wait their turn for their application to be processed. The advent of small desktop computers led to a change in attitude exemplified by the name of these devices: the personal computer (PC). The idea was that each person would have his or her own computer, and falling hardware costs made it economical to allocate ever cheaper computing resources to making computer use less effortful and less confusing. The resultant features, such as graphical user interfaces, made computers accessible for continually widening groups of less technically trained computer users. PCs that were networked together, first within organizations and later across the world via the Internet, led to our current state of the networked PC with Web access and a variety of mechanisms to support not just personal but also collaborative computer use in the contexts of work, learning, play, and everyday life.

The next stage is to move from a vision of one (networked) computer per person to very many (networked) computers per person. This is the idea of ubicomp—where computers are so cheap that they become mere resources to be drawn on as needed in a fast, lightweight, ad hoc, rapidly changing manner that people configure and reconfigure as their needs and activities change from moment to moment. A useful analogy may be to think of this transition as paralleling that of certain kinds of production, from the blast furnace (like a mainframe, one big piece of technology needing lots of people for its operation and itself operating in turn on huge projects) to the electric-powered lathe operated by a single skilled machine tool operative (PC), and on to office furniture and supplies—a panoply of chairs, tables, flipcharts, whiteboards, stickies, pens, highlighters, and markers that, like ubicomp, are technologies assembled and reassembled minute by minute and are so plentiful that they are left lying around in abundance in the hope that at times they might be useful resources for human creativity.

Concepts Used in Ubiquitous Computing Research

Mark Weiser is generally credited as the founder of ubicomp in a series of papers in the 1990s (Weiser 1991, 1993; Weiser and Brown 1996). Particular aspects of ubicomp differentiate it from conventional computing, at least in terms of emphasis. Some of these are outlined below and can be useful in considering how they might inform our consideration of ubiquitous learning.

BEYOND THE DESKTOP

Ubicomp considers uses of computing resources that are not just located in a person's desktop PC. A ubicomp-enabled room might contain many computational resources that the person may want to make use of at different times, including large, wall-mounted displays, horizontal tabletop displays, laptops, PCs, tablets, handheld devices, and cell phones, as well as control over audio speakers, lighting, and heating. Conventionally, we consider each of these as separate devices, but within a ubicomp perspective, they are all computational resources that may be combined and recombined in many different ways as people's activity changes minute by minute. Thus we go from a consideration of software to roomware (Prante, Streitz, and Tandler 2004). Although all the devices may be connected together into a single network, the people using them should not have to think of them as a vast, complex whole but rather as a set of combinable, configurable parts.

MOBILITY

Another part of a consideration of computer use beyond the desktop is the acknowledgment that people move around at work—within a room, from room to room, sometimes from building to building, and even out of doors. This blindingly obvious fact seems to have been somewhat overlooked in much traditional work on PC applications that, upon reflection, seem to have a built-in assumption that users work all the time at a single desk. A consideration of computer use beyond the workplace and into the domestic and social spheres merely emphasizes this truism of innate mobility. How can technologies and applications support various kinds of mobility? We already see indicators in the ever-growing popularity of cell phones, handheld devices, and laptop computers. Another aspect is the growth of wired and, especially, wireless connectivity that enables people to access both public and private resources from a range of different locations rather than only when sitting in front of a particular PC.

SOCIABILITY

The personal computer that came into widespread use in the 1980s was in many ways a device supporting applications that seemed to assume a rather solitary form of living and working. The field of "computer-supported cooperative work" that developed in the late 1980s explicitly challenged these assumptions and investigated how networked PCs could encourage more collaborative forms of working, acknowledging that much work was in any case already inherently collaborative. Computer-supported cooperative work research drew not just on computer science but also on other disciplines, such as sociology and anthropology, to inform the design of applications that were truly useful, usable, and acceptable in aiding collaborative interactions between people. The research area of "computer-supported collaborative learning" drew on computer-supported cooperative work theory and applications and combined it with insights on collaborative aspects of learning from educational theory. As computer-supported collaborative learning drew productively on computer-supported cooperative work, so may ubiquitous learning be able to draw productively from ubiquitous computing.

MIXED REALITY

A consequence of acknowledging mobility and sociability is a recognition that use of technology should not be divorced from where it happens and the other resources around it. In order to integrate technologies into their lives, people need to integrate them with other things. This includes paper, whiteboards, buildings, and other physical devices. A tighter integration allows people to enjoy the advantages of both digital and physical artifacts. In particular, there is a growing body of ubicomp work that looks at the potential of tangible computing—a range of input and output devices that exploit our senses of touch, position, orientation, muscle memory, and kinesthetics both to allow very precise control of physical tools and gestures for the benefit of others.

Multiple tangible computing devices can serve a variety of different complex purposes while retaining the relative simplicity in use that comes from each device's being designed for a single purpose. Thus, in educational settings, rather than using a single piece of software to run on a PC or laptop, children learning environmental science may be given a number of different devices that separately act as light and moisture probes, that aid in plant identification, that support data collection and analysis, and that support communication and discussion about evolving conceptualizations (Rogers et al. 2004). Findings from use studies show that it is in fact relatively easy to learn and use a multiplicity of devices (because each device only does one or a few simple things) and that the various devices in concert encourage (even enforce) a more collaborative and reflective approach to learning through their coordinated use. Embodying computational elements in physical elements such as wooden blocks and pieces of card allows for the development of augmented reality systems that combine the ease and sociability of combining and rearranging physical elements with the added functionalities and alternative visualizations that computation can provide (Price et al. 2003; Price and Rogers 2004).

SENSORS, NETWORKS, DATA, AND DISPLAYS

As devices become ever cheaper, it becomes feasible to instrument the world with millions of data sensors (Greenfield 2006). This allows for more intelligent use of energy in buildings and various kinds of safety monitoring, as well as new ways to undertake science, as each small monitor's output is networked and integrated with those of thousands of others over, say, an entire river system. Vast amounts of data can then be collected very economically, which creates new challenges for storing and interpreting it, using yet more ubicomp devices to support various kinds of visualization and collaborative interpretation.

DATA CAPTURE AND ACCESS

It is not just information about the physical world that can be collected and stored. So too can information about human activity—what you have seen, which data you used, who you talked to, and what was said. The growth of e-mail archives and security camera data are early indicators of possible uses—and their consequences both for good and for ill. Such accumulations of data, their indexing, and ease of access open up opportunities for very beneficial data mining and the augmentation of human memory, as well as more dystopian losses of privacy, security, and trust. Something as seemingly benign as videorecording a lecture and allowing students to rapidly index the instructor's speech, PowerPoint slides, drawings, and text question-and-answers can be a great enhancement to learning by enabling students to concentrate on the rich picture and allowing more focused review of just those parts of a lecture that they need to attend to. Yet it can also be a risk for some learners, perhaps leading to a complete absence of note-taking and a disengagement from the learning experience (Abowd 1999; Brotherton and Abowd 2004).

CONTEXT AWARENESS

Devices that can use information from sensors can respond more appropriately in different settings. Location is one kind of context awareness receiving much attention, but there are many others, including a sense of time or of other people and devices present. With location awareness, it becomes possible for a handheld device to provide information to a tourist about nearby buildings. With additional information gathered over time, the system may tailor the information presented in response to the user's reactions to that information.

RECONFIGURABILITY

People will need to incorporate all these devices and resources into their lives, combining devices in perhaps unanticipated ways in order to achieve their real life goals. The technological infrastructure needs to support arbitrary combinations and reconfigurations of resources, as people appropriate technologies for their own purposes, using them in ways that the developers need not have originally planned. This support needs to be able to cope with the frequent appearance of yet more devices, some of which are enhanced versions of older ones while others offer new kinds of input, processing, or output. In this way, end users become codevelopers of their computing spaces rather than passive consumers of preplanned technologies. Of course, this is still mostly science fiction, but developers acknowledge that people will need the ability to reconfigure ubicomp resources in their homes and offices just as they have the ability to reconfigure their rooms' furniture and paper-based informational resources. Much current work in this area focuses on interconnection standards and "middleware": software that allows devices to communicate and share resources. The next challenge is to develop interfaces so that end users can exploit this potential for rapid, lightweight, dynamic reconfiguration.

AMBIENT COMPUTING

As computers become progressively cheaper and more plentiful, it becomes possible to conceive of more "wasteful" uses for them. In the early days of computing, processor time was so valuable that humans were expected to work hard to maximize the value extracted from the computer, which consequently demanded their full attention, often just to keep it running. Ambient computing is the opposite extreme—where hardware and processing and display resources are so low-cost that it makes sense to provide information on the off-chance that a person might be interested. Early examples already in widespread (and almost unconsidered) use include clocks, traffic reports, and informational kiosks.

EVERYDAY COMPUTING

Everyday computing (Abowd and Mynatt 2000) considers the more diffuse uses of computing resources over far longer stretches of time (days, weeks, and years rather than seconds, minutes, and hours). In these timeframes, people are doing many different things, but each of these individual activities is part of larger activities that persist and interweave. In such a view, it can help to consider people having a densely interwoven skein of multiple continuing uses of computer applications for different work, personal, family, health, financial, social, and other purposes, which keep interrupting each other and being resumed. This very different view leads to a very different perspective on the design of interfaces and functionalities from the more precisely drawn activities that have a clear beginning, middle, and end that have been the focus of much optimization in workplace computing to date.

BLURRING BOUNDARIES

Even in these early days of ubicomp, we see interesting blurring of boundaries. Widespread adoption of computers, cell phones, and high bandwidth networks has already led to greater porosity of our work and domestic lives. We may work from home, we may shop at work, and we may be expected to be on call at all times. Students are offended if we fail to reply to an e-mail sent at 5 P.M. on a Friday before 9 A.M. on a Monday. Such porosity clearly has many advantages and disadvantages. And we are only just beginning. What happens as we acknowledge the far greater intermingling of learning, work, and play? We already have learning organizations, as well as organizations channeling playfulness into innovation and design of new products and services. Computer games may be learning devices, training devices, even military recruitment devices. We find serious games conferences, serious play, serious leisure, amateur historians, and older people adopting "hobbies" to stay intellectually alert and interested in life as they contemplate thirty or more years of activity after conventional retirement ages. "Hobby" seems a misnomer for an activity if you devote twenty years to it—even if you may not have formal qualifications in it. What emerges as we consider interactions as being almost always mixtures of learning, work, and play whose proportions might be manipulated?

From Ubiquitous Computing to Ubiquitous Learning

What can some fifteen years of research in ubiquitous computing contribute to a discussion of ubiquitous learning? Many of the issues translate fairly straightforwardly.

MORE DEVICES, MORE POSSIBILITIES

Traditional education can be enhanced by more computational resources, including those currently only affordable in research labs. This is the same route that stand-alone PCs have followed, becoming every year more powerful, but this time it applies to a multiplicity of different devices. New kinds of learning experiences can be developed by combining resources: large displays and tablet PCs, remote sensors and powerful data visualizations, always-available digital libraries and collaborative applications. As personal devices such as cell phones (Mitchell, Race, and Clarke 2005), handheld devices, iPods, and their inevitable successors become more prevalent, it becomes possible to consider educational experiences that use not just a particular one of these technologies but interesting combinations of them (Moher et al. 2005; Moher 2006).

FROM ROOMWARE TO CLASSROOMWARE

Work on "roomware" in workplace settings can be drawn on to consider the potential for "classroomware" in educational settings, where both consider how a variety of different input and output devices can be flexibly and rapidly combined and recombined to meet different purposes, such as smooth transitions between individual work, small meetings, larger plenaries, and back on a minute-by-minute basis (Peiper et al. 2005).

RECONFIGURABILITY

Just as current teachers draw on a rich set of noncomputational educational technologies and resources amassed in a regular classroom—and the supplies cupboard—so may teachers in a ubicomp environment rapidly assemble a set of technological, physical, and informational resources for a particular classroom activity and then reassemble them for a different activity. Skilled teachers drawing on a wealth of personal and professional practice have been able to do this with a mass of paper and artifactual resources for decades. Currently doing anything similar with arbitrary collections of computational resources is beyond the capability of even the most skilled and well-resourced hacker. But as with ubiquitous computing, so ubiquitous learning will require radical reconfigurability if it is ever to be successful.

SENSORS

Cheap sensor data can be shared easily and cost effectively, should the people collecting it so desire. Also, as sensors continue to become cheaper, it is possible for schools to acquire them both for their own use and as part of a larger, federated research endeavor. These falling costs, potentially leading to a ubiquity of data, create new educational opportunities for more kinds of people, including students to be involved in research activities.

SOCIABILITY AND TANGIBILITY

Collaborative software allows for more kinds of projectlike learning activities, exploiting the configurable resources noted above (Hwang 2006). Mobile devices with appropriate context awareness create the potential for highly tailored situated learning experiences (Ogata and Yano 2004). This aligns with approaches in educational theory dating at least back to John Dewey. However, educational technologies, and particularly technologies appropriated for educational use, do not necessarily fit ideally into a use context without further refinement. A piece of chalk in the hand of a gifted teacher is not merely an input device used to apply marks onto a large output display unit called a blackboard. It also serves as a means of gesture and emphasis, and its use is interwoven with speaking, pointing, moving, glancing, and so forth. Chalk has its problems, but it is much more flexible in use than many current computational tools intended for educational purposes, where the focus is clearly limited to a sole application that requires instructors to concentrate most of their attention on enabling the product to do something amazing. The challenge in designing for ubiquitous learning is to consider how ubiquitous computing tools can be incorporated but may need to be changed. A tool that is optimal for computer-supported cooperative work may be suboptimal for computer-supported collaborative learning because the goals are different. In the former, the participants know how to do the task and want to do it as quickly, safely, productively, and as well as possible. In the latter, the participants need to learn about the task and how to do the task, and perhaps doing the task slowly and badly while thinking about what happened is the more efficient learning activity even when it is not the most efficient working activity.

BEYOND THE DESKTOP AND THE CLASSROOM

There is a rich tradition of innovative educational computing at a desktop in a computer lab. Ubicomp can provide additional resources to add to such experiences, but it can also encourage us to consider applications supporting use in other locations: elsewhere at school, on field trips, at home, and in yet more settings (Halloran et al. 2006; Schnädelbach et al. 2004). Ever-smaller devices permit the integration of computing applications (and hence potentially learning) into small niches of time, such as while waiting or while using public transport. As e-learning led to a reconsideration of learning from other locations than the classroom (but still desk-based), so m-learning provides additional options for some kinds of learning to occur in even more mobile settings (Keegan 2002).

There is also great potential for supporting different kinds of learning in different kinds of context: not just formal education (K–PhD) but also workplace learning, leisure learning, serious play, learning for the elderly, and learning in domestic contexts of family health, finance, politics, and environmentalism. Just as ubicomp leads to notions of more informal everyday computing, how might "ubilearn" lead to notions of more informal everyday learning? Some of this learning may itself be very lightweight, perhaps even ambient, but much of it will be characterized by the sustained mental concentration that we more commonly attribute to the acquisition of knowledge. However, any theory of "ubilearn" must acknowledge that this process gets interrupted and interwoven with other activities and may perhaps be more usefully considered in the longer timeframes that ubicomp has been forced to address.

LEARNING TO USE UBICOMP ITSELF

This is an issue that deserves far greater attention than it currently receives. It can get overlooked both by computer scientists and by educational researchers. The former may be more interested in the functionality of the system or in how people use the system in their lives after initial learning has (somehow) happened, while the latter may be more interested in the use of the technology to support the learning of another more important topic (physics, literature, medicine) than in how people learn how to use the technology itself.

Nevertheless, the learning *of* ubicomp applications is just as interesting a challenge as learning *with* ubicomp applications. It is likely to remain a challenge, perhaps even a growing one, for a number of reasons: as new devices are developed for new uses, employing new ways of interacting, people will have to learn how to use them. Despite the best efforts of human–computer interaction researchers, few interfaces are as "intuitive" as they are claimed to be. The term "intuitive" is itself somewhat problematic—few people actually intuit how to use the interfaces. They normally employ some learning process that is often overlooked. Applications are also upgraded with slightly different features and interfaces and are also replaced by rival products. Adding to the complexity, as ubicomp devices are tailored and combined in new ways, those uses-in-combination must be learned as well.

Clearly, good interface design can lower some of the barriers to learning, but it is unlikely to completely obliterate them, particularly as access to devices is broadened to a wider audience. A variety of learning methods should be supported, including individual learning (ranging from consulting manuals, help systems, hints, and wizards, to fiddling and experimenting with the device) as well as more social learning. Social learning in turn can range across several levels of formality—from organized training sessions, to various kinds of local and remote technical support that use a variety of communications media (telephone, bulletin board, instant messaging), to informal help and advice from peers or family members.

Over-the-Shoulder Learning

Over-the-shoulder learning (OTSL) is a body of work that examines informal peer help-giving; it initially concentrated on interactions between adults in the workplace (Twidale 2005). Extensions of the work have looked at similar interactions in formal learning, for leisure, among children, and in "virtual" contexts (Twidale and Ruhleder 2004a, 2004b; Twidale, Wang, and Hinn 2005; Singh, Twidale, and Rathi 2006). The claim is that a consideration of informal learning-teaching and help-giving such as this grows in importance as computing becomes more ubiquitous.

The focus of OTSL is informal help on how to use computer applications. People seek informal help both when they initially learn to use an application and in subsequent incremental learning of more sophisticated uses. Clearly, OTSL is a kind of computer-supported collaborative learning, but it is also in many ways substantially different from the typical applications and interactions of this model. The ideal interaction is incredibly brief (minutes, even seconds) and deeply interwoven into a larger (usually work) activity.

OTSL is an easily recognizable phenomenon—one that many people spontaneously engage in. It can be as simple as calling over a friend and asking for help on formatting a page in Microsoft Word and then being shown or talked through a series of interaction steps. In studies of OTSL in a variety of different workplaces, the most minimal yet still effective help noted was the yelling of a single word across a corridor between offices—the name of the command in the application that would do the action that the help-seeker had asked about.

The following transcript from a videotape made early in my associates' and my research illustrates OTSL in action. The recording shows one colleague (T) helping another (L) to create and upload a Web page. Our decision to videotape the session for the purpose of deeper analysis means that the interaction was less spontaneous than those observed in our ethnographic studies, but the interaction itself was very similar to the more authentic ones we observed in a variety of settings. The participants had been planning to take part in the help activity and scheduled it when videotaping was possible.

L: . . . So if I'm going to put this up, I need to convert it into HTML.

T: Yes.

L: And I've got to convert it . . . then (mutters) I have to take it across to the B server . . . Save. OK. Now, I better get to the B server, haven't I?

T: Yes.

L: So that's my next . . . H tried to help me a couple of times. She showed me once, and I just got completely confused. So. (Types in name and password on the server.) I got to bring up my own Web page, haven't I?

T: Well, there's different ways, but I want to see what you've done before so I can explain it.

L: I'm trying to remember. OK. I do this. I go to FTP.

T: Right. That's the way I do it, so that's good.

L: I go FTP (types in more). Now, I go to FTP and My Documents. Now, the other thing I kept doing wrong is that I got to get onto the public, I got to get onto the public site.

T: That's not helping. I've got an idea of how. (Points.) Now click on "close," which closes the connection. Now click on "connect again." Now that gets you into B; just click on that to see if there are other ways . . . Are these your files?

L: Well, that's a login. I don't want that. I don't know what that is.

T: Well click on that and see what comes up. Yeah, that might work. Try typing in your password. (L does so.) No.

L: No, that doesn't do that. Well, let's connect again. Well let me just do B again. Get into . . .

T: There we go. There's A (a different server) . . .

L: Oh, should I do . . .

T: No, not that one, the one below it (pointing). Do you have a different . . .

L: Yes, a different password.

T: Type in your A password.

L: (Not working, retypes.) I must have done something wrong.

T: Do you have the same username between B and A?

L: Yes. Right. Oh there. It's there.

T: So it seems that if it's not there, it's in the A one.

L: And I have to move it between the A and the B.

T: I don't know that you do, actually. Click on public. So, in general, everything that you want to put on the Web is going to be somewhere underneath here (points). Now while we're here (points), let's switch back to the Web and open a new window.

L: File, new window.

T: Now go to your homepage.

L: Oh, I should have, could I have opened the window and converted the files in there?

T: There are ways of doing that, but I think the way you've done it is one of the simplest.

L: So simple is the name of the game.

T: (Points.) Now that's your official and there's your personal. We can do this in several segments, and I think we should do that bit last. So first of all we'll get the file you've created up on the Web, and we'll test if that works.

L: And then we'll link it.

T: And then we'll link it. So when we first put it up, only people who know its exact URL will be able to get to it. But then we can link to it from this page (points), which will make it much more accessible. We're now going to go . . .

L: Back to FTP.

T: That's right.

L: Right. So, this is . . .

T: It's that one (points), ".htm."

L: So I just click on that and it goes across.

T: You click on it and then you click on that (points).

L: It's on (mumbling). (Makes a series of clicks.)

T: I didn't know you knew how to do that!

L: Oh, yeah!

T: Ahhh!

L: Well, I remembered that.

T: Very nice. Right, so it's there, so let's test if it's really there or not. So if you go back into this here . . . that's right. Click on that one (points), that window you're in. Now if we can edit this URL . . . just move the cursor to the end of this (points again) and click again . . . so . . . no, don't click . . . just click on the cursor again, that's right. And now I want you to delete up to that slash there, OK. Now type in "filename.htm."

L: It isn't there . . .

T: Oh, you need to (points out typo in URL, L retypes).

L: Isn't there a way of calling this up so that we can have a window that lets you choose the file? Because I always forget what I call these things.
T: Yes, there is; this is just a quick test. So press return . . .
L: Oh dear.
T: It says it hasn't found it. So let's go back to FTP to see what went wrong.
L: Is it case sensitive?
T: Um, it might be . . .
L: Oh, I know, don't we have to refresh or something like that?
T: Sometimes you do, but go back here. I don't think the refresh in this case because . . . Let's try . . . Of course I can't remember if the "htm" was capitalized or not, so click on the FTP. See if it was.
L: No, it wasn't.
T: Hey, we just got rid of it again.
L: So it won't accept things in lowercase then.
T: Type it in again, I'm a bit suspicious. I don't know why it lost those capitals.
L: Oh, there it is.
T: Oh, there it is . . . you were right; it is case sensitive. So now, have a look at this; see if you like the look.
L: So this in . . .
T: This is in html.
L: It's awfully wide.
T: That's okay. It expands to fill the size of the screen.
L: Oh, okay. I probably should have broken it up, but that'll do for now.
T: That'll do for now. So I think the thing to do now is switch back to this. Let's . . . It's a bit confusing because of this case, so I would say it's probably better to rename everything to lowercase just so you don't have any confusion in the future. So if you select it (points) and click on rename. (L does so.) That's right. (Points.) That's the one that's stored on your machine that's up on the Web.

It is worth noting that the interaction is far more free-form than a conventional education or training process. The help-seeker has a task he wants to do, and the help-giver is guiding him through it. So the help-giver is not really delivering a classic syllabus but is using her expertise to guide and scaffold the interaction and to explain some additional aspects of the meaning of some of the steps. The interactions observed are very rarely simple, instructional monologues of the form: "Do that, do that, do that . . . there, you're done." Interactions were much more conversational and dynamic. Also, things often go wrong. Sometimes the teaching/helping is suboptimal and has to be revised. Sometimes the advice is wrong or something happens that needs to be corrected. This can be due to an error on the part of the help-giver or some external artifact making the desired goal more complicated to achieve than first expected. Often this occurs because of earlier, failed attempts at doing the task prior to asking for help that have added to the complexity of the solution. Now it is necessary to undo prior incorrect, often misremembered or forgotten steps, as well as to perform the correct ones.

As we discovered as our study progressed, this transcript contains elements that recurred in many interactions and that were not quite what we had expected to find. We had anticipated seeing teaching episodes of varying quality and effectiveness, helped or hindered in various ways by the functionality and interface of the application under discussion, that would in turn inform our analysis and allow us to design better support technologies and best practices for help giving. In particular, we were sensitive to people's struggling to remember the help they had been given. We certainly saw those issues, but we also observed learning–teaching interactions merging back and forth with collaborative problem solving, plus considerable use of multiple applications, which added to the complexity of the interaction. Additionally, the transcript reveals issues we encountered at several other sites where people had to cope with navigating multiple virtual locations and having multiple online logins, identities, and passwords—the "where am I and who am I?" problem (Twidale and Ruhleder 2004b). These issues become even more pronounced in ubicomp settings. The transcript gives a flavor both of the messiness and the power of informal help giving that we observed throughout our study.

Although fast, fluid, flexible, and deeply contextualized, OTSL often has to battle to compensate for poorly designed applications. Sometimes this is a matter of overcoming poor interface design, such as an interaction explaining which icon to click on to achieve the desired effect and an associated warning not to click on a very similar-looking icon that does something different. With better user testing and analysis, the need for that kind of interaction could have been obliterated, by the user's guessing and learning from an interface with better designed icons and more informative hover-text. However, the need for approaches like OTSL is likely to remain, owing to the highly contextualized nature of work. For example, a request for help with creating a sales report can involve not just a discussion of which sequence of buttons to click in Microsoft Word but also aspects of the corporate culture and expectations about the content of the report that even the most expert Microsoft technical support hotline could not possibly address.

Furthermore, the study revealed a substantial use of multiple applications in order to do a given task. A report may be written in Microsoft Word but involve data copied and pasted from a spreadsheet, some from public Web pages, and other items from corporate databases and intranets, as well as files e-mailed back and forth that contain modifications by colleagues. This means that a request for help may necessitate a diagnosis of a problem that extends over two or more applications as well as a consideration of the operating system and the file system. The explanation may be a sequence of actions in different applications or even the opening of yet another application in order to construct a workaround. This reminds us that even in very conventional desktop applications, users do not passively consume software. They innovate in their use of applications by composing flows of work and by copying and pasting resources between applications. This is done even by people who vociferously claim to be "no good at computers" and yet are making use of computational resources in innovative ways without the need or the ability to program. Again, we see this as a foreshadowing of the potential of ubiquitous computing—provided people can learn how to use and innovate with a large set of resources.

An OTSL episode can veer unpredictably between teaching, collaborative problem solving, and co-discovery. The help-seeker may have approached a particular colleague because he expects that she already knows the answer, but it can turn out that they both have to work together to solve the problem, both learning as they do so. This kind of informal peer learning/teaching/helping can be considered as yet another example of "wikification" (Tapscott and Williams 2006)—the growing awareness of a widespread phenomenon (predating computers, let alone Web 2.0 technologies) of informal mechanisms coexisting with formal ones. In the case of ubiquitous learning, it leads us to consider how such informal kinds of learning do not and should not replace formal education and training, but can powerfully supplement it. Currently, however, the informal and formal learning episodes are rarely studied by the same people, using a similar set of analyses and theories, and so are rarely used to inform each other in terms of pedagogic strategies and computational design implications.

DESIGNING FOR COLLABORATIVE LEARNABILITY

One challenge for designing human–computer interaction in a world of ubicomp is to consider how to support not just its conventional focus on individual learnability but also collaborative learnability. Presently, we have some applications that seem to support collaborative learnability by accident rather than by design. For example, text messaging on cell phones has exploded in usage since its first introduction. From the perspective of traditionalist individualist human–computer interaction, the interface to text messaging is highly problematic—on most phones it is fiddly to learn how to use it effectively, indeed at all. The fact that hundreds of millions of people have bothered to learn (while other hard-to-learn applications are ignored or abandoned) shows its utility and how this can compensate for poor usability.

However, if we consider the interface from the perspective of how it affords collaborative learnability, it does have powerful compensatory features. It may be fiddly to learn on your own, but it is much easier to learn socially if someone shows you and sends you messages to practice on. The very portability of cell phones affords microlearning episodes in settings far removed from formal classrooms—sitting together on a sofa or in a café or bar, for example. Similarly, Unix has many rather surprising affordances for collaborative learning, despite being highly problematic in terms of individual learning (Twidale 2005).

As noted, as computer applications have been extended in their uses and context, computer scientists have worked with more kinds of disciplines in order to support design. With a move toward PC applications for nonexperts, cognitive psychologists have added to our understanding of human–computer interaction. With a consideration of collaboration, sociologists and anthropologists have added to our understanding of how people interact with each other. With a growing awareness of the learning burden implied by a flood of new technologies and new applications, and an awareness that "intuitiveness" is an aspiration but not something we can reliably construct, there is at least the possibility that experts with a background in education, learning, and teaching can help inform the design of more learnable, particularly socially learnable, applications.

Conclusion

Ubiquitous computing is emerging as a body of research in computer science that draws on many other research traditions to inform its analysis. It is much more than a study of novel gadgetry. Much of the research is innovative and playful, exploring the potential of radically new technologies by developing weird and wonderful proofs of concept that at times seem designed almost as pieces of conceptual art—pieces intended to provoke a reaction, change perspectives, and initiate debates—rather than as polished final products. Many of these early proofs of concept will turn out to be research dead ends and yet may inspire more fruitful applications and conceptualizations.

All this lively exploration and experimentation is in part an acknowledgment that as computing pervades people's work, personal, and social lives, traditional, reductionist, lab-based research methods are insufficient, and the very methods of doing research need to be redesigned along with the technologies that the research is intended to inspire—and indeed is inspired by.

This raises many interesting opportunities for reconsidering how learning has a role to play in this ferment. Ubiquitous learning can be about adopting or appropriating ubicomp technologies for use in traditional educational settings such as classrooms, or it may be about the alignment of ubiquitous computing with more ubiquitous contexts of learning outside the formal classroom: in the workplace, in the home, in public places, everywhere. These are not new ideas for educational theorists; indeed, they are issues that have been raised by progressive educators for decades. The ideas are still big—it's just the gadgets that have gotten smaller.

Readings and References

The concept papers by Mark Weiser are an excellent way to understand the ideas behind ubiquitous computing. These papers continue to influence the thinking of researchers in the field. A good accessible overview is Adam Greenfield's *Everyware.* Most work in ubiquitous computing is initially published in rigorously peer-reviewed proceedings of conferences. These include *PerCom, Pervasive,* and *UbiComp.* Useful journals include *Personal and Ubiquitous Computing* and *IEEE Pervasive Computing.* Not surprisingly, researchers in this area typically make papers, preprints, and technical reports accessible and searchable online via various digital libraries, scholarly repositories, and personal and departmental Web pages.

Abowd, Gregory D. 1999. "Classroom 2000: An Experiment with the Instruction of a Living Educational Environment." *IBM Systems Journal* 38(4): 508–30.

Abowd, Gregory D., and Elizabeth D. Mynatt. 2000. "Charting Past, Present, and Future Research in Ubiquitous Computing." *ACM Transactions on Computer-Human Interaction* 7(1): 29–58.

Brotherton, Jason A., and Gregory D. Abowd. 2004. "Lessons Learned from eClass: Assessing Automated Capture and Access in the Classroom." *ACM Transactions on Computer-Human Interaction* 11(2): 121–55.

Greenfield, Adam. 2006. *Everyware: The Dawning Age of Ubiquitous Computing.* Berkeley, Calif.: New Riders.

Halloran, John, Eva Hornecker, Geraldine Fitzpatrick, Mark Weal, David Millard, Danius Michaelides, Don Cruickshank, and David De Roure. 2006. "The Literacy Fieldtrip: Using UbiComp to Support Children's Creative Writing." In *Proceedings of 5th International Conference for Interaction Design and Children,* 17–24. New York: ACM Press.

Hwang, Gwo-Jen. 2006. "Criteria and Strategies of Ubiquitous Learning." In *Proceedings, IEEE International Conference on Sensor Networks, Ubiquitous, and Trustworthy Computing.* Vol. 2, *Workshops,* 72–77. Washington, D.C.: IEEE Computer Society.

Keegan, Desmond. 2002. *The Future of Learning: From eLearning to mLearning.* Hagen, Germany: Fern University Institute for Research into Distance Education.

Mitchell, Keith, Nicholas J. P. Race, and Michael Clarke. 2005. "uLearn: Facilitating Ubiquitous Learning through Camera Equipped Mobile Phones." In *Proceedings of the IEEE International Workshop on Wireless and Mobile Technologies in Education,* 274–81. Washington, D.C.: IEEE Computer Society.

Moher, Tom. 2006. "Embedded Phenomena: Supporting Science Learning with Classroom-Sized Distribution Simulations." In *Proceedings of CHI 2006,* 691–700. New York: ACM Press.

Moher, Tom, Syeda Hussain, Tim Halter, and Debi Kilb. 2005. "RoomQuake: Embedding Dynamic Phenomena within the Physical Space of an Elementary School Classroom." Extended abstracts, in *Proceedings of CHI 2005,* 1,655–68. New York: ACM Press.

Ogata, Hiroaki, and Yoneo Yano. 2004. "Context-Aware Support for Computer-Supported

Ubiquitous Learning." In *Proceedings, 2nd IEEE International Workshop on Wireless and Mobile Technologies in Education*, 27–34. Washington, D.C.: IEEE Computer Society.

Peiper, Chad, David Warden, Ellick Chan, Roy Campbell, Sam Kamin, and Tim Wentling. 2005. "Applying Active Space Principles to Active Classrooms." In *Proceedings of 3rd IEEE International Conference on Pervasive Computing and Communications Workshops. PerCom 2005*, 97–102. Washington, D.C.: IEEE Computer Society.

Prante, Thorsten, Norbert A. Streitz, and Peter Tandler. 2004. "Roomware: Computers Disappear and Interaction Evolves." *IEEE Computer* 3(12): 47–54.

Price, Sara, and Yvonne Rogers. 2004. "Let's Get Physical: The Learning Benefits of Interacting in Digitally Augmented Physical Spaces." *Journal of Computers and Education* 43(1–2): 137–51.

Price, Sara, Yvonne Rogers, Mike Scaife, Danae Stanton, and Helen Neale. 2003. "Using 'Tangibles' to Promote Novel Forms of Playful Learning." *Interacting with Computers* 15(2): 169–85.

Rogers, Yvonne, Sara Price, Geraldine Fitzpatrick, Rowanne Fleck, Eric Harris, Hilary Smith, Cliff Randell, Henk Muller, Claire O'Malley, Danae Stanton, Mark Thompson, and Mark Weal. 2004. "Ambient Wood: Designing New Forms of Digital Augmentation for Learning Outdoors." In *Proceedings of Interaction Design and Children*, 3–10. New York: ACM Press.

Schnädelbach, Holger, Boriana Koleva, Michael B. Twidale, and Steve Benford. 2004. "The Iterative Design Process of a Location-Aware Device for Group Use." In *Proceedings of Ubicomp 2004, Lecture Notes in Computer Science* 3205: 329–46.

Singh, Vandana, Michael B. Twidale, and Dinesh Rathi. 2006. "Open Source Technical Support: A Look at Peer Help-Giving." In *Proceedings of the 39th Annual Hawaii International Conference on System Sciences*. Washington, D.C.: IEEE Computer Society.

Tapscott, Don, and Anthony D. Williams. 2006. *Wikinomics: How Mass Collaboration Changes Everything*. New York: Portfolio.

Twidale, Michael B. 2005. "Over the Shoulder Learning: Supporting Brief Informal Learning." *Computer Supported Cooperative Work* 14(6): 505–47.

Twidale, Michael B., and Karen Ruhleder. 2004a. "Over-the-Shoulder Learning in a Distance Education Environment." In *Learning, Culture and Community in Online Education: Research and Practice*, ed. Caroline Haythornthwaite and Michelle M. Kazmer, 177–94. New York: Peter Lang.

———. 2004b. "Where Am I and Who Am I? Issues in Collaborative Technical Help." In *Proceedings of CSCW '04*, 378–87. New York: ACM Press.

Twidale, Michael B., X. Christine Wang, and D. Michelle Hinn. 2005. "CSC*: Computer Supported Collaborative Work, Learning, and Play." In *Computer-Supported Collaborative Learning 2005: The Next Ten Years!* ed. T. Koschmann, D. Suthers, and T.-W. Chan, 687–96. Mahwah, N.J.: Lawrence Erlbaum Associates.

Weiser, Mark. 1991. "The Computer for the 21st Century." *Scientific American* 265(3): 94–104.

———. 1993. "Some Computer Science Issues in Ubiquitous Computing." *Communications of the ACM* 36(7): 75–84.

Weiser, Mark, and John Seely Brown. 1996. "The Coming Age of Calm Technology." In *Beyond Calculation: The Next Fifty Years of Computing*, ed. Peter J. Denning and Robert M. Metcalfe, 75–85. New York: Springer-Verlag.

PART B

Contexts

8

Ubiquitous Learning

Educating Generation I

EVANGELINE S. PIANFETTI

Understanding Ubiquity and Generation I

Technology has the power to inspire us to transform the way we live, the way we teach, and the way we learn. It is the impact of technology on every facet of our lives, known or unknown, that defines its ubiquity. And yet, as we look at the majority of classrooms, the way we teach and the way we learn have not changed over the past several hundred years. The basic principles and tenets that are followed still define a standard for what it means to be educated. For example, teachers still aim to ensure that children can read, write, and conduct basic mathematical operations. We see that in the majority of classrooms students need to interact with others, to learn certain facts and skills, and to receive feedback and assessments on their learning.

Our challenge as educators is how we balance these basic principles for a generation that has grown up immersed in technology and for whom the expectations of the workforce have changed. We have spent so much time trying to close the achievement gap and making sure that "no child is left behind," that we may be failing to understand what our students need to thrive in a twenty-first-century society. Wallis and Steptoe (2006) identify characteristics that will define our future workforce. They will be people who can think across disciplines and whose quest for learning allows them to construct their own knowledge path while teachers facilitate their experiences. They will use new approaches to solve problems in ways not previously possible. These individuals think creatively and rapidly process information. Schools need to shift their focus to ensure that students not only gain core knowledge but also possess portable skills that will allow them to be successful in the workforce.

And for no group is this more critical than Generation I, a generation that has grown up never knowing a time when the Internet did not exist or that certain technologies such as smart phones, digital cameras, blogs, and wikis were not always a part of mainstream society. Generation I students are *digital* learners because of the ubiquity of technology that surrounds them. If we consider the notion of situated computing as defined by Cope and Kalantzis (2008), the power of these ubiquitous technologies affords Generation I students the ability to define interrelationships between what is learned in the classroom and what is needed to function without our society. This permits a student to transform common facts into ideas of inquiry and inspiration. It is Generation I that now asks questions such as, What would have happened if the South had won the Civil War? and who can use technologies to re-create and re-envision a world where the facts are altered and knowledge is redefined. Ubiquitous learning, for a generation whose comfort and competencies with technologies increases without effort, means that they are redefining how they come to know and what it is they want to know. Coupled with the idea that learning can now occur anywhere, owing to the portability and interconnectedness of technologies, the challenge presented by ubiquitous learning is how we may come to define expertise and creativity and how we as educators will be able to reach a generation so well defined by its technologies and how we connect to the world.

Consider this: it is estimated that the average student from Generation I will graduate college having played more than ten thousand hours of video games (Fisch 2003), having spent over ten thousand hours talking on cell phones, and having watched about twenty thousand hours of television (Prensky 2001). In 2004, the Institute for Social Research suggested that children and teenagers would spend at least 2.75 hours a week using a home computer and projected that this would increase as the cost and efficiencies offered by personal computers became more accessible to the average family. We see that an estimated 70 percent of children between the ages of four and six have used a computer (Fisch 2003). The statistics are steadily increasing. Technological devices are defining how students remember, understand, apply, analyze, evaluate, and create their own knowledge path (Anderson et al. 2001). And the vital force of these technological devices is their ubiquity. Generation I's "www" is wherever, whenever, and whatever (Wesch 2007).

Ubiquitous learning through the integration of technology allows for reflection, questioning through inquiry-based practices, meaningful learning through context-rich instructional environments, and problem solving in which students engage in critical thinking. The Generation I classroom will be defined by paperless homework, school-to-home portals, e-books, online learning, and ubiquitous access to resources. For Generation I, iPods, wikis, blogs, Facebook, and

MySpace will be common tools for learning, and yet, even though 90 percent of schools have Internet access, only 20 percent of teachers feel prepared to use it for instructional practices or to involve students through its use. The challenge that we now face is not a new one. We need to ensure that our teachers are connecting with students in a manner such that learning is authentic, creative, and transferable to different domains of knowing. The danger that we see coming from ubiquitous access to technology, as it helps to define ubiquitous learning, is that our teachers are unprepared to engage a generation who have come to expect that ready-access to, and meaningful use of, technology defines that curriculum.

The TIMeS Project

The TIMeS project is a model for improving instruction in high-needs schools. For more than three years at the University of Illinois at Urbana-Champaign, the Office of Educational Technology and the Office for Mathematics, Science, and Technology Education in the College of Education, along with instructors from the departments of mathematics and physics, have implemented a statewide professional development project with several Illinois school districts as part of the Technology-Intensive Mathematics and Science (TIMeS) project. This project was designed to increase teachers' content-area knowledge in math and science through the use of technology, with the goal to improve student achievement in those areas. This way, all three foundational subjects can be strengthened at the same time. The TIMeS project is built on the tenets of ubiquitous learning, in which concepts are situated within contexts that are relevant and meaningful to students. It affords educators a chance to explore new ways of teaching in order to reach a generation that has come to define new ways of learning (Richardson 2006).

The TIMeS Model has six major components:

Participant training: The TIMeS model has two training cohorts, one face-to-face (grades K–2 teachers) and one online (to accommodate the teachers in grades K–8).

Access to technology: Teachers are not able to effectively integrate technology unless they have the hardware and software on which they were trained. The TIMeS model provides technology to all the participants to use in the classroom.

Classroom implementation: Both of the cohorts of teachers are required to implement their new knowledge/skills in their classrooms.

Sustained support: Participant teachers have access to the TIMeS staff and equipment for help in planning, implementation, or troubleshooting. The TIMeS staff provides scaffolded support to participating teachers so that they subsequently become their own layered support for their schools.

Evaluation/reflection/collaboration: Teachers are asked to participate in an online discussion board about their successes and failures with attempts to effectively integrate technology.

Pre-service connection: Student teachers at the UIUC College of Education have access to TIMeS staff, training, and equipment.

There are clear indications that these elements are instrumental in enabling educators to transform their instructional practices from a teacher-centric model to a teacher-as-facilitator model where inquiry-based learning through ubiquitous access to technical resources is the capstone of the classroom. For example, one of the most significant changes in the structure of learning tasks took place in a fourth-grade classroom where no one wanted to write. Students hated writing; their writing assignments reflected that fact (including those done by pupils with good writing skills), and the teacher hated correcting them because they were so fraught with errors and basic lack of effort. As a participant in the TIMeS project, this fourth-grade teacher decided to redesign the assignment to include digital images and video to help assist with writing. For example, in four-square writing, the writing technique used in the district, the students write an introductory paragraph, supporting detail paragraphs, and a concluding paragraph. In teaching her students to work through these steps as a process, this instructor had students take cameras home and film the things that they did during the morning, afternoon, and evening every day. This activity could be used prior to writing to help students visually organize the steps in a day and then write the paper to go with the images, or to illustrate the paper they had already written.

The students' work improved significantly. For example, students were asked to choose from among several experiments that exemplified concepts that would be covered in the science curriculum during the year. They illustrated the scientific method by photographing each step of the experiment that they had chosen to do. Students then created PowerPoint slides that explained the experiment in terms of the scientific method. The students' digital images were also embedded in the slides to enhance the explanation of the scientific process. Students then shared the presentations, thus exposing all the class members to several examples of the real-life application of the scientific method.

Another indication that teachers were transforming their pedagogy could be seen in a classroom where graphing calculators and small robots were used to make the ordering of mathematical operations into an inquiry-based lesson. Students were given a series of mathematical expressions that had no parentheses and were asked to solve them based on their guess about how the steps should be sequenced. The answers were entered into a program in the small robot. If their answers were correct, the robot would follow a predetermined path that had been laid out by the teacher. Wrong turns indicated wrong answers. After making corrections so the robot would follow the correct path, students were able to contribute to an introductory discussion of the order of operations.

Ultimately, the TIMeS model allows teachers the freedom to try without fear of failure. When success is obvious, pedagogy coupled with technology becomes an integral part of instructional practices, student work, and assessment. The changes in pedagogies exhibited by TIMeS teachers are well suited for educating Generation I. Generation I students require that their learning be closely aligned with future workforce expectations. This includes the ability to collaborate with others to solve problems and to cross between disciplines, such as the experience gained by the students who worked with digital media to explain the scientific method. The use of technology to denote missteps in thinking, as indicated by the graphing calculator and robots example, is also a critical skill needed by Generation I learners. Unlike other generations that may use technology as a means to come to an answer, Generation I will use technology as a vehicle through which they come to discover a solution or question the validity of an answer. Without employing such pedagogies as inquiry-based instruction or project-based learning, teachers will not reach Generation I students at the level that will make them prosper intellectually and in the workforce.

Toward an Agenda for Ubiquitous Learning

Technological resources are helping to define a generation for whom the pursuit of knowledge is framed by their own construction of meaning and understanding. For Generation I, the pursuit of learning comes by asking critical questions and establishing the means by which knowledge is gained through authentic learning activities. As educators, it is imperative for us to engage students at their level. This includes designing educational environments that integrate technology through authentic learning tasks. Learning should be framed by critical thinking through the solving of real-life problems. We need to start looking at the ubiquity of technology that is defining our society and translating the "common uses" of technology into meaningful learning experiences. It is by accepting the interconnectedness of technologies and our daily lives that we will be able to fully integrate the multimodalities of learning.

This means we should not shun the use of technological resources such as cell phones or gaming consoles in the classroom, but rather embrace them for the new dimensions and perspectives on learning that their users bring to the process. We need to start redefining the common notions of literacy to include the digital learner. Consider that the average student graduating college today has read and responded to more than two hundred thousand e-mails since first using e-mail as a communication tool, possibly as early as middle school. How will this make us rethink literacy and how we approach the fundamentals of reading and writing in the digital age? We need to map a research agenda in which we articulate both the promises and the challenges that will redefine what it means to be educated as a member of Generation I. We cannot risk robbing our children of the potential that is found in each of them because we do not rethink what it means to teach and to learn in the information age. As educators, we need to be agents of change by establishing and/or participating in sustained professional development activities; developing quality digital content from which our students learn (such as podcasts); and we need to collaborate and network with each other so that we garner strength through our content and technical expertise. In the end, we must be able to provide students not only with the tools and skills that they need to succeed but also with the belief that their ideas can inspire innovation and creativity in our society. This will be the lasting legacy of Generation I—ideas, inspiration, and innovation.

Readings and References

For those wanting to learn more about the intersection between education, technology, and professional development, the best strategy is to survey a variety of ideas articulated by some key leaders in the field. Recommended sites for these readings are as follows:

Vicki Davis, http://coolcatteacher.blogspot.com
Stephen Downes, http://www.downes.ca
Edutopia, http://www.edutopia.org/professionaldevelopment
James Farmer, http://incsub.org/blog
Wes Fryer, http://www.speedofcreativity.org
Doug Johnson, http://doug-johnson.squarespace.com/blue-skunk-blog
Alan Levine, http://cogdogblog.com
Scott McLeod, http://www.dangerouslyirrelevant.org
Sheryl Nussbaum-Beach, http://21stcenturylearning.typepad.com/blog
Marc Prensky, http://www.marcprensky.com/writing
Will Richardson, http://weblogg-ed.com
David Warlick, http://davidwarlick.com/2cents
Tim Wilson, http://technosavvy.org (he spoke at the ICE conference)

Anderson, Lorin W., David Krathwohl, Peter W. Airsia, Kathleen A. Cruikshank, Richard E. Mayer, Paul R. Pintrich, James Raths, and Merlin C. Wittrock, eds. 2001. *A Taxonomy for Learning, Teaching and Assessing: A Revision of Bloom's Taxonomy of Educational Objectives.* New York: Addison Wesley Longman.

Cope, Bill, and Mary Kalantzis. 2008. "Ubiquitous Learning: An Agenda for Educational Transformation." In *Ubiquitous Learning.* Urbana: University of Illinois Press.

Fisch, Karl. 2003. *Did You Know?* Video. Kaiser Family Foundation. Available at YouTube, http://www.youtube.com/watch?v=pMcfrLYDm2U.

Prensky, Marc. 2001. "Digital Natives, Digital Immigrants." *On the Horizon* 9(5): 1–6.
Richardson, Will. 2006. "The New Face of Learning: The Internet Breaks School Walls Down." *Edutopia* 2(7)(October): http://www.edutopia.org/new-face-learning.
Roblyer, Margaret D., and Elizabeth B. Kirby. 2001. "The Fifth Literacy: Research to Support a Mandate for Technology-Based Visual Literacy in Preservice Teacher Education." *Journal of Computing in Teacher Education* 17(2)(Fall): 8–15.
Wallis, Claudia, and Sonja Steptoe. 2006. "How to Bring Our Schools out of the 20th Century." *Time*, December 10, 50–56.
Wesch, Michael. 2007. "A Vision of Students Today." YouTube, http://www.youtube.com/watch?v=dGCJ46vyR9o.

9

Ubiquitous Learning with Geospatial Technologies

Negotiating Youth and Adult Roles

LISA BOUILLION DIAZ

As elaborated by Bertram Bruce and others in this volume, ubiquitous, or "anytime, anywhere," learning is a concept that has a long intellectual history within education. The question before us is how ubiquitous computing and digital media afford new opportunities for implementing and supporting the social practices associated with that learning paradigm. Geographic information systems and related geospatial tools are a compelling example of how technology has become a pervasive presence in our lives. Historically designed for workplace applications such as city planning, programs like Google Maps have introduced GIS to a broader public as an everyday tool for planning trips and finding resources in the community.

This chapter examines the potential for geospatial technologies to create ubiquitous learning environments, drawing from examples of community mapping projects within the University of Illinois Extension 4-H Youth Development Program and related 4-H activities around the nation. These mapping projects represent youth–adult partnerships and collaborative activity that spans school and out-of-school time. These case studies will be used to argue the importance of redefining teacher and learner roles within a ubiquitous learning framework. Subsequent analysis will suggest related principles for considering new social arrangements that support sharing of expertise and mutuality in interactions that cross the borders of youth and adult worlds of practice.

4-H Community Mapping

Founded in 1902, 4-H is a youth development program currently serving more than 6.5 million young people in the United States. This program is delivered through the Cooperative State Research, Education, and Extension Service (CSREES) that connects land-grant universities across the fifty states. The 4-H clubs are facilitated by adult volunteers and provide a supportive out-of-school context in which youth have an opportunity to explore a wide range of topics through experiential-based projects (e.g., cooking, small machines, animal science, photography).

Youth between the ages of eight and eighteen are learning about geospatial technologies through a new 4-H curriculum called Exploring Spaces, Going Places. Supported through grants from the ESRI company, more than four hundred 4-H clubs around the nation are also using geographic information systems (GIS) software to collect and map data about their communities. Using global positioning system (GPS) devices, handheld computers, digital cameras, and other mobile technologies to collect data, these young people are working in partnership with diverse adult partners to investigate questions related to their communities.

Community mapping projects start with a discussion among youth and adults to answer the question, "What is included in our community?" Further questions include: What are its defining features? What do we want to examine in our community? What questions do we want to ask? What data would be relevant to answering those questions? What is the best way to collect that data? A key feature of GIS maps is the ability to layer diverse data sets within the same map view.

In one community mapping project, youth collaborated with staff from a local forest preserve to create informational materials for visitors. Using GPS and GIS technology, a map was developed for use in a brochure to better mark the locations of the interpretive signs that could be found along the preserve trails. Additional datasets were subsequently collected, drawing on the interests of both youth and the adult partners. Those data included the location of local green spaces, bike paths, hiking trails, and related conservation resources in the area. In this case, youth contributed knowledge of conservation resources that would be of interest to their peer group, as well as prior experience with using GPS and GIS technologies. The adult partners contributed their knowledge of resources within the preserve and experience with visitor interests.

Reflecting a diversity of neighborhood needs and partnership opportunities, other 4-H youth mapping projects have collected data on things such as the location of after-school programs, vacant lots, sites of illegal trash dumping, fire hydrants and other water sources, emergency evacuation sites, cell towers and signal strength, public computer access points, and historic landmarks. These data are collected and shared in partnership with a range of adults representing schools, city councils, departments of housing and social services, chambers of commerce, libraries, police and fire departments, hospitals, and local businesses.

Redefining Youth–Adult Roles

Traditional boundaries of space and time are traversed as 4-H youth engage in mapping activities across school and out-of-school time and collect related data across different physical spaces in the community. But more centrally, these projects illustrate the way in which ubiquitous learning brings together youth and adult worldviews and interests, as well as technology and information literacy practices previously situated within more discrete home, work, and education contexts. Learning and collaborative work that cross these borders illustrate a "new relational order" (Haythornthwaite, chapter 4 of this volume) in which questions of expertise, standards of practice, and educational purpose must be reexamined.

In discussions about the question "What defines our community?" youth and adult responses often reflect different perceptions, interests, and areas of expertise. The model of "youth as learner" and "adult as teacher" no longer fits within a framework of ubiquitous learning. At least three dimensions of expertise or knowledge that are brought together within youth–adult partnerships for community mapping include the following: (1) tool expertise, (2) content expertise, and (3) context expertise. Take, for instance, the example of a project that maps emergency evacuation sites. Youth may bring knowledge of how to use handheld technologies for data collection (e.g., digital cameras and GPS devices), while an adult partner may bring tool expertise related to GIS software used to visualize the data. Another adult partner may contribute content knowledge regarding the criteria that define a suitable emergency evacuation site, while youth bring knowledge of their community context. The mix of contributed knowledge varies from project to project, but in each case the roles of teacher and learner are fluid across youth and adult participants.

This fluidity of roles is further shaped by the affordance of handheld data collection technologies to create portable, socially interactive, context-sensitive, and individualized learning experiences (Klopfer and Squire 2008). These data collection devices include GPS units, PDAs, cell phones, and video cameras. In the context of community mapping projects, youth move with these technologies from their club meeting, to the streets of their city, to the workplace of partner organizations. Just as the lines between youth and adult worlds are increasingly blurred, so are the lines between when we are playing, working, and learning with these technologies. Diverse experiences brought together within the context of collaborative community mapping require negotiation of new standards of use for these tools that no longer fit neatly within home, work, and education contexts of practice. Central to this negotiation are questions about data accuracy and reliability. What is the measure of accurate data? How much data are needed to reliably answer questions about the community?

As youth and adults bring together different knowledge of their community within mapping projects, they also bring different standards of use for the technologies utilized in these efforts. For instance, the standards of accurate information within the context of using geospatial data to conduct a treasure hunt, or "geocache," may be quite different from the standards for using geospatial data to inform decisions about the location of emergency evacuation sites (see figure 9.1). Harvey and Chrisman (1998) outline a framework of GIS technology as a "boundary object," socially constructed through negotiation across a web of social relationships. As boundary objects, GIS maps serve to distinguish differences while also providing common points of reference among collaborators. The design features of GIS technology that afford its role as a boundary object include online and asynchronous editing of shared objects, layering of diverse datasets, multimodal representations, and customizable units of analysis. These features align with several of the "moves" within ubiquitous learning outlined by Cope and Kalantzis in chapter 1 of this volume (see table 9.1).

Principles of Mutuality within New Social Arrangements

The central proposition of this chapter is that border crossing, as in the example of collaborative community mapping projects, challenges traditional youth and adult roles. This central move within ubiquitous learning calls on us, as educators and designers, to better understand how to facilitate mutuality within these new arrangements for youth–adult interactions. The word "mutual," in this case, describes a relationship of reciprocal dependence, action, or influence in which

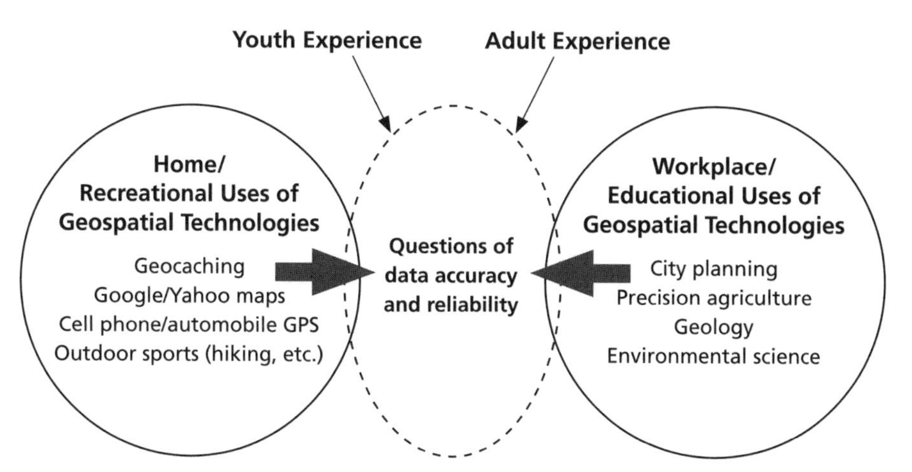

Figure 9.1. Negotiated standards of technology use within collaborative community mapping projects.

Table 9.1. Geographic Information Systems (GIS) Affordances for Ubiquitous Learning

GIS Features/Affordances	Moves toward Ubiquitous Learning*
Online access to shared objects Asynchronous and distributed editing	Blur traditional institutional, spatial, and temporal boundaries of education
Layers of diverse datasets representing different viewpoints and interests on the same geographic space	Use differences among learners as a productive resource
Customizable unit of analysis that situates data of interest within larger, collectively constructed framework	Connect one's own thinking to distributed cognition and collective intelligence
Multimodal representations (geospatial view, spreadsheet view, address data points, video data points, etc.)	Broaden the range and mix of representational modes

*See chapter 1 of this volume.

there is shared contribution and shared gain. As Fielding describes, "the accepted roles of student and teacher become less mutually exclusive, more open to extension and reversal, more open to mutual learning, more welcoming of a radical collegiality" (2001, 108).

The concept of mutuality is not new to education and can be found within research that connects positive youth outcomes to relationships with caring adults (Benson et al. 1998; Eccles and Gootman 2002; Grossman and Johnson 1999; Hererra et al. 2000; Jekielek et al. 2002; Paisley and Ferrari 2005; Peterson 2001; Pittman 1992; Scales and Gibbons 1996; Sipe 2000) and attributes improved student and school outcomes to programs that promote student voice (Costello et al. 2000; Fielding 2001, 2004; McLaughlin 1999; Mitra 2004; Takanishi 1993).

Classrooms and programs that seek to connect learning experiences for youth to the practices of adult communities often claim a goal for "real-world" or authentic learning. The curricular models loosely categorized under this umbrella reflect varied design approaches, including project-based or problem-based learning (Hmelo, Gotterer, and Bransford 1997), anchored instruction (Cognition and Technology Group 1990), workplace apprenticeships (Fuller et al. 2005; Hamilton 1990), and service learning (Youniss and Yates 1997). Many of these curricular designs trace their inspiration to work by John Dewey (1938) and other situative learning theorists (Brown, Collins, and Duguid 1989; Vygotsky 1978) who argue the importance of context, discourse, community tools, and social interaction as scaffolds for learning. The rhetoric of real-world learning is a prominent theme within educational reform (Petraglia 1998), yet the assumptions about what we recognize as real-world learning and how we expect to support those learning experiences remain undertheorized (Radinsky et al. 1999).

"Third space" research—across anthropology, education, psychology, and human–computer interaction—offers a promising framework through which to advance our understanding of the measure of mutuality within learning environments that seek to achieve ubiquity by crossing borders between youth and adult communities of practice (see figure 9.2). Defined as the overlapping space of two communities, "third space" is characterized by the hybridity of knowledge, practice, and viewpoint offered by the diverse participants (Bhabha 1994). The attributes of activity within this space—such as decentered authority, ill-defined tasks, diverse perspectives, and a need for negotiation and dialogue to bridge differences—are connected to opportunities for mutuality within learning environments (Bouillion and Gomez 2001; Gutiérrez, Baquedano-Lopez, and Tejeda 1999; Moje et al. 2004). As diverse literatures are considered together, it is interesting to note the similarity between characterizations of "third spaces" and characterizations of authentic learning activities, which include ill-defined and complex tasks completed over a period of time, opportunities for collaboration, opportunities to examine tasks from different perspectives, and opportunities for reflection (Reeves, Herrington, and Oliver 2002).

While the framework of third space is useful in characterizing principles of mutuality, it leaves us with many questions about how to productively and successfully sustain activity between youth and adults within an overlapping space that is reflective of both communities and retains true hybridity. As previously outlined, the space of hybridity is characterized as unpredictable, ill-defined, and potentially contentious. Many "real-world" constraints have the potential to shape youth–adult collaborations in ways that privilege or reflect one community of practice over the other, making it difficult to achieve youth–adult partnerships of mutual benefit (Bouillion and Gomez 2001; Radinsky et al. 1999). For instance, when the adult(s) is involved primarily for altruistic reasons and has a limited stake in the content or product outcome, the activity is more likely to reflect and be shaped by youth interests, knowledge, and practices. Although youth engagement and ownership are potential gains in this scenario, they come

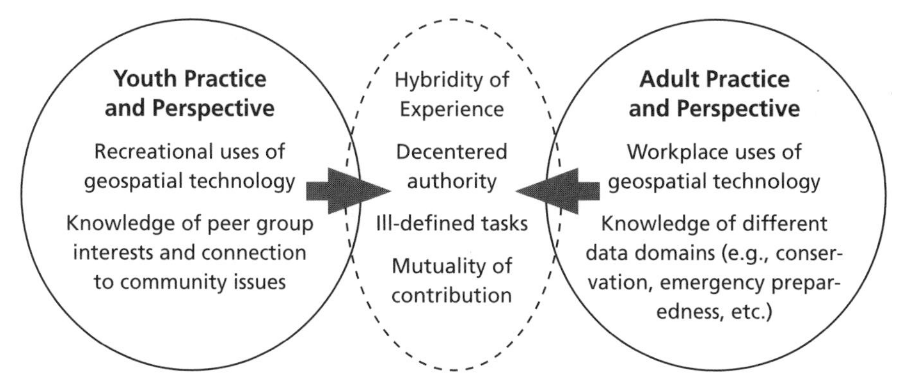

Figure 9.2. Features of collaborative community mapping as a "third space."

with a potential trade-off in lack of rigorous content and/or application of that content to adult worlds of practice. On the other hand, youth–adult activities may privilege adult expectations and experience, particularly when the adults have a high-stakes investment in the content or product outcome (e.g., standardized test scores or a time-specific workplace need for the activity product). The potential gain is that youth may develop a deeper understanding of content and practice related to the adult community. The trade-off is the risk that youth will fail to see the relevance and meaning of this activity to their own lives.

The ubiquity of digital technologies in our society is chipping away at the borders of what we define as youth and adult practice, while also challenging us to reconsider how we define activities of education, work, and play. The design challenge before us is to identify and create new social arrangements that support sharing of expertise and mutuality in interactions that cross these borders. As illustrated in the example of collaborative community mapping, geospatial technologies afford such opportunities.

Readings and References

For further reading on promising practices in youth–adult relationships, see the January 2005 special issue of the *Journal of Community Psychology* and Karen Pittman (1992), *Defining the Fourth R: Promoting Youth Development through Building Relationships.* For further exploration of "third space" applications, see the 2006 special issue of *Mind, Culture, and Activity* and the literature review by Michael Muller (2003), also available at IBM Watson Research Center, http://domino.research.ibm.com/cambridge/research.nsf/0/56844f3de38f806285256aaf005a45ab?OpenDocument. For further reading on boundary objects, see John Seely Brown and Paul Duguid's 1994 article, "Borderline Issues: Social and Material Aspects of Design," *Human–Computer Interaction* 9(1): 3–36, and Theresa D. Anderson's 2007 review, "Settings, Arenas and Boundary Objects: Socio-material Framings of Information Practices," *Information Research* 12(4): available at InformationR.net, http://InformationR.net/ir/12-4/colis/colis10.html.

Benson, Peter L., Nancy Leffert, Peter C. Scales, and Dale A. Blyth. 1998. "Beyond the 'Village' Rhetoric: Creating Healthy Communities for Children and Youth." *Applied Developmental Science* 2(3): 138–59.

Bhabha, Homi K. 1994. *The Location of Culture.* London: Routledge.

Bouillion, Lisa, and Louis Gomez. 2001. "Connecting School and Community with Science Learning: Real World Problems and School–Community Partnerships as Contextual Scaffolds." *Journal of Research in Science Teaching* 38(8): 878–98.

Brown, John Seely, Allan Collins, and Paul Duguid. 1989. "Situated Cognition and the Culture of Learning." *Educational Researcher* 18:32–42.

Cognition and Technology Group at Vanderbilt. 1990. "Anchored Instruction and Its Relationship to Situated Cognition." *Educational Researcher* 19(5): 2–10.

Cole, Michael, and Yrjö Engestrom. 1993. "A Cultural-Historical Approach to Distributed Cognition." In *Distributed Cognitions: Psychological and Educational Considerations,* ed. Gavriel Salomon, 1–46. Cambridge: Cambridge University Press.

Costello, Joan, Mark Toles, Julie Spielberger, and Joan Wynn. 2000. "History, Ideology and Structure Shape the Organizations That Shape Youth." In *Youth Development: Issues, Challenges, and Directions,* ed. Natalie Jaffe, 185–231. Philadelphia: Public/Private Ventures.

Dewey, John. 1902. *The Child and the Curriculum.* Chicago: University of Chicago Press.

———. 1938. *Experience and Education.* New York: Collier Books.

Eccles, Jacquelynne, and Jennifer Appleton Gootman, eds. 2002. *Community Programs to Promote Youth Development.* Washington, D.C.: National Academy Press.

Fielding, Michael. 2001. "Beyond the Rhetoric of Student Voice: New Departures or New Constraints in the Transformation of 21st Century Schooling." *Forum* 43(2): 100–110.

———. 2004. "Transformative Approaches to Student Voice: Theoretical Underpinnings, Recalcitrant Realities." *British Educational Research Journal* 30(2): 295–311.

Fuller, Alison, Heather Hodkinson, Phil Hodkinson, and Lorna Unwin. 2005. "Learning as Peripheral Participation in Communities of Practice: A Reassessment of Key Concepts in Workplace Learning." *British Educational Research Journal* 31(1): 49–68.

Grossman, Jean B., and Amy Johnson. 1999. "Assessing the Effectiveness of Mentoring Programs." In *Contemporary Issues in Mentoring,* ed. Jean Baldwin Grossman, 25–47. Philadelphia: Public/Private Ventures.

Gutiérrez, Kris D., Patricia Baquedano-Lopez, and Carlos Tejeda. 1999. "Rethinking Diversity: Hybridity and Hybrid Language Practices in the Third Space." *Mind, Culture, and Activity: An International Journal* 6(4): 286–303.

Hamilton, Stephen F. 1990. *Apprenticeship for Adulthood.* New York: Free Press.

Harvey, Francis, and Nicholas Chrisman. 1998. "Boundary Objects and the Social Construction of GIS Technology." *Environment and Planning* 30(9): 1,683–94.

Herrera, Carla, Cynthia L. Sipe, Wendy S. McClanahan, with Amy J. A. Arbreton and Sarah K. Pepper. 2000. *Mentoring School-Age Children: Relationship Development in Community-Based and School-Based Programs.* Philadelphia: Public/Private Ventures.

Hmelo, Cindy E., Gerald S. Gotterer, and John D. Bransford. 1997. "A Theory-Driven Approach to Assessing the Cognitive Effects of PBL." *Instructional Science* 25(6): 387–408.

Jekielek, Susan M., Kristin A. Moore, Elizabeth C. Hair, and Harriet J. Scarupa. 2002. *Mentoring: A Promising Strategy for Youth Development.* Washington, D.C.: Child Trends Research Brief.

Klopfer, Eric, and Kurt Squire. 2008. "Environmental Detectives: The Development of an Augmented Reality Platform for Environmental Simulations." *Educational Technology Research and Development* 56(2): 203–28.

McLaughlin, Milbrey. 1999. *Community Counts: How Community Organizations Matter for Youth Development.* Washington, D.C.: Public Education Network.

Mitra, Dana L. 2004. "The Significance of Students: Can Increasing 'Student Voice' in Schools Lead to Gains in Youth Development?" *Teachers College Record* 106(4): 651–88.

Moje, Elizabeth B., Kathryn M. Ciechanowski, Katherine Kramer, Lindsay Ellis, Rosario Carrilo, and Tehani Collazo. 2004. "Working toward Third Space in Content Area Literacy: An Examination of Everyday Funds of Knowledge and Discourse." *Reading Research Quarterly* 39(1): 38–70.

Muller, Michael. 2003. "Participatory Design: The Third Space in HCI." In *The Human-Computer Interaction Handbook*, ed. Julie A. Jacko and Andrew Sears, 464–81. Mahwah, N.J.: Lawrence Erlbaum Associates.

Paisley, Jessica E., and Theresa M. Ferrari. 2005. "Extent of Positive Youth–Adult Relationships in a 4-H After-School Program." *Journal of Extension* 43(2): article no. 2RIB4. Available at Journal of Extension, http://www.joe.org/Joe/2005april/Rb4.Shtml.

Peterson, William. 2001. *National 4-H Impact Assessment Project.* Tucson: University of Arizona Cooperative Extension.

Petraglia, Joseph. 1998. *Reality by Design: The Rhetoric and Technology of Authenticity in Education.* Mahwah, N.J.: Lawrence Erlbaum Associates.

Pittman, Karen. 1991. *A New Vision: Promoting Youth Development; Strengthening the Role of Youth-Serving and Community Organizations.* Washington, D.C.: AED Center for Youth Development and Policy Research.

———. 1992. *Defining the Fourth R: Promoting Youth Development through Building Relationships.* Washington, D.C.: Academy for Educational Development, Center for Youth Development and Policy Research.

Radinsky, Josh, Lisa Bouillion, Elaine Lento, and Louis Gomez. 1999. "Mutual Benefit Partnership: A Curricular Design for Authenticity." *Journal of Curriculum Studies* 33(4): 405–30.

Reeves, Thomas Charles, Jan Herrington, and Ron Oliver. 2002. "Authentic Activities and Online Learning." In *Quality Conversations: Research and Development in Higher Education,* ed. Allan Goody, Jan Herrington, and Maria Northcote, 25:562–67. Jamieson Centre, Australia: Higher Education Research and Development Society of Australasia.

Scales, Peter C., and Judith L. Gibbons. 1996. "Extended Family Members and Unrelated Adults in the Lives of Young Adolescents: A Research Agenda." *Journal of Early Adolescence* 16(4): 365–89.

Sipe, Cynthia L. 2000. "Mentoring Adolescents: What Have We Learned?" In *Contemporary Issues in Mentoring,* ed. Jean Grossman, 10–23. Philadelphia: Public/Private Ventures.

Takanishi, Ruby. 1993. "Changing Views of Adolescence in Contemporary Society." In *Adolescence in the 1990s: Risk and Opportunity,* ed. Ruby Takanishi, 1–7. New York: Teachers College Press.

Vygotsky, Lev. 1978. *Mind in Society: The Development of the Higher Psychological Processes.* Cambridge, Mass.: Harvard University Press.

Youniss, James, and Miranda Yates. 1997. *Community Service and Social Responsibility in Youth.* Chicago: University Of Chicago Press.

10

Digital Divide and Higher Education in Sub-Saharan Africa

FAZAL RIZVI

The Commonwealth of Nations is a most curious international organization. It is a voluntary association of more than fifty independent sovereign states, most of which were once British colonies, but which now hold strong postcolonial aspirations. It has lofty goals, which include the promotion of democracy, human rights, and good governance, but little wealth in common with which to pay for its ambitious plans. The interests of the richer Commonwealth countries, such as Australia, Canada, and Britain, seem to lie elsewhere—with the more influential international groups, such as the Organisation for Economic Co-operation and Development—while its poorer members are relegated to the margins of the global political system. Yet the Commonwealth heads of government meet regularly, even if little is achieved at these meetings beyond pious rhetoric about the need for cooperation. It is difficult to point to any significant outcomes resulting from these meetings, in any policy area.

Perhaps a notable exception to this is education, where cooperation among Commonwealth countries has ranged from such international scholarship programs as the Colombo Plan to its more recent initiatives in open learning and distance education. The Commonwealth has always viewed education as fundamental to social and economic development. This sentiment was reiterated by the Commonwealth ministers of education at their meeting in December 2006, held in Cape Town, South Africa. Much of their discussion centered on globalization and the implications of the new information economy on educational policy and practice. Given its location, the meeting explored the potential that the new technologies had for expanding access to education, particularly higher education, especially in the sub-Saharan countries. Much of this debate focused on the idea of a "digital divide." Repeatedly, the ministers argued that information technology had become a fundamental tool of development and that the issues pertaining to the digital divide were now urgent. With one voice, they insisted that Africa had no alternative but to participate in the global flows of information and communication.

In this chapter, I want to examine the idea of the digital divide, as it is commonly used to characterize global inequalities, and discuss some of the initiatives that have been taken for overcoming it. In particular, I want to consider the case of the African Virtual University (AVU), sponsored initially by the World Bank but now supported by both the Commonwealth and a range of other international organizations. AVU is designed to provide greater access to higher education in sub-Saharan Africa. Its business model is predicated on a number of assumptions. It regards online learning as not only an affordable, flexible, and effective means of delivering higher education within the African context but also a way of preparing Africans to participate in the global economy. It thus underlines the university's potential to bridge the digital divide. I want to assess these claims, and I will argue that initiatives such as AVU are based on a very limited conception of the digital divide and that unless they broaden their view of learning, in ubiquitous terms as defined in this collection, they risk reproducing and perhaps even extending the problems of global inequalities in higher education that they seek to address.

Although the term "digital divide" is little over ten years old, it has quickly become part of a new global slogan system—so much so that it now masks more than it elucidates the nature of the stratifications between those who are and those who are not digitally networked. Just the same, the idea of the digital divide does point to something significant in the ways in which social and economic development has now become highly dependent on a country's capacity to participate in the new information economy. This new economy, as Manuel Castells (2000), among others, has pointed out, is characterized largely by its articulation of scientific and technological processes, the shift from material production to information processing, the emergence and expansion of new forms of networked industrial organizations, and the rise of socioeconomic globalization. Castells argues that economic productivity is now linked to the quality of information and its management in the processes of production, consumption, distribution, and trade. This is so because information processing industries such as health care, banking, software, biotechnology, media, and of course education have now become dominant, and because global trade now involves global circuits of knowledge exchange and data processing.

If participation in information-rich industries has become fundamental to economic development, then the idea of the digital divide implies lack of access to those technologies that enable such participation. However, given the complexity of "informationalism," as Castells calls it, the digital divide cannot simply refer to the uneven distribution of the technological hardware across communities. It is a much more complicated and multidimensional phenomenon that incorporates a whole range of factors, from access to computers to the manner in which knowledge is now produced and distributed. Pippa Norris (2001) has, for example, suggested that the idea of the digital divide encompasses three distinct chasms: first, a global digital divide, which refers to the unequal Internet access between industrialized and developing societies; second, a social divide, which describes the separation between information-rich and information-poor sectors in each nation; and finally, and more significantly, a democratic divide, which signifies the differences between those who do and do not use the enormous and growing resources of the Internet to engage, mobilize, and participate in public life.

But even this corrective does not fully capture the complexities surrounding the idea of the digital divide. With the size of the online community doubling every year (van Dijk 2005), it is now clear that the Internet is transforming the way people live, work, interact, and play. Few now doubt that digital technologies have dramatically increased the flow of capital, goods, and services within the global marketplace. The Internet has not only become an important component of economic activity but also a ubiquitous source of information. For the developing countries, however, the Internet in particular and the digital technologies in general bring into play both risks and benefits. On the one hand, the digital technologies provide the developing countries opportunities to leapfrog various stages of economic and social development, while, on the other hand, the digital economy fundamentally favors information-rich societies. The voices of the developing countries on the Internet are almost entirely absent. As Ferguson (2006) notes, in the neoliberal world order, sub-Saharan Africa has been pushed further into what he calls the "global shadows." Africa is inextricably linked to the global economy, yet in ways that further marginalize its voices.

The Internet age thus has the potential to extend the disparities between the postindustrial economies at the core of the global economic system and the developing societies at the periphery. The richer economies are able to use the digital technologies to boost productivity, while the poorer societies are left in a position to play catch-up, which they can seldom do, owing to the fast-changing nature of these technologies. The Commonwealth ministers in Cape Town were fully aware of the always shifting nature of the new technologies and recognized the potential they had to reinforce the patterns of stratification in the new economy. Indeed, they acknowledged that the network society was creating uneven communication systems: one for those with income, education, and literal connectivity and the other for those without the connectivity and rich information upon which the new economy is clearly based. The problem of the digital divide is thus linked to the structural exclusion of most sub-Saharan nations from the information economy, where know-how and data have replaced land and capital as the basic drivers of economic growth and productivity. But what the ministers did not fully appreciate was the need to understand the digital divide in *relational* terms, rather than in terms of deficit of both equipment and skills.

In their policy deliberations, the ministers continued to interpret the idea of the digital divide as largely a matter of access to technological hardware and Internet connectivity. To overcome the digital divide, their policy proposals thus remained centered on initiatives that sought the provision of computers and connectivity. It has become increasingly clear, however, that the issues of access to equipment and connectivity can be solved by higher levels of investment and the availability of inexpensive computers. For instance, the MIT Media Lab's much-publicized $100 computer, now referred to as XO-1, will soon be a reality, as might be the ways to solve the problems of broadband. Nevertheless, these initiatives by themselves will not close the digital divide, because even if all students throughout sub-Saharan Africa were given free computers, they might still be unable to use them in pedagogically effective ways. The problem of literacy and technical skills required to access the information and services available on the Internet would still remain. As Warschauer (2003) suggests, the debate about the digital divide must now shift from the concern about the uneven provision of equipment to a focus on the challenges facing the effective integration of technology into communities, institutions, and societies. What is important, he argues, is not so much the physical availability of computers and the Internet but rather people's ability to make use of those technologies to engage in meaningful social practices.

The Commonwealth ministers in Cape Town were of course not unaware of this basic point. They therefore reiterated the importance of access to higher education, both in overcoming the digital divide and in taking advantage of the opportunities offered by the new digital economy. Indeed, they maintained that if the failure to access and use new technologies implied an even greater marginalization from the world economy, then the developing nations had no other option but to invest in forms of higher education that contributed to the development of competencies and skills appropriate for the successful participation in the new knowledge economy. Furthermore, they favored those programs that used the new technologies to meet the fast-growing demand for higher education in sub-Saharan Africa, a region very much lacking public resources for building and developing university campuses. They maintained that the new technologies had the potential to increase efficiency in the provision and quality of higher education through more flexible forms of delivery, and they favored those initiatives that used these technologies to "scale-up" the delivery of online programs, as long as new policies were also developed to coordinate the accreditation, recognition, and quality assurance of online programs, especially when these were offered across national borders.

An example of such an initiative to expand access to higher education to students throughout sub-Saharan Africa, widely discussed at the Commonwealth meeting in Cape Town, is the African Virtual University. As described by Juma (2006), AVU was established in 1996 as a World Bank project and was originally conceptualized as a technology-based distance education network to bridge the digital divide in Africa, especially by building capabilities in science, computer studies, and engineering. It was designed partly to meet the fast-growing demand for higher education in Africa and was viewed as an alternative to the traditional and expensive methods required to build and run brick-and-mortar universities. AVU's delivery model sought to make extensive use of satellite and Internet technologies, allowing it to offer online programs from around the world, while taking into account the infrastructural limitations prevailing in Africa. In this way, AVU did not feel compelled to develop its own distinctive programs. Rather, it purchased content that was already developed elsewhere, offering it to its students under license through a network of learning centers.

In the first phase of its operations (1997–99), AVU offered short courses developed at institutions in the United States, Ireland, and Canada, as well as the World Bank. During the second phase (1999–2002), it established thirty-one learning centers in seventeen African countries, which helped students to complete the learning requirements of the courses offered. During this period, AVU viewed its efforts in improving connectivity among the AVU's central campus and learning centers, the host African universities, and the mostly Western universities that had developed the content as a way of bridging the digital divide (Juma 2006, 350). Because this training involved regional and global interconnectivity, AVU expected its programs to also serve as a catalyst for new investment and economic development in sub-Saharan Africa. During the current phase (2002–7), the number of learning centers has expanded significantly, and AVU now offers degree programs in computer science and management. For example, AVU provides two degree programs, which it has purchased from the Royal Melbourne Institute of Technology (RMIT) and Curtin University of Technology in Australia. It now possesses its own Very Small Aperture Terminal (VSAT), a satellite communications system that handles data, voice, and video signals.

In fewer than ten years, AVU has thus taken major strides in providing programs to countless numbers of students who would not otherwise have had access to higher education. Its short courses, in particular, have built the capacity of many people in different occupations. In addition, it has managed to develop an impressive array of partnerships with overseas universities and various institutions such as the African American Institute, the Australian Agency for International Development, and the Association of Canadian Universities and Colleges. Moreover, it has encouraged, albeit to a very small degree, resource mobilization and sharing across the sub-Saharan region. It has also arguably generated among African scholars a greater interest in ICT-enhanced learning and the ways in which technology could be used to improve the quality of teaching and learning. And finally it can claim to have encouraged greater participation of African women in science and engineering.

Despite these achievements, however, AVU has been beset by a range of administrative, technical, and academic problems, as Juma (2006) has noted. To begin with, it has had to follow administrative policies and processes that are in line with local accountability requirements, making decision-making processes both slow and often inflexible and coordination across national systems cumbersome and difficult. The African partner universities in the network have often perceived AVU as a competitor rather than as a partner. The attempts by AVU to secure national and international accreditation for its courses have been complex and have taken years. Costs have also been a problem, not only in terms of the license fee charged by international partners but also in relation to the technology infrastructure required to teach the courses. Despite its obvious advantages, the costs of delivering programs via satellite technologies have become prohibitive. For example, delivering the required twelve hours of instruction per week per course costs $US 12,000 (Juma 2006). This higher delivery cost has of course been transferred to the students' tuition fees, making AVU courses accessible only to the African elite. Many AVU students have transferred their enrollment to the cheaper public universities as soon as they have been able to. Not surprisingly, then, AVU has consistently failed to reach its enrollment goals, and its graduation rates have been uniformly poor.

However, beyond these practical problems, it is perhaps more important to look at AVU's operating model and ask to what extent it represents a way forward and has the potential to bridge the digital divide. Here we encounter a number of conceptual concerns that reveal AVU's philosophy to be underpinned by a narrow view of access to higher education, a flawed understanding of the sources of the digital divide, and a limited view of the nature of learning. In organizational terms, AVU functions on a model that seeks to tap the best international resources, programs that would otherwise be inaccessible to African students. It pays a license fee for the course content with the expectation that this content will be modified to suit the local conditions. This model is based on the assumption that a skilled and entrepreneurial labor force developed through international programs is more likely to generate economic investment and productivity than the local programs, and that the "brain drain" will be reduced because Africans will have international educational resources within Africa.

Now, each of these assumptions can be questioned. There is no guarantee, for example, that armed with international qualifications, the graduates of AVU will not still want to emigrate to Western countries where their professional competencies are equally valued, and where there exists a clearly identified need for their skilled labor. That international qualifications will generate greater economic investment in Africa is also a highly questionable assumption, based on a deficit view of the quality of the programs that the existing African universities already offer. Such an assumption reproduces a hoary colonial view of the capacity of Africans to develop their own effective programs appropriate to the local needs and conditions and to their engagement with the global economic processes. AVU had hoped that its international programs would be modified as a result of local input, but this has been resisted both by African students who want what they regard as an authentic overseas qualification and by international partners who consider this task an additional burden for which they are not adequately recompensed.

It is clear that the AVU operating model is based on a market logic that does not view transnational collaboration as intrinsically good but as a service that is purchased from an international content developer under certain licensing arrangements. Thus, it is not surprising that earlier courses by leading American institutions, like MIT, were not sustained beyond the first few years. Their contributions were replaced instead by the more commercially motivated operators like Australia's RMIT and Curtin universities. In its current phase, AVU has become a corporate entity. As a nonprofit organization with its headquarters in Nairobi, Kenya, it is now concerned more with its financial sustainability than with the broader issues of educational disadvantage in Africa. AVU has not only commodified its programs, but it now also competes for a greater share of the educational market with local and international providers. Within this market logic, it clearly provides access to online programs, but only to those students who are able to pay. It thus works with a very narrow conception of educational access, inadequate for meeting the broader challenges of the digital divide in sub-Saharan Africa.

Perhaps even more significant, the AVU educational model appears to be based on a fundamental distinction between the development of the course content and its delivery. The course content is developed by international academics who are not themselves involved in teaching it and who often have little knowledge of the African context. It is left up to the tutors at the local learning centers to communicate the significance of the content to local students. While this cultural translation always involves processes of interpretation—appropriate and active negotiation of content on the part of the tutors and students—the fact remains that this pedagogic model embodies an assumption of unmediated reception of content that is often assumed to be culturally neutral. But as a number of recent learning theorists in the sociocultural tradition have pointed out, this is a fundamentally misguided view of how knowledge is acquired. The contexts of content design and its delivery cannot be so easily separated, and education is most effective when learners are not only consumers of knowledge, but also its active creators.

This observation is fundamental to the conception of learning that lies at the heart of the idea of ubiquity. As Bill Cope and Mary Kalantzis argue, online programs that simply reproduce "heritage classroom and book-oriented approaches" fail to explore the new possibilities afforded by the digital media. Despite good intentions, AVU's model of learning remains trapped within the "old pedagogical practices of didactic teaching, content delivery for student indigestion, and testing for the right answers" (Cope and Kalantzis, chapter 1 in this volume). Its learning management system and its network of learning centers reproduce, albeit in a new medium, older models of communication and forms of pedagogic relationships. In short, the potential of digital technologies to afford new modes of learning that can seriously address issues of the digital divide is not realized.

The idea of ubiquitous learning holds greater promise. It seeks to blur the traditional institutional, spatial, and temporal boundaries and shifts the balance of agency. The student is no longer in a subordinate position to the content developer and is thus able to challenge culturally biased constructions of knowledge. It permits lateral student-to-student communication as well as the development of new epistemic communities that have the potential to dispute, in the case of the developing countries, colonial assumptions that are often embedded in the content produced in the developed world. AVU's pedagogic model is based fundamentally, as I have already noted, on a distinction between knowledge makers and knowledge users, as well as on a particular conception of pedagogic power. Ubiquitous learning, on the other hand, undermines such a relational order, as Haythornthwaite calls it in this volume, releasing new possibilities of learning based on principles that recognize learners' differences and that view them as a productive resource.

Insofar as the traditional models of online learning continue to privilege content over pedagogy, they fail to recognize that knowledge is produced and utilized in a range and mix of representational modes. If the participation in the global information economy is not simply about formal access to higher levels of education but about negotiating and working with the complex architectures of knowledge in ways that are both creative and critical, then effective learning in this new media requires the development of new capacities that are defined by "a peculiar conceptualizing sensibility, sophisticated forms of pattern recognition, and schematization" (Cope and Kalantzis, chapter 1 in this volume). But beyond this, such learning requires building collaborative cultures through which it is possible for groups of students to understand and challenge global inequalities, using a whole range of knowledge traditions and sources.

AVU's approach to bridging the digital divide appears restricted to the desire to increase the number of students enrolled in online programs. What the idea of ubiquitous learning suggests, on the other hand, is that this approach is based on a very limited view of the potential afforded by new digital media. If the digital divide is not simply about access but also about pedagogic relations and critical capacities, then any serious attempt to address it demands African scholars and students to build their own epistemic communities that draw on both African and other knowledge traditions to engage with the dominant knowledge that is circulating in the global media, and that is often embodied in the content of the course developed in the Western metropole. The thrust of initiatives to bridge the digital divide should not be, as Besser (2001) has pointed out, to create a new body of digital age consumers, but rather, people who are able to become active participants in global communication systems and who are able to produce knowledge that is appropriate to the local conditions and needs. Without the development of this capacity, Africans are likely to remain trapped within an asymmetrical global knowledge system, which while it connects the whole world into a series of networks of flows, does so selectively, and which reproduces the patterns of existing power relations.

The current global system of knowledge is decidedly skewed toward the West. Much of the content on the Internet is produced in the developed countries, where English is the dominant language. As Castells (2000) has pointed out, the developed countries are able to leverage the opportunities offered by the information economy to further reinforce their economic power. He has argued that while the fault lines of marginality might not necessarily follow the current divide between North and South, it is difficult to see societies where education is grossly underfunded and where there is far too much reliance of knowledge products imported from abroad, closing the gap between themselves and those societies already at the core of the information revolution. It is more likely that experiments like AVU will produce segments within African countries that are integrated into the global information economy, while the bulk of their population remains outside its scope.

What this analysis suggests is the need for a different pedagogic model for Africa, into which global and local knowledge traditions are integrated. If the digital divide is to be challenged in a serious fashion, then such a model would seek to draw on the enormous reservoir of knowledge available on the Internet, some of which is free as a result of such democratic initiatives as Open Source and Creative Commons, but would seek, at the same time, to develop in students a capacity to critically interrogate them for their local relevance and utility. There is a huge gap at the moment in the appropriateness of online content for marginalized populations of the world, which threatens to reproduce and perhaps even greatly increase economic and social disparities. These disparities cannot, of course, be overcome by education alone, but they can be more effectively challenged by the inherently democratic principles of ubiquitous learning.

Readings and References

Besser, Howard. 2001. "The Next Digital Divides." *Teaching to Change LA* 1(2): http://www.tcla.gseis.ucla.edu/divide/politics/besser.html (accessed July 2007).

Castells, Manuel. 2000. *The Rise of the Network Society.* 2nd ed. Oxford: Blackwell.

Ferguson, James. 2006. *Global Shadows: Africa in the Neo-liberal World Order.* Durham, N.C.: Duke University Press.

Juma, M. N. 2006. "Kenyatta University: African Virtual University, Kenya Developments since 2003." In *The Virtual University,* ed. Susan D'Antoni, 97–110. Paris: UNESCO.

Norris, Pippa. 2001. *Digital Divide: Civic Engagement, Information Poverty, and the Internet Worldwide.* Cambridge: Cambridge University Press.

van Dijk, Jan. 2005. *The Deepening Divide: Inequality in the Information Society.* Thousand Oaks, Calif.: Sage.

Warschauer, Mark. 2003. *Technology and Social Inclusion: Rethinking the Digital Divide.* Cambridge, Mass.: MIT Press.

11

Cyberenvironments

Ubiquitous Research and Learning

JAMES D. MYERS AND
ROBERT E. MCGRATH

Over the past fifteen years, the World Wide Web has evolved from a tool created to support scientific research to a ubiquitous social infrastructure. The Web has had an enormous impact on society in terms of changes in practices and culture, in the emergence of new businesses and career paths, and in the extent to which our lifestyles have become dependent on its existence. Yet a mechanistic description of it—that it greatly simplifies sharing of text and multimedia information and enables links between documents—provides no more than a hint of its transformative power. Nonetheless, the Web has revolutionized our notion of how information is created and by whom. Wikis, blogs, and related tools enable personal publishing and the community development and evolution of resources (Wesch 2007), in stark contrast to traditional authoring and publishing. Who would have imagined when the first browser appeared that we would be able to access encyclopedias created by thousands of individuals (e.g., Wikipedia), and further, that we would be able to contribute our own knowledge back to them, from our home computers, in real time?

In science and engineering, adoption of the Web has been just one part of the broader adoption of cyberinfrastructure—high performance computing, instruments, data, networks of sensors, and analysis and visualization services all available via the Internet (Atkins et al. 2003; National Science Foundation Cyberinfrastructure Council 2007). Riding on the exponential increases in computational, data storage, and networking technologies, the development of "grids", "e-science", "science gateways", and "community databases," has given researchers access to more, and more powerful, resources than ever before, with a direct effect on scientific productivity.

However, we believe that cyberinfrastructure is also beginning to foster change in our conceptualization of research and learning processes in ways analogous to the Web's impact on our notion of information authoring and publishing. The availability of directly accessible data, instruments, and computational resources supports and is helping to catalyze a shift in scientific research toward multidisciplinary, systems-oriented studies and to close coupling of computational modeling with experimental observation. Researchers are also increasingly publishing data and experimental procedures independently, in addition to writing papers to summarize their work, which is enabling their colleagues to quickly assemble the data, instrumentation, and computational resources needed to reproduce results quickly and to extend the work in new directions. Similar to the way the Web enabled linking across Web sites, scientists can now link instruments, models, and analyses in computational workflows. Instead of a creating a text-centric encyclopedia, researchers are coordinating at the community level to collaboratively create reference databases that can feed data directly into workflows.

The National Center for Supercomputing Applications (NCSA) has coined the term "cyberenvironments" to describe systems designed to support both traditional research activities and the evolution of these types of new collaborative practices. Rather than focusing solely on *access to* advanced resources, cyberenvironments emphasize the continual creation of new resources, the dynamic integration of these shared resources into projects, and the direct publication of the new resources created in projects back into the community-level scientific context. Cyberenvironments are intended to support researchers in efficiently discovering, accessing, and integrating resources to explore new ideas and in disseminating their work, in a detailed and actionable form, to their colleagues.

How does this impact learning? First, working across disciplines and making use of shared resources requires much more just-in-time, agile learning and emphasizes packaging of resources with all the information needed to understand them (using technologies from the Semantic Web, for example). Thus a model made available as a service will link to the paper in which it is described, to sample data and outputs, to analyses in which it has been used, to notes about its quality and applicability for certain problems, to alternate models, and so forth. Knowing who created, annotated, and used the model in turn provides connections to a network of experts who may be able to answer questions. As researchers couple their own work with models or data created by others, and the type of rich metadata described above becomes available, researchers will increasingly view learning as a continual process that occurs as one works rather than a prework exercise (or something that ends with formal schooling). Such a model becomes very scalable once seeded, as each researcher's explorations add new metadata and new resources to the mix.

Such changes will not be limited to practicing researchers but will expand, just as the Web has, to impact students and the general population. Weather forecasts on the Web already link to the underlying radar and satellite data used to create them. We are entering an era where every news story and every textbook can link to the data and models behind them and, further, can provide a "live" cyberenvironment in which students and the public can question the assumptions in the analyses, add their own data, change models, and form their own conclusions. In the same way that researchers will pull relevant subsets of data from sensor networks and databases, and select models and tools that address their interests at the appropriate level of abstraction, students and the public will be able to find, or create, cyberenvironments appropriate for their current level of understanding. Students might, for example, model the damage expected from historical or potential future earthquakes using relatively simple assumptions that can be discussed in a classroom, refine the model on their own, run the current state-of-the-art model developed by researchers, and compare the results of each with the actual impacts of historic earthquake events. At any point in time they would have the option to discover pertinent information, other models, local experts, and related projects at other schools. Ultimately, it may be through exploration in such environments that students discover courses and textbooks that they may see as useful supplements to their self-guided inquiries.

Without the example of the Web, such a vision of ubiquitous and coupled research and learning could be dismissed as idle, utopian dreaming. We could not possibly define all the required data, modeling, and other infrastructure needed and coordinate a centralized project to create such a system. However, in the same manner that the Web provided a basic framework for content creation and a linking mechanism, which in turn enabled community-scale coordination and provided social and economic feedback mechanisms to allow identification of "what works," cyberinfrastructure and cyberenvironments can also be designed to enable decentralized efforts and harness network effects and "crowdsourcing" (Brabham 2008) to build incrementally toward the best solutions.

Scientific resources—data, instruments, models—are individually more structured, more complex, and generally more costly than the texts and images from which the Web is built. Furthermore, scientific theories and conceptual models are more complex than, for example, a list of favorites, and more precise than general recommendations. Both of these differences add some complexity and lead to requirements beyond what the current Web provides, but research, particularly within the Grid and Semantic Web communities, is identifying the appropriate interfaces, protocols, design patterns, and infrastructure that will be necessary. There are also a wide range of projects, two of which are discussed below as examples, that are demonstrating the value of cyberenvironments and the potential for ubiquitous research and learning practices.

Software Architecture: "Design for Innovation"

To act as a driver for new models of research practice and as an enabler of ubiquitous learning, cyberenvironments must be built to allow extensibility and evolution directly by end-users. As with the Web, this will require the development of cyberinfrastructure that separates how one creates and connects scientific resources from the specifics of what the resources are. In addition, cyberenvironments must make resources "actionable" in the same way that Web addresses (URLs) allow one to access any resource that is referenced. We will also need a mechanism that makes it possible, once given a reference, to query a database, run an instrument, or perform a computational experiment. In developing these capabilities, we must also recognize that, while scientific results may be relevant for centuries to come, the projects in which research work is done often last for only a few years. Thus the design of cyberenvironments must explicitly address the fact that resources may move over time and that, as a consequence of data owners' differing concerns, a wide range of access control policies will be applied to different resources and to individual resources.

While the technical details of what is needed are beyond the scope of this article, it is important to note that the required technologies do exist and are being combined into a usable framework today. Moreover, the required "design principles" are easy to state succinctly and, as with the Web, a mechanistic description of how cyberenvironments work will be broadly understandable. We have sketched the general architecture and technologies involved in cyberenvironments (Myers and Dunning 2006). At the highest level, the necessary mechanics include the following:

Semantic content management extends the Web concept of URLs as a way to retrieve content and access services with a mechanism to retrieve arbitrary metadata about these resources and a way to move resources over time (and be able to recognize resources at different URLs as copies).

Process management uses the notions of workflow and provenance to separate the overall pattern of activities and data involved in a process from the specifics of what mathematical/logical processing occurs in each step. This enables generic mechanisms for running processes and for tracking, for example, the fact that one dataset was created from another.

Virtual organization-based management separates concerns related to security, preferred vocabularies, standard practices, group organization, and related details into middleware from applications and resources. This would allow, for example, a workflow engine to be used with strict access controls for medical research and reused, with public data and nonproprietary algorithms, in a classroom—without change to the engine itself.

These design patterns can be seen as examples of "reflection" and "virtualization," techniques that have been used broadly in software development to enable rapid evolution and extension of systems by independent third parties (Myers and McGrath 2007).

In short, these mechanisms allow the creation of a cyberenvironment that would allow researchers or students to find data in community repositories; discover what it means (e.g., that the numbers represent speeds in meters per second); explore how it was created (e.g., that it was derived from sensors deployed at certain locations, that the sensors were calibrated using specific procedures, that the data are consistent with a particular model, and that bad values from broken sensors have been removed); feed it into a model developed elsewhere and pipe the output to the users' favorite visualization tools; and directly publish their findings and any new data or computational procedures they develop. The critical point is that these mechanisms work in all sorts of situations—observation and modeling of supernovae, assessing the impact of earthquakes, investigating chemical reactions, or understanding the impacts of global warming. Such a framework enables independent people to publish data, instruments, methods, and software services and for others to then "mash" them together to address specific issues and explore new directions. In the same way that we can now post videos to YouTube (http://www.youtube.com) and embed them in our own Web pages or add our own data to Google maps (http://www.google.com/apis/maps), we will soon be able to combine live scientific resources as needed to perform research, explain principles, and explore.

Case Study: Cyberenvironments for Science and Engineering

While the concept of cyberenvironments will take time to mature, there are already projects that incorporate aspects of their design and architectural patterns to provide novel functionality. The National Center for Supercomputing Applications (NCSA) and other groups are engaged with a number of communities driving toward end-to-end cyberenvironments tailored to their specific disciplines. Even at this stage, it is clear that cyberenvironments are not simply allowing researchers to accelerate their current practices. They are also allowing new types of research and collaboration that enable study of more complex systems.

THE COLLABORATORY FOR MULTI-SCALE CHEMICAL SCIENCES (CMCS)

CMCS is a U.S. Department of Energy–funded effort, led by Sandia National Laboratories and begun in 2001, that was designed to enhance information transfer between chemistry subdisciplines, including quantum chemistry, thermochemistry, kinetics, and combustion modeling (CMCS 2007; Myers et al. 2005; Schuchardt et al. 2005). CMCS has attracted international groups in a number of subfields who are coordinating their research efforts and acting as community "expert groups" to publish new reference data and models backed by rich information about their creation and ranges of validity. These distributed groups associated with CMCS have used the base content management and service integration capabilities of the system to assemble and curate computational and experimental data, to transparently exchange data between modelers who use different software with different file formats, and to stage data for use with newly developed tools. Through CMCS, they have statistically analyzed networks of thermochemical data and generated reduced kinetic mechanisms that run efficiently on high-performance computers.

In the area of thermochemistry, this new ability to gather data from researchers around the globe and statistically analyze it together has resulted in a tenfold improvement in the precision of our knowledge of the properties of important chemical species (Ruscic et al. 2005). Furthermore, any group wishing to understand this work, or to repeat or extend it, can (with permission) access the data, tools, and discussions that occurred, see the specific analyses that were performed, and create their own space to work in CMCS and perform "what-if" analyses that include new data.

Other groups using CMCS have likewise made chemistry advances, despite the fact that the core framework of CMCS has no chemical knowledge built in; CMCS just provides a framework in which chemists can assemble the data, tools, and expertise needed to address their research interests.

ENVIRONMENTAL CYBERINFRASTRUCTURE DEMONSTRATOR (ECID)

The ECID project at NCSA has developed components incorporating the design principles outlined above and has created an end-to-end cyberenvironment prototype targeting use cases in the context of environmental research and planning activities related to the Water and Environmental Research Systems (WATERS) Network (WATERS 2007). ECID incorporates a collaborative portal, workflow and modeling capabilities, the ability to connect to streaming data sources, metadata and data provenance management, and a social networking–based recommender system. The basic collaboration capabilities of ECID are being used to support the planning activities of the WATERS National Project Office. More advanced capabilities that enable the creation of "digital observatories" that synthesize underlying observational data and modeled results and provide an overall sense of the functioning of, say, a watershed, river, or bay are being piloted, as part of a follow-on effort, in research related to the causes and effects of pollution in different water systems (e.g., Corpus Christi/Nueces bays in Texas and the Illinois River basin).

ECID has also been used to demonstrate scenarios envisioned for future national environmental observatory efforts involving, for example, the ability to develop workflows for streaming sensor data analysis on the desktop and to then publish them to run on back-end servers to create new derived data products for the community. ECID is also exploring the use of data provenance and social network analysis (Contractor 2005) to provide alerts and recommendations about relevant data and new techniques that are relevant to a researcher's current efforts and to provide a dynamic, "always-on" overview of community activities.

Looking at ECID as a model for future cyberenvironments, one can identify several key aspects. First, ECID reduces the differences in working with local and remote data and computational resources by, for instance, allowing local and remote data to be brought into workflows using the same interface and by allowing workflows to be moved from desktop to remote resources. Second, ECID blurs the roles of end-user and contributor in that any user can be given permission to add data, documents, workflow templates, or new workflow processes to the system such that they become accessible to others in the same way as the original content. Third, ECID uses a number of strategies, from the basic use of workflow (which helps make the logic of a program more explicit to new users), to the incorporation of group spaces and collaboration tools, to the global use of metadata, provenance, and network browsing and recommendation capabilities to expose tacit knowledge and integrate learning and work activities into a seamless whole. These capabilities enable researchers to explore analyses and view recommendations for tools and data that have been used in similar problems in the past. In addition, users may dynamically create work groups (virtual organizations) around problems of interest. These groups can generate data, workflows, and documentation and publish this information directly to other researchers and students who can browse, use, and build on them.

Agenda: Ubiquitous Cyberenvironments for Learning

The examples discussed above provide some sense of how cyberinfrastructure and cyberenvironments are enabling new types of scientific coordination and allowing researchers to expand their studies to more complex systems and directly address problems of societal interest. We argue that these capabilities are not limited to science and engineering, nor to large, formal organizations. Similar collaborative activities are needed for business, public affairs, disaster management, education, and entertainment. Furthermore, they support many of the "moves" toward ubiquitous learning outlined in chapter 1.

MOVE 1: BLUR THE TRADITIONAL INSTITUTIONAL, SPATIAL, AND TEMPORAL BOUNDARIES OF EDUCATION

Students and informal learners at all levels will have access to actual datasets, experimental tools, computational models, provenance trails, and other scientific resources through cyberenvironments, at any time from any location. Scientific data, literature, methods, instruments, and experts will be accessible in any context, not just in science class or the laboratory. All participants will play the role of teacher and learner throughout their active lives.

MOVE 2: SHIFT THE BALANCE OF AGENCY

Cyberenvironments allow students to actively engage in research and to create their own experiences, exploring as far as they like—from simplified explanations to the cutting edge of understanding. Student work will be captured and can be published for the benefit of others, making each student an active scientist and teacher. Furthermore, all participants will be able to contribute to the cumulative knowledge as citizen scientists. In these environments, the notions of teacher versus student, scientist versus citizen, and professional versus amateur become less distinct.

MOVE 3: USE DIFFERENCES AMONG LEARNERS AS A PRODUCTIVE RESOURCE

Cyberenvironments are designed to enable "innovation at the edges" and to enable people with different disciplinary perspectives and different learning and work styles to share common infrastructure while creating customized environments that fit their unique perspectives.

MOVE 4: BROADEN THE RANGE AND MIX OF REPRESENTATIONAL MODES

Cyberenvironments for science and engineering will provide ubiquitous access to a unique and unprecedented array of content, including live and historic data from instruments and sensors (covering the entire planetary system), datasets and computational models, and literature and expert commentary. Ubiquitous learners will synthesize and repurpose these resources, inventing new representations and new paths through knowledge as they explore, possibly quite far from the original purposes of the investigations.

MOVE 5: DEVELOP CONCEPTUALIZING CAPACITIES

One way to characterize cyberenvironments is to say that they will add depth to the Web; every scientific result will be backed by the data and experiments used to derive it, and will, at multiple levels be re-derivable. Ubiquitous access to such infrastructure will lead to broader, more direct comprehension of the scientific method and to the development of general skills to apply scientific thinking and cyberinfrastructure to the exploration and mastery of new concepts.

MOVE 6: CONNECT ONE'S OWN THINKING TO DISTRIBUTED COGNITION AND COLLECTIVE INTELLIGENCE

Participation in a cyberenvironment will connect the users to the social mind of their virtual communities, both as a consumer and as a content producer. Moreover, cyberenvironments will allow such virtual communities to engage with each other and the public in data- and model-supported dialogue. Thus, they will promote very rich conversation across disciplinary boundaries and between researchers, students, and citizens.

MOVE 7: BUILD COLLABORATIVE KNOWLEDGE CULTURES

Cyberenvironments have developed out of the needs of collaborative science and engineering, which are prime exemplars of "knowledge cultures." Cyberenvironments promote participation in virtual communities, providing ubiquitous tools and services to enable the creation and accumulation of new knowledge, and they will foster a learn-by-doing mentality. These technologies will enable construction of collaborative cultures of many types, formal and informal.

We believe cyberenvironments represent an opportunity for ubiquitous learning to be based on real data and live instruments and to engage students in authentic research activities. At the same time, we expect the concept of ubiquitous learning to be increasingly critical to the advancement of science and engineering. Scientists and other information workers can no longer remain isolated in the ideas and methods of their own disciplines. Society faces grand challenges that are inherently multidisciplinary, such as those related to environmental sustainability and human health. To address such challenges, researchers must work as part of broad, multidisciplinary teams and take advantage of shared technological resources. Of necessity, they will have to learn about data, tools, and concepts outside their formal discipline and will need to do so just-in-time as they apply their talents to particular problems. Indeed, new career paths are likely to appear as cross-disciplinary researchers mine results from other experiments and act as community coordinators rather than pursuing their own independent efforts.

Multidisciplinary scientific and engineering research, and other highly creative endeavors, will ultimately require a very organic set of learning aids, ranging from relatively static material that focuses on theory, to examples and exercises that are updated as often as new data and new analysis processes appear, to in-process capture of researchers' tacit knowledge. Individuals working in these fields will dynamically transition between the roles of researcher/creator, teacher, and learner, using cyberenvironments for the following purposes:

1. Discussion and social networking, to design studies and recruit necessary expertise
2. Discovery of community resources, including techniques, tools, data, and human knowledge
3. Iterative development of complex processes, based on best practices, evaluation of alternatives, and collaborative assessment
4. Publication of data, techniques, and results
5. Integration of information across disciplines, from professional researchers and citizen scientists
6. Continuous interactive learning, as researchers explore beyond the bounds of their training to understand data and models connected to their own interests

In such an open, evolving, "mashed up" situation, people will play an active role in the cyberenvironment: not as "users" and "providers," but as participants—creating, evolving, evaluating, and integrating resources as they explore and interact with colleagues. Participants will continuously learn what methods and data are recommended to answer certain questions (and why), what questions should be asked, and, ultimately, what "works." While novices will not all become experts, there will be no sharp boundary between professional work and learning. All participants will play the roles of teacher and learner throughout their active lives, and the means to learn, research, and teach will be available to everyone.

Cyberenvironments will support ubiquity in another sense as well. True ubiquity requires easy knowledge transfer between tasks and situations. The generic, subject-independent mechanisms of cyberenvironments will, like the Web, define a skill set that, once mastered, will create a level of "literacy" sufficient to both participate in and initiate collaborative problem solving. For example, experience as part of a collaborative chemistry project in school will transfer directly to other online collaborations, such as an environmental science investigation in a job, or to exploration of the science behind news stories on cures for diseases, global warming, and other topics of general interest.

Conclusion

Direct access to data, instruments, and computational resources are fueling a shift in scientific research toward multidisciplinary, systems-oriented studies and to close coupling of computational modeling with experimental observation. Cyberenvironments, which emphasize the integration of these shared resources into projects and the integration of new resources created in projects back into the community-level scientific context will support and catalyze this trend.

The "content" of this new ubiquitous cyberenvironment will include research results, such as papers, processes, data, and new instruments and computational tools, and formal and informal learning materials and exercises, all of which must be conveyed through the cyberinfrastructure in actionable form with enough information about themselves to be incorporated into further research work. We argue that the existence throughout the infrastructure both of this type of self-description and the ability to move quickly from reading to doing will change practices: researchers will come to expect that training materials will be directly linked to the data and models in the cyberinfrastructure, and that they can contribute, Web-style, to the body of research and to training materials, examples, and exercises about shared resources. Increasingly, researchers will learn about new resources just-in-time, in the context of work activities. Such practices will be indispensable in multidisciplinary research settings but will also blur the boundaries between research, formal learning, and everyday life.

Cyberinfrastructure and cyberenvironments will ultimately be as pervasive as personal computers and Internet connections are today, in schools, in homes, in libraries, and virtually any space. We believe cyberenvironment literacy will be seen one day as Web literacy is today and that it will be a foundation for ubiquitous lifelong learning supporting professional scientists and engineers and society as a whole.

Readings and References

The Atkins report to the U.S. National Science Foundation (along with similar efforts globally) has defined a vision for ubiquitous cyberinfrastructure (Atkins et al. 2003). This has led to the establishment of an Office of Cyberinfrastructure and a concerted national and global effort to deploy ubiquitous, reliable cyberinfrastructure (National Science Foundation Cyberinfrastructure Council 2007). Myers and Dunning (2006) consider the whole research process in order to define what is needed for collaborative cyberenvironments. Myers and McGrath (2007) discuss software architecture principles and the importance of reflective design in cyberenvironments. The broad literature connected with the terms "e-science," "semantic grid," and "collaboratory" may also be of interest.

Atkins, Daniel, Kelvin K. Droegemeier, Stuart I. Feldman, Hector Garcia-Molina, Michael L. Klein, David G. Messerschmitt, Paul Messina, Jeremiah P. Ostriker, and Margaret H. Wright. 2003. *Revolutionizing Science and Engineering through Cyberinfrastructure.* Arlington, Va.: National Science Foundation.

Brabham, Daren C. 2008. "Crowdsourcing as a Model for Problem Solving: An Introduction and Cases." *Convergence: The International Journal of Research into New Media Technologies* 14(1): 76–91.

CMCS. 2007. Collaboratory for Multi-scale Chemical Science, http://cmcs.org (accessed 2007).

Contractor, Noshir S. 2005. "The Role of Social Network Analysis in Enabling Cyberinfrastructure and the Role of Cyberinfrastructure in Enabling Social Network Analysis." Paper presented at the National Science Foundation workshop on Cyberinfrastructure for the Social Sciences, Warrington, Va., March.

Myers, James D., Thomas C. Allison, Sandra Bittner, Brett Didier, Michael Frenklach, William H. Green, Yen-ling Ho, John Hewson, Wendy S. Koegler, Carina Lansing, David Leahy, Michael Lee, Renata McCoy, Michael Minkoff, Sandeep Nijsure, Gregor von Laszewski, David Montoya, Luwi Oluwole, Carmen Pancerella, Reinhardt Pinzon, William Pitz, Larry A. Rahn, Branko Ruscic, Karen Schuchardt, Eric Stephan, Al Wagner, Theresa Windus, and Christine Yang. 2005. "A Collaborative Informatics Infrastructure for Multi-Scale Science." *Cluster Computing* 8(4): 243–53.

Myers, James D., and Thom H. Dunning. 2006. "Cyberenvironments and Cyberinfrastructure: Powering Cyber-Research in the 21st Century." Paper presented at the Foundations of Molecular Modeling and Simulation conference, June 9–10.

Myers, James D., and Robert E. McGrath. 2007. "Cyberenvironments: Adaptive Middleware for Scientific Cyberinfrastructure." Paper presented at the Adaptive and Reflective Middleware conference, Newport Beach, Calif., November 26.

National Science Foundation Cyberinfrastructure Council. 2007. "NSF's Cyberinfrastructure Vision for 21st Century Discovery." Arlington, Va.: National Science Foundation.

Ruscic, Branko, Reinhardt E. Pinzon, Gregor von Laszewski, Deepti Kodeboyina, Alexander Burcat, David Leahy, David Montoy, and Albert F. Wagner. 2005. "Active Thermochemical Tables: Thermochemistry for the 21st Century." *Journal of Physics: Conference Series* 16(1): 561–70.

Schuchardt, Karen, Carmen Pancerella, Larry A. Rahn, Brett Didier, Deepti Kodeboyina, David Leahy, James D. Myers, Olumwole Oluwole, William Pitz, Branko Ruscic, Jing Song, Gregor von Laszewski, and Christine Yang. 2005. "Portal-Based Knowledge Environment for Collaborative Science." Paper presented at Grid Computing Environments (GCE) 2005: Workshop on Grid Computing Portals, Seattle, November 18.

WATERS. 2007. Waters Network Home Page. http://www.watersnet.org (accessed 2007).

Wesch, Mike. 2007. "The Machine Is Us/Ing Us." YouTube, http://youtube.com/watch?v=NLlGopyXT_g (accessed 2007).

12

Immersive Environments for Massive, Multiperson, Online Learning

ALAN B. CRAIG, STEVE DOWNEY, GUY GARNETT, ROBERT E. MCGRATH, AND JAMES D. MYERS

The majority of instruction offered via the Internet to date is Web-based and largely asynchronous in nature; immersive technologies, on the other hand, present new opportunities for shared, collaborative, and synchronous educational experiences. Furthermore, as these physically immersive environments and technologies evolve, the line increasingly blurs between what is physical versus what is virtual. As a result, there is an ever-increasing opportunity for delivering engaging situated learning and promoting increased interaction between learners, teachers, the content, and each other. This chapter discusses how massive, multiperson, online learning environments extend the concept of ubiquitous learning and can change the very nature of online instruction.

Owing to their highly interactive, persistent, and collaborative nature, massive, multiperson, online learning environments provide exceptional opportunities for advancing research and educational practices associated with a variety of learning theories, including situated learning, interactive learning, participatory learning, spatial learning, temporal learning, and intuitive learning as discussed in chapter 1. Such systems are also evolving toward supporting heterogeneous hardware devices and user interfaces, including cellular telephones, gaming consoles, multimodal virtual reality interfaces, and others.

As an illustration of these ideas, we discuss as a case study a course, Art in Virtual Worlds (2006), in which students at the University of Illinois at Urbana-Champaign worked together in an online virtual world, called Second Life (SL).

We have observed that virtual worlds are easy to learn and fun to experience, so students are likely to spend more time there. Unlike other shared spaces (such as Web-based ones), shared virtual worlds enable safe, easy contact with large communities. The encounter is similar to Web-based collaboration, but with a greater sense of user presence: you get to see, speak to, and text chat with other users (or at least their avatars) while you are in the shared space. You can also work on projects together, much as you could if you were actually in the same room together. At the same time, because the experience is mediated through the computer, students can experiment with self-presentation and expression with less anxiety than face-to-face interactions might generate.

Realizing the promise of these environments will require ubiquitous, scalable infrastructure of the sort discussed in chapter 11. In addition, we will need open frameworks—under the control of teachers and educational institutions (rather than for-profit companies)—with flexible mechanisms for creating content and diverse worlds as well as further work on instructional frameworks for ensuring sound pedagogical principles and engaging learning activities.

Revolutionary New Ways to Teach and Learn

Most of today's teaching on the Internet is Web-based and asynchronous. While this affords great flexibility for learners to access materials when and where they want, its comparatively static and solitary nature leaves learners isolated from both their peers and instructors, and disengaged from the content itself. Immersive environments deviate from this model. They enable interactive engagement between subject matter experts (who at times are learners) and learners (who at times are subject matter experts), and they make the content more interactive and experiential. These attributes combine to make the virtual world better approximate the real world and to increase the ability of the virtual world to positively impact learning through virtual experiences. While synchronous interaction (e.g., between experts and learners) does not scale to very large groups, the spontaneous development of informal social organizations such as "guilds" in the online game World of Warcraft suggests mechanisms that enable the spread and retention of expertise in immersive environments. In these ways, immersive environments not only blur the traditional institutional, spatial, and temporal boundaries of education (move 1 from chapter 1), but they can also shift the balance of agency (move 2) in that the teachers and learners are engaged in a common experience, rather than teachers bestowing great knowledge on learners who absorb information from them like a sponge.

In the future, three-dimensional, immersive environments will further break down the borders of what is "virtual" and what is "real," blurring the distinction between that which exists in the physical realm and that which lives only in the digital domain. This blending of the digital with the "real" will enable situated, experiential learning to take place outside of the actual physical situation. Real-world objects can already be scanned and brought into the digital space, environmental data of all kinds can be captured with sensors, and digital objects can be "printed" as three-dimensional solid objects. As these techniques become cheaper, easier, and more widespread, they will enable more, and more realistic, virtual experiences that can be used for teaching and learning.

Many virtual worlds are also persistent, meaning that they are always there and your actions affect the world. It also means that the world continues to evolve whether or not any humans are engaged with it. Persistence allows learning to occur anytime and, potentially at least, allows learners to pick up where they left off. With the continued development of technology, these worlds soon will be accessible not only through desktop computers but also through a variety of mobile and ubiquitous interfaces. The important point is that the virtual world is persistently available, regardless of the means of interfacing with it. This allows these enduring virtual worlds to provide different channels through which learning can occur and to be ubiquitously available via multiple, diverse modes of interaction.

This chapter presents this new approach for delivering instruction via the Internet that capitalizes on the affordances such persistent virtual worlds offer as a ubiquitous learning framework that can build on the successes of massive, multiperson, online environments such as World of Warcraft (http://www.worldofwarcraft.com), Second Life (http://secondlife.com), and Lineage (http://www.lineage.com). In presenting this new model, we discuss the vision foreseen for these new environments, an instructional framework for engaging learners, and the technical drivers and challenges accompanying these worlds.

"Virtual Worlds": Persistent Immersive Environments

Current online learning environments are woefully inadequate in two key areas—interactivity and situating of instructional activities (Ogata and Yano 2004). Web-based environments fail to convey the real-world environmental challenges associated with, for instance, collecting samples of offshore plants, or transmitting remote musical performances of students in an online music composition course. Immersive, multiperson, online learning environments provide visual and simulated physical affordances that more accurately mirror the actual environments in which the knowledge is to be applied. In doing so, they provide opportunities for situated learning and increased interactions between and among the learners and the content. In the near future, these environments will be more widely accessible through mobile devices and more physically engaging through immersive technology, thereby enabling users to participate bodily in these interactions.

It is important to draw a distinction between mental immersion and physical immersion. Mental immersion is the state in which a person is cognitively absorbed in the content of some virtual world, regardless of the medium in which that virtual world is manifested. For example, a person can be mentally immersed in a good novel, or a movie, or an online gaming environment. Physical immersion, on the other hand, substitutes, or augments, the stimuli to one or more of a person's senses. Thus, to be physically immersed in a virtual world, technology must provide a synthetic stimulus to the end user in a manner that is appropriate for the simulated condition. By providing multiple representations and delivery mechanisms, immersive environments, especially those that are physically immersive, can broaden the range and mix of representational modes (move 4) (Burbules 2004; Sherman and Craig 1995, 2003).

It is not always necessary, or desirable, to occlude the "real" (physical) world from the participant. It is sometimes advantageous to integrate synthetic stimuli in registration with real-world stimuli to augment the physical world by superimposing the virtual on it. For example, a participant could visit a museum and have annotations and extra information about the exhibits displayed as overlays on the real exhibits. In addition, some participants may be physically immersed, while others might be interacting via a two-dimensional interface on a computer or via their cell phones.

Today, full physical immersion is available only in a few special installations. However, contemporary entertainment industries have driven commercial technology toward extremely high-quality graphics and sound systems, connected by high bandwidth channels in homes and desktops. Massively Multiplayer Online Games (MMOG) have evolved into complex "synthetic worlds" (Castranova 2005), shared, persistent, immersive three-dimensional environments in which people live out fantasy and reality. This technology presents tremendous opportunities for creating flexible and diverse collaborations, new forms of understanding, and compelling educational experiences. Furthermore, the success of contemporary online games offers a model for how to create persistent, shared, immersive environments. We would like to exploit and extend this successful technology and associated metaphors to create high-quality, low-cost software that is accessible to a broad range of users.

As physically immersive environments and technologies evolve, the line blurs increasingly between what is physical and what is virtual. From these technical developments persistent virtual worlds are emerging, providing greater opportunities for situated learning and increased interactions between learners and the content, and among one another. The following case study illustrates the experience-driven nature of these online learning worlds and how these sensory-rich environments compel learners to explore and become engaged in their world and their lessons.

Case Study: Art in Virtual Worlds

One of the authors (Garnett) conducted a class at the University of Illinois called Art in Virtual Worlds. This section gives informal impressions from the perspective of a teacher.

> In the evening after dinner on the day of our first class, in which I introduced the merest rudiments of travel and interaction in the virtual world called Second Life, I decided to check in and see how—or even if—the students were getting along in it. To my surprise, I was immediately hailed on the Second Life internal chat (a kind of instant messaging service for people in that world) by an excited student, a young woman I will refer to as "S." S. told me I simply *had* to come see what she had found. In our afternoon class I had merely suggested to students that they wander around Second Life and explore on their own, but to be prepared to report back to class on anything "interesting" they had found. Well, S. insisted we fly off right then and there to a place she had already landmarked (the Second Life equivalent of a browser bookmark). After a brief teleport (the fastest way to travel long distances in Second Life) we materialized at a telehub and covered the remaining distance by flying (the second fastest way to get around in Second Life is to have your avatar leap into the air and travel in the direction desired, à la Superman). Confidently, S. led us directly to the object of interest she had identified: a luscious and elaborate garden. I was taken immediately by the lifelike fluttering of butterflies from one blossom to another. As we entered, to a constant stream of chat from S. describing all the wonderful details—including sounds of birds and frogs—we came upon the chief attraction of this particular garden: a twenty-five-foot high waterfall cascading over granitic rocks.

This experience illustrates, on a number of levels, some of the significant advantages and qualitative changes brought about by teaching in a virtual world. On one level, there was a very personal sense of excitement and anticipation as teacher and student flew toward what obviously was a very exciting discovery by the student. The teacher could observe firsthand the degree of skill the student had attained in a very short time, mastering navigation, flying, and chat. On another, more qualitative, level, the teacher was amazed by how different this experience was from the "reports" expected in the next class session: there was little need for S. to describe what she had found; rather, student and teacher were brought into a direct coexperience.

That experience is qualitatively different from the many e-mails containing URLs that teachers receive from students pointing to one page or another of class-related research or news; it is even substantially different from the instant messaging and other real-time chat that are now fairly commonplace in educational experiences. It is fairly certain the garden and waterfall would not have been remembered so viscerally, in such detail, not to mention which student had discovered it and shared it, if it had been a simple text-based class report, even if it had included graphics. This shared sense of presence is a critical attribute of virtual worlds. It heightens the participant's experience and leads to greater retention. It is not so much that the boundary between virtual and real is blurred; it is that the boundary disappears entirely. In this case, the student and teacher were not two people engaged in some kind of computer-mediated communication: they were two people involved in one shared experience.

This sense of shared experience continued throughout the semester in Second Life. Students and teacher almost always resorted to such direct experience when students presented their projects (see figure 12.1), even in the classroom. In fact, the students would often be logged in to Second Life during class, while the teacher's avatar's point of view was displayed on the class projector, with student avatars coming on screen to point something out or materialize something (usually) rel-

Figure 12.1. Students showing their "sculpture" project in Second Life.

evant from their inventory (a kind of storage system that allows avatars to carry things around with them, ranging in size from text files to cars and houses).

Another key aspect of the class was to form collaborative teams: students from computer science, music, art, and a variety of other majors joined together to plan, design, and create their work. The online interactions turned collaborative class projects into nightly social events. Students checked in to Second Life to see what the others were doing, to chat, to share some new find, or generally just to hang out. As they worked, they naturally discovered each other's strengths, and no doubt weaknesses as well, and learned from each other and taught each other. Rather than the usual collaborative tactics that rely heavily on the "most motivated" person in a group to make sure things happen, they built objects together, in shared virtual space. The students met much more than they usually would get together in real space. Convenient access was one reason for this high level of participation: even if someone was out of town, visiting family on a weekend for example, he or she still often managed to log in to Second Life. It was also far easier for students to log in from their dormitories than it would have been to go in to the lab, especially late at night. Another motivation was sheer curiosity: students wanted to keep up with their classmates' activities, and not having to walk or get a campus bus over to a lab made it far easier to do so with little or no planning and minimal consequences.

One other aspect of teaching in Second Life was completely surprising. The class, including the teacher, interacted with a far wider range of people who were not in the class. This included friends, and sometimes family, of students, but it also included random passersby in Second Life who saw the students building something intriguing and came over to have a look and chat with them. These passersby were from all over the world, and in reality were in fact somewhere else in the world at the moment, connected only by the Internet. We realized that just as a university may be embedded in a larger community (engendering the familiar tension between "town and gown"), our "virtual lab" had become part of a larger community, a vast and varied "town" that was completely autonomous from our "gown." Yet this ad hoc community of strangers was able to lend the students both appreciation and advice during the process of creating art in a virtual world. Thus, students, students' families, and others immersed in the simulated world were actually spontaneously engaging and building a collaborative knowledge culture (move 7), as well as connecting their thinking to the social norms of the immersive environment. In this way, by drawing on other resources in the environment (both human and nonhuman), their thinking became connected to the social mind of distributed cognition (move 6).

From this experience, we have drawn a number of important implications about the use of virtual worlds for pedagogic purposes:

Time invested: Because it is easy to learn and fun to do, students are likely to spend more time in the virtual world than in traditional collaborative settings online or face to face. This hypothesis is consistent with a poll of MMOG users who spent an average of three to four hours per day in the virtual worlds of massive, multiperson, online environments (MMORPG 2002). In our experience, at least up to a certain point, the more time they spend, the more they learn. More complex activities take more time and skill, but simple tasks are easily accomplished.

Networking: The nature of such a space (such as SL) enables easy contact with a larger community, resulting in mostly positive feedback and the sense of participating in something larger and paradoxically more "real" than a classroom project. The sense of presence and electronic mediation contributes to feelings of comfort and control, which may reduce anxiety about both the technology and interpersonal interactions. Furthermore, it is relatively easy to find kindred spirits, advertise your work, and connect to new communities.

True collaboration: Unlike other shared spaces (such as those that are Web-based), shared virtual worlds enable a greater sense of presence: you get to see, speak to, and chat online with other users (or at least their avatars) while you are in the shared space. In the Art in Virtual Worlds project, this facilitated sessions from home or dormitory and led to more concrete collaboration. Rather than simply breaking large projects up into subprojects that could be worked on individually, students spent more time actually interacting together.

Instructional Framework for Ubiquitous Learning in MMOLEs

The shift toward ubiquitous learning is leading to a new model for lifelong learning, community building, and learner engagement. These mentally immersive, massively multiperson, online learning environments (MMOLEs) provide radically better and new features for three different categories of learning:

Experiential learning: The strong sense of user presence and naturalistic interactions enable rich, pseudorealistic experiences for situation-based learning.

Collaborative learning: The presence of multiple people and actors, along with a shared, persistent "world," promotes collaborations and community building.

Creativity: The ability for all participants to create and share content, up to and including whole "worlds," enables new kinds of learning through visually compelling self-expression and creativity by learners.

Because of their highly interactive and collaborative nature, MMOLEs provide exceptional opportunities for advancing research and educational practices associated with a variety of constructivist learning theories: inquiry-based learning (Dewey 1964; Edelson et al. 1999), situated learning theory (Lave 1988), and social development (Vygotsky 1978). Compared with Web-based collaboration, immersive environments have more modes of interaction and presentation, combined with the scale and location independence of the Web. Techniques that work face-to-face or in Web-based environments could be reconsidered for immersive environments. The nature of interactivity and collaboration afforded by such environments will require new learning theories and "best practices" to capitalize on their capabilities. Many of these soon-to-emerge practices will reflect the shifting roles of instructors and learners (move 2) and will tap into the immense power of social cognition (move 6) and knowledge cultures (move 7) to establish new forms of instruction and learning possible only through a ubiquitous approach to education.

To that end, a preliminary instructional framework is proposed (Downey 2008) that incorporates elements from each of the three theory bases mentioned while remaining extensible in order to allow educators to integrate their own unique contributions based on the instructional content and needs of their learners. It also incorporates the notion of the "quest" from role-playing games described below. Briefly stated, the framework employs five stages: (1) engage the learner, (2) provide a learning quest, (3) engage the content, (4) assemble knowledge, and (5) evaluate progress. In stage 1, learners are first engaged by stimulating their curiosity, exposing them to problems and scenarios they are likely to experience in their real lives, and motivating them to begin exploring situations and asking questions. In stage 2, learners are given specific tasks to complete. In the form of a quest, learners are presented with directed-learning activities, similar to a game quest, stating their learning goal and providing instructions for discovering needed information and possibly forming collaborations with their peers. Using their learning quest instructions, in stage 3 learners embark on their activities, navigating their virtual world, discovering and accessing data and information needed for their quest, sharing knowledge with their peers, and observing and interacting with the context and situation surrounding their learning activity.

Another crucial element from games enters in here, one that is critical for maintaining student interest: the pursuit of the learning quest must be engaging, and its solution must be rewarding. At stage 4, "assemble knowledge," learners formalize the initial ideas and mental constructs they have established for their learning quest by interpreting information, assembling knowledge, testing hypotheses, and generating solutions. Finally, the quality of the learner's knowledge is assessed and feedback is provided to guide him or her to areas of improvement and/or provide connections to additional learning quests that build on the learning completed and lead to a whole new level of curiosity, inquiry, and experiential learning. Each of these learning stages can be present in varying degrees; they need not be rigorously sequential and discrete.

While the state of the virtual world is dynamic and the collaborations are synchronous, the learning quests and content may be either synchronous or asynchronous: as in games, some quests may require coordination and collaboration with other learners. Therefore, learners can access their learning quests and collaborate with their peers at any time and from any location from which a network connection is available.

Technical Challenges

In order to provide ubiquitous, physically immersive spaces, numerous technical hurdles must be overcome. Perhaps one of the most critical is devising a means to provide wide area tracking of the physical location and posture of participants. All aspects of creating truly immersive spaces need higher fidelity, which requires bandwidth, computing power, and higher-resolution transducers (both temporal and spatial). Even given solutions to these technical issues, widespread adoption of such a MMOLE paradigm requires an order-of-magnitude increase in the flexibility and tools available for teachers and others to create engaging and pedagogically sound virtual worlds for learners.

Game engines have adopted a few standardized approaches to integrating graphics, networks, databases, physical models (physics), networking, scripting, and game play. These approaches may be used in straightforward, obvious ways but need to be extended to enable interactive learning and research. For example, the notion of "physics" in games allows us to define how scientists, teachers, and student avatars could interact with data and its visualization, which could in turn be used to represent many different aspects of the data model in a tangible manner.

Current synthetic worlds are constrained in ways that prohibit the full range of activity and interactions needed for ubiquitous learning. In particular, none of them is scalable in the ways we envision; none has the high levels of data and transaction security that are necessary for some applications; and none supports the input, display, and manipulation of large amounts of diverse, time-critical, real-world data from databases, sensors, imaging systems, or other sources. There are further challenges in meeting the requirements for manipulation and interaction necessary for experimentation while maintaining the social affordances of the environment. Specifically, learners may need to control the temporal dimension of their interaction with a virtual space and be able to discover or create alternative realities/alternative histories for the same physical space from within the environment itself. For example, studying different phenomena within a simulated ocean bay may require interacting with it on vastly different timescales, which would make it difficult to chat with others occupying the same space. Similarly, if quests involve manipulation of the space (e.g., raising the temperature to observe the effect on glacial melting), indicators may be needed to show when results accurately represent the real world or are based on scientific consensus versus simply being a "what-if" exploration, and learners may need to find and compare alternative scenarios.

Realizing the full promise of these environments will require open frameworks with flexible mechanisms for creating content, which will be built on ubiquitous, scalable infrastructures, such as those discussed in chapter 11.

Conclusion

"Virtual worlds" are rapidly emerging as a social phenomenon and are already called on to serve as a medium for learning and teaching. Enormous potential is evident even in today's primitive systems, such as Second Life.

To realize the full potential of this technology for ubiquitous learning will require technological and pedagogical developments. This presents some key technological challenges of interfaces, software architecture, and cyberinfrastructure. We also emphasize the need for better understanding of teaching and learning in these environments, best practices, and toolsets to enable broad participation and unleash the creativity inherent in a ubiquitous learning environment.

This infrastructure will facilitate many of the "moves" toward ubiquitous learning presented in chapter 1.

MOVE 1: BLUR THE TRADITIONAL INSTITUTIONAL, SPATIAL, AND TEMPORAL BOUNDARIES OF EDUCATION

Students and informal learners at all levels will "inhabit" virtual worlds. While traditional boundaries may be maintained in these worlds, it is equally possible to create wholly different experiences, social roles, and identities. As described earlier in this chapter, these experiences could be accessible to learners through a wide range of devices and interfaces across spatial and temporal boundaries.

MOVE 2: SHIFT THE BALANCE OF AGENCY

In these environments, the notions of teacher versus student, scientist versus citizen, professional versus amateur become less distinct. Students may play the role of teacher, experts may collaborate directly with novices, and ordinary people may create their own "schools" if they desire.

MOVE 4: BROADEN THE RANGE AND MIX OF REPRESENTATIONAL MODES

Persistent, three-dimensional worlds are a new representational mode, and within them a broad range of representations may be mixed. These virtual worlds may become the default delivery medium for mixed media of many kinds. Their manifestations may follow traditional conventions (e.g., users are represented by humanoid avatars mimicking our natural behaviors and appearance), or they may take on totally new forms of abstract idea presentations and interactions befitting a conceptual domain.

MOVE 6: CONNECT ONE'S OWN THINKING TO DISTRIBUTED COGNITION AND COLLECTIVE INTELLIGENCE

Participation in a virtual world is a shared experience, more compelling and immersive than Web-based collaborations. The sense of co-presence enabled by virtual worlds promotes collaboration and the development of shared ideas, communicated through visual and auditory as well as verbal communications.

MOVE 7: BUILD COLLABORATIVE KNOWLEDGE CULTURES

A virtual world is, in itself, a collaborative culture. Within these cultures, participants build their own social networks, collaborative communities, and knowledge cultures. As with traditional cultures, these cultures are born, grow, thrive, decline, and dissolve.

Acknowledgments

The National Center for Supercomputing Applications is funded by the U.S. National Science Foundation under Grant No. SCI-0438712. Any opinions, findings, and conclusions or recommendations expressed in this material are those of the authors and do not necessarily reflect the views of the National Science Foundation.

Readings and References

Sherman and Craig (2003) give a broad view of virtual reality technology and research. Castranova's *Synthetic Worlds* (2005) is a groundbreaking discussion of virtual worlds as a site for the creation of new cultures. Downey (2008) addresses issues for education in these environments.

Burbules, Nicholas. 2004. "Rethinking the Virtual." *E-learning* 1(2): 162–83.

Castranova, Edward. 2005. *Synthetic Worlds: The Business and Culture of Online Games.* Chicago: University of Chicago Press.

Dewey, John. 1964. "Science as Subject Matter and as Method." In *John Dewey on Education: Selected Writings,* ed. Reginald D. Archambault, 182–95. Chicago: University of Chicago Press. (Orig. pub. 1910.)

Downey, Steve. 2008. "Instructional Framework for Massive Multiperson Online Learning Environments." Unpublished paper.
Edelson, Daniel C., Douglas N. Gordin, and Roy D. Pea. 1999. "Addressing the Challenges of Inquiry-Based Learning through Technology and Curriculum Design." *Journal of Learning Sciences* 8(3–4): 391–450.
Lave, Jean. 1988. *Cognition in Practice: Mind, Mathematics, and Culture in Everyday Life.* Cambridge: Cambridge University Press.
MMORPG. 2002. "How Many Hours per Day Do You Play MMORPGs?" MMORPG, http://www.mmorpg.com/features.cfm/view/polls.
Ogata, Hiroaki, and Yoneo Yano. 2004. "Knowledge Awareness Map for Computer-Supported Ubiquitous Language-Learning." Paper read at Wireless and Mobile Technologies in Education conference, Shongli, Taiwan, March 23–25.
Sherman, William R., and Alan B. Craig. 1995. "Literacy in Virtual Reality: A New Medium." *Computer Graphics* 29(4): 37–42.
———. 2003. *Understanding Virtual Reality: Interface Application and Design.* San Francisco: Morgan Kaufmann.
Vygotsky, Lev. S. 1978. *Mind in Society.* Cambridge, Mass.: Harvard University Press.

13

Let's Get Serious about E-games

A Design Research Approach toward an Emerging Perspective

WENHAO DAVID HUANG
AND TRISTAN E. JOHNSON

Ubiquitous learning, as described in previous chapters, is the most recent interpretation of how we can and should learn in the era of knowledge economy. Learning can be experienced anywhere, anytime, and via any media. Advancement of technology has made information and knowledge more accessible to the population at large; thus educators today are trying to figure out the best way to take advantage of technology in order to enhance the creation, transition, transformation, and utilization of knowledge. But so far the outcome is not as good as anticipated. This seems to be a case of déjà vu if one recalls the history of instructional and learning technologies over the past one hundred years. There is a pattern to how formal education systems cautiously, if not reluctantly, responded to newly developed learning technologies such as Sidney Pressey's teaching machine, instructional radio, cable television for teaching, and the computer (e.g., PLATO system mentioned in chapter 1). Educators often felt uncertain about being early adopters of new learning technologies for various reasons, although the times and circumstances might then have allowed for such diffidence.

Today, however, being watchful, late adopters confers little advantage for three reasons. First, globalization has leveled the field of competition when it comes to workforce development. Our students are no longer competing with the neighboring counties, cities, or even states for jobs and economic growth. Instead, talents from all over the globe are the competition, and their technology preparedness often is better than what we have offered to our students in the United States. Second, the influx of information and knowledge exchange provided by powerful information and communication technology changes our lives and work constantly and rapidly. Being hesitant could cause a regrettable loss of opportunities. Third, existing technology infrastructures and the next generation workforce already have profound experiences in applying new technologies to solve complex problems outside of formal education systems. The gap between what the workforce is demanding and what formal education systems can provide will keep widening if we continuously ignore societal and social changes stimulated by creative utilizations of technologies.

To address the aforementioned factors influencing the adoption of new learning technologies, this chapter proposes a sustainable approach that encourages educators in formal education systems to better utilize contemporary learning technologies for instructional purposes. In particular, it focuses on the adoption of e-games for teaching and learning, owing to their increasing popularity among next-generation learners. The first section will identify the latest trend seen in society in the context of e-games. Next, the linkage between e-games and learning will be discussed. The third section will describe ten interrelated e-game characteristics based on exhaustive literature reviews. Fourth, we will propose a cognitive load-based instructional design model to link games' multidimensional characteristics with desired learning outcomes and hope to promote the utilization of e-games in formal education settings. Finally, we will conclude with a discussion on the emerging perspectives on educational e-games design and its potential impact on the attainment of ubiquitous learning.

E-games' Omnipresence Is Inevitable

Advanced communication and information technology has made e-games ubiquitous by lowering the manufacturing costs of computers and game consoles (e.g., PlayStation, Nintendo Wii, etc.), increasing compatibility between e-games delivery platforms (e.g., offline and online), and streamlining the process of game development. For the scope of this chapter, e-games encompass all games that require computer processors to deliver the game-playing process and game environments. They could be computer games delivered from networked PCs and Macs, console games delivered through televisions, or mobile games delivered by cell phones. Playing e-games is no longer an expensive recreational activity, but one relatively affordable for everyone.

Furthermore, this trend is observable across generations, directly affecting the delivery of formal and informal learning. Learners who are now in the pipeline of our formal education systems are playing e-games, and, more important, learners who are about to enter the K–16 education system will have grown up with e-games. With the introduction of Nintendo Wii™ technology, older generations too can easily interface with e-games for various learning purposes (e.g., physical rehabilitation to help patients relearn lost abilities) (Miller 2007). Playing e-games, whether within or outside the classroom, has become part of many people's daily lives, and the inevitable reality is that it soon will become a preferred means of interaction heavily utilized by future generations.

E-games for Learning

E-games can be described from two perspectives: the game-playing process perspective and the game component perspective. E-games' playing process is essentially the same as that of non–e-games (e.g., board games, card games). E-games' components, however, are more complicated than those of their counterparts, owing to the interactions involved, particularly for the purpose of enhancing learning experience.

From the game-playing process perspective, e-games are entertaining. Although players need to follow rules in the game (e.g., online chess), it is equally important for them to experience freedom, uncertainty, and unpredictability (Caillois 1962). Abt (1970, 7) defines the process of game playing as "contests among adversaries or teammates operating under constraints for winning an objective." Suits (1990, 55) summarizes it as the "voluntary effort to overcome obstacles." Some might argue, however, that the term "contest" does not fully describe the fun and entertaining aspects of playing games (Gredler 1994). The playing of e-games could also be a less entertaining and more serious activity in the context of learning. This requires players to make a series of decisions to achieve predetermined game objectives (Abt 1970). In 2002, the Woodrow Wilson International Center for Scholars launched the Serious Games Initiative (2007) to promote the benefits of using games delivered via computers or game consoles as training and educational tools to develop complex skills in various industries (e.g., the military, higher education, health care). The Federation of American Scientists (2006) further advocates that educators should better utilize video games' powerful effect in educational settings to enhance intended learning processes.

From the game component viewpoint, Crawford (1982) identifies four independent yet interconnected computer game components: *representation, interaction, conflict, and safety.* The representation of the game system consists of all participating agents (players, system interface, game rules, and game objectives), which enables intended interactions. Conflict could be the means and/or the end of interactions, which requires players to dissolve complicated situations. The safety component allows players to experience the outcome of their game-playing actions without experiencing any real harm. To confirm the complex components of e-games, Amory (2007) suggests that games should include *game space* (play, exploration, authenticity, tacit knowledge); *visualization space* (critical thinking, storylines, relevance, goals); *elements space* (fun, emotions, graphics, sounds, technology); *problem space* (communication, literacy level, memory); and *social space* (communication tools and social network analysis) in order to fully harness e-games' effect on learning.

In summary, e-games for learning should be entertaining to play, while players aim to attain serious game objectives with actions guided by rules. Furthermore, the intended game-playing process requires purposeful design of interactions aligned with learning and afforded by complex game structure.

E-games' Multidimensional Characteristics

In addition to the convenient access to e-games, their multidimensional characteristics play a pivotal role in engaging players in this ubiquitous trend. Ten interconnected game characteristics have been repeatedly reported in the existing literature:

1. Challenge
2. Competition
3. Rule-bound actions
4. Goal- and task-oriented play
5. Fantasy and modified reality
6. Storyline or representation
7. Stimulation of engagement and curiosity
8. Role playing
9. Player control
10. Heavy utilization of multimodal presentation

CHALLENGE

A challenging activity is achievable, unpredictable, clearly defined, and designed to stretch and flex players' existing knowledge or skill levels (Baranauskas, Neto, and Borges 2001; Belanich, Sibley, and Orvis 2004; Bennett and Warnock 2007; Csikszentmihalyi 1990; Garris, Ahlers, and Driskell 2002; Malone 1981; Malone and Lepper 1987; McGrenere 1996; Rieber and Matzko 2001). For example, the difficulty levels inherent in the different stages of Mario Brothers® challenge players' problem-solving skills and console controlling skills whenever players move to the next level.

COMPETITION

Competition equates to contest, which implies the application of rules to identify winners. Players may compete with the game system (e.g., arcade game with a single player), individual players, or teams to achieve the game objectives. Players develop and refine their skill levels by fully participating in the competitions (Baranauskas, Neto, and Borges 2001; Crawford 1982; Csikszentmihalyi 1990; Rieber and Matzko 2001). Chess is an exemplary example of players competing with each other in a constrained-by-rules environment.

RULE-BOUND ACTIONS

Game players follow rules to carry out every move in the game. Playing games without rules makes the entire process meaningless. The constraints of game rules ensure fair play for all players, and they can be an explicit or implicit translation of intended instructional messages (Bennett and Warnock 2007; Björk and Holopainen 2003; Garris, Ahlers, and Driskell 2002; Hays 2005). For example, players need to throw the dice to determine how many steps they can move in the Monopoly game.

GOAL- AND TASK-ORIENTED PLAY

Game goals explicitly identify the desired game outcome in various forms (e.g., final scores) to guide game players' actions. They also serve as the criteria for players' final performance assessment (Bennett and Warnock 2007; Björk and Holopainen 2003; Csikszentmihalyi 1990; de Felix and Johnson 1993; Gredler 1996; Hays 2005; Malone 1980). Game tasks are the building blocks of game goals. Players need to accomplish a series of game tasks, in predetermined sequence, in order to reach the final goal stage. Game tasks also can be considered as the formative evaluation of players' skill development process (Björk and Holopainen 2003; Gredler 1996; Hays 2005). In the game of Monopoly the goal is to be the wealthiest person among players. The player can only achieve that goal by accomplishing series of tasks such as purchasing railroads, managing real estate, profiting from investment, and so forth.

FANTASY AND MODIFIED REALITY

Games enable players to experience fantasy. In other words, players might have an experience that is impossible for anyone to acquire in reality (e.g., Star Wars games). This particular characteristic sets games apart from simulations (Bennett and Warnock 2007; Garris, Ahlers, and Driskell 2002; Kirriemuir and McFarlane 2006; Malone 1981; Malone and Lepper 1987). Modified reality in games mimics the real world to certain extents, but not entirely. Players might be placed in a different context (e.g., role, time, space, culture) to experience the process (Belanich, Sibley, and Orvis 2004; Björk and Holopainen 2003; Crawford 1982; Csikszentmihalyi 1990). For example, World War II combat games enable players to reenact part of history.

STORYLINE OR REPRESENTATION

The storyline or representation in games provides the overview of the entire game-playing process and guides actions. It adds contextual references to the game environment. The storyline also helps players make sense of the game goals, tasks, and rules (Rieber and Matzko 2001). The storyline of D-day in World War II, for example, immediately sets the tone of the game for players, which consequently might facilitate the game-playing process.

STIMULATION OF ENGAGEMENT AND CURIOSITY

Games engage players by allowing them to immerse themselves completely in the game-playing process. Players no longer consider themselves external to the game. Instead, they are part of the game, and they are intrinsically motivated. Competition, curiosity, and mystery are often injected into games to enhance the games' ability to engage players (Asgari 2005; Bennett and Warnock 2007; Csikszentmihalyi 1990; Malone 1980; Malone and Lepper 1987; McGrenere 1996).

ROLE PLAYING

Role playing is essential and relates closely to the challenge, fantasy, storyline, and engagement of games. Players stretch themselves in all aspects if asked to role-play a game character. Role playing further enhances games' effects to allow players to experience fantasy (Björk and Holopainen 2003; Gredler 1996). Console games based on real sports, for example, allow players to be the most valuable players (MVPs) of certain seasons, for a higher level of engagement.

PLAYER CONTROL

Games provide a wide array of control options to help players establish identities in the game. For example, e-game players usually create avatars to represent themselves. Players can design the avatars' hair styles, eye colors, clothing, and accessories. Furthermore, the game control encourages players' full participation by allowing them to take ownership of their plays (Belanich, Sibley, and Orvis 2004; Bennett and Warnock 2007; Csikszentmihalyi 1990; Garris, Ahlers, and Driskell 2002; Gredler 1996; Malone 1981; Malone and Lepper 1987; McGrenere 1996).

HEAVY UTILIZATION OF MULTIMODAL PRESENTATION

This characteristic is at its best in e-games. Multimedia representations are heavily utilized in computer and video games. Such applications, in addition to enriching the game-playing experience by making it more appealing and authentic, also help players develop visual and spatial skills (Bennett and Warnock 2007; Björk and Holopainen 2003; de Felix and Johnson 1993; McGrenere 1996).

The Missing Pedagogical Link

E-games are reaching the tipping point of impacting how future generations learn, with three interacting elements. First, playing e-games has been recognized as a socially acceptable activity across generations. Soon it will become a necessity of communication, corroborated by the fact that the hardware needed to deliver e-games is now more readily available than ever. Second, e-games, with their multidimensional characteristics, are especially capable of engaging learners. Their potential to enhance learning experience in general, and to facilitate the development of complex skills, is eminent (Federation of American Scientists 2006). The third element, or the pedagogical link, however, is still missing. The question at hand is how educators can efficiently and systematically integrate e-games into learning processes. The lack of an empirically proven educational e-games design model requires educators, e-games designers, learning scientists, and e-games players' immediate attention. Simply replicating e-games' complex and interaction-rich structures in learning environments without considering their pedagogical impact might hamper the process of learning by too greatly increasing learners' cognitive load (Ang, Zaphiris, and Mahmood 2007).

In order to preliminarily establish the missing link, educators, learning scientists, and game designers must take theoretically grounded approaches to purposefully align e-games' characteristics with intended learning outcomes (Gagné and Driscoll 1988). Post hoc analyses of existing e-games' effects on learning may further our understanding to some extent. However, researchers still seldom confidently identify the correlative or causal relationship between certain game characteristics and learning outcomes (O'Neil, Wainess, and Baker 2005). Without such practical knowledge in place, the design process of educational e-games would be inevitably inefficient. Given that the primary purpose of designing educational e-games is to enhance learning experiences while engaging learners with e-games' appealing characteristics, a design research methodology guided by existing instructional design models is desperately needed. This will help us address the missing pedagogical link. The selection of instructional design models should meet the following criteria:

Capability to design complex interactions and learning environments across platforms such as e-games

Scalability to accommodate various scopes of design projects and e-game characteristics

Flexibility to design linear, nonlinear, branched, and webbed learning sequences seen in e-games

Grounding in learning theories to align with intended learning outcomes

Ability to sustain performance transfer to help learners transition from gaming environments to real performance settings

AN EXAMPLE

The four components/instructional design model (4C/ID-model; van Merriënboer, Clark, and de Croock 2002) fits the aforementioned selection criteria in an exemplary manner. This model's learning tasks design approach matches well with e-games' emphasis on game goals and tasks. Other game characteristics can also be easily implemented into the design model (see figure 13.1).

The 4C/ID-model consists of four nonlinear, interrelated design components: *learning tasks, supportive information, just-in-time (JIT) information, and part-task practice.* All design processes focus on the learning tasks component.

Learning tasks are concrete, authentic, whole-task experiences that are provided to learners to promote schema construction for nonrecurring

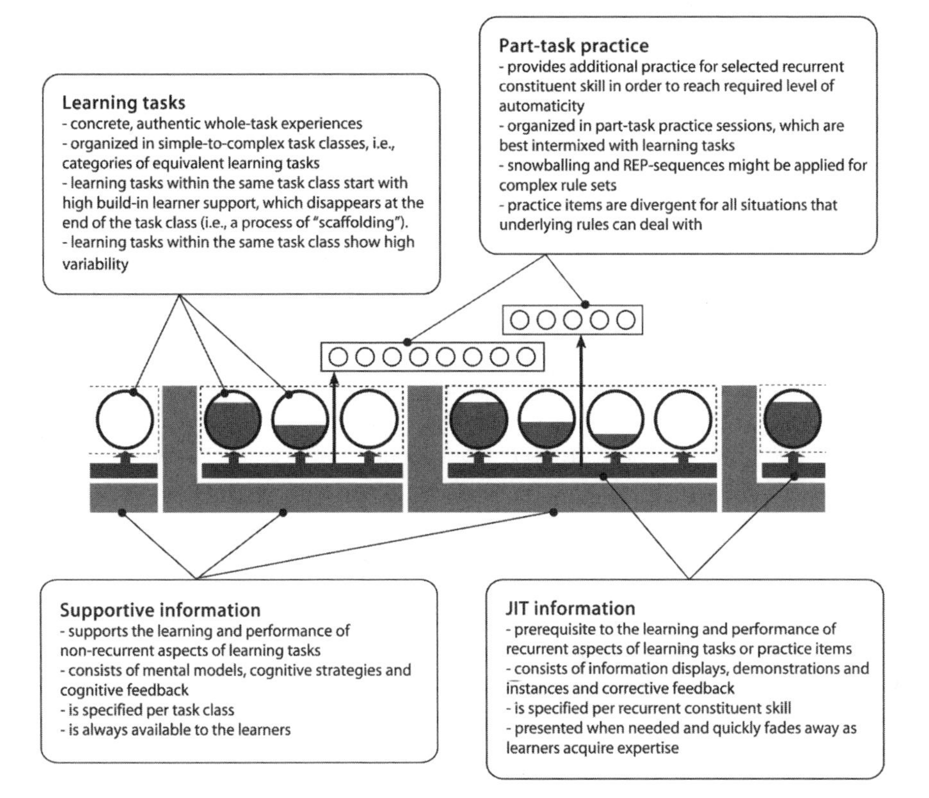

Figure 13.1. The 4C/ID-model. (From van Merriënboer, Clark, and de Croock 2002, 44.)

aspects of tasks and rule automation. Learning tasks must be complex and require the coordination and integration of all constituent skills. Task classes are used to define simple-to-complex categories of learning tasks on the basis of the body of knowledge (i.e., mental models and cognitive strategies). Learners are required to elaborate on their existing knowledge base when presented with a higher task class. Supports are also available for learning tasks to facilitate problem-solving processes.

Supportive information about concepts and theories aids in the learning and performance of nonrecurring aspects of intended tasks. It should promote learners' cognitive effort to relate new information to existing schema structures.

Just-in-time information helps learners develop automated responses. Rules and principles are essential to this design module. Demonstrations and examples, for example, are often applied in this component.

Part-task practice promotes rule automation for selected recurrent aspects of the intended complex task. The design approach aims to gradually develop learners' ability to automate the performance of recurrent skills via small task building blocks.

The main design goal for adapting 4C/ID-model for educational e-game design is to situate learners in authentic and complex learning environments represented as games. With regard to integrating game characteristics into the 4C/ID-model design components, the learning tasks could encompass the e-game goals, rules, tasks, challenge, and competition, while supportive information could readily provide the fantasy element or game storyline. Another important aspect of the e-game design achievable by the 4C/ID-model is its emphasis on the nature of the interactions among all design components. This model has great potential to design complex e-game learning environments enriched with fluid interactions, concrete and interconnected learning tasks, abundant active and experiential learning activities, and multimedia presentations, thus enabling learners to transfer desired performance beyond the context of e-games.

Moving toward an Emerging Perspective

Not all existing instructional design models are appropriate to be adapted for educational e-game design. The adaptation process must be subject to rigorous and empirical design research, guided by contemporary design theories. Currently, the emerging perspective about system design based on observations of ant colonies, human cities, molecular biology, and computer science (Johnson 2001) seems to best respond to the improvement of conventional instructional design's centralized approach and supports a more flattened, multilateral, and interaction-rich educational e-games design process. The emerging perspective advocates a design process that does not require centralized, top-down control. Instead, it uses the interaction and feedback generated by all design components to forward the design process, which is considered an efficient method for creating technology-rich learning environments such as video games (Irlbeck et al. 2006). This new system design approach further reminds us not to preclude the possibilities of creating interdisciplinary design models to overcome the challenge presented by educational e-game design.

Conclusion

The adoption of an existing instructional design model for educational e-game design proposed in this chapter has provided a sustainable approach to encourage more educational e-game usage in formal education settings. The idea is to help educators demystify the complexity of designing educational e-games while maintaining the necessary equilibrium between educational e-games' pedagogical soundness and their ability to provide an engaging learn-and-play process. We hope that such an efficient-model adoption approach eventually will be practiced by more educators for all innovative learning technologies. Thus, formal education systems will also be able to catch up with the change brought by technological advancement.

Furthermore, the emerging perspective on design discussed in this chapter implies several pathways to forward the concepts, understanding, and community practice of ubiquitous learning. First, interdisciplinary collaboration is the winning formula. Experts from computer science, interactive system design, learning science, and information and communication technology should collaborate with those who have expertise in liberal arts and social sciences in order to make the design of "tools" and "technology" more relevant for educational purposes. Second, interactions among all elements and entities of learning (e.g., learners, teachers, instructional materials, social contexts, cultural issues, knowledge exchange, community-building via Web technologies) that occurred before, during, and after any formal and informal learning experience should inform the design, development, and evaluation of ubiquitous learning environments throughout their lifespan. It should be a fluid and dynamic process afforded by real-time information exchange. Technology available today has enabled us to do so effortlessly.

As a result, we envision the ubiquitous learning environment to become an organic entity for all types of formal and informal learning, one that is not only based on volumes of learning theories and models but also responds with meaningful solutions to the realistic needs of our students, parents, educational systems, governments, and societies around the world.

Readings and References

For fundamentals of game design and instructional design theories and models, interested readers can explore Charles M. Reigeluth, ed., *Instructional-Design Theories and Models: II. A New Paradigm of Instructional Theory* (Mahwah, N.J.: Lawrence Erlbaum Associates, 1999); Andrew Rollings and Ernest Adams, *On Game Design* (Indianapolis: New Riders, 2003); and Katie Salen and Eric Zimmerman, *Rules of Play: Game Design Fundamentals* (Cambridge, Mass.: MIT Press, 2004), as well as the following titles, listed below: Federation of American Scientists 2006; Gredler 1994; Johnson 2001; and van Merriënboer, Clark, and de Croock 2002.

Abt, Clark. 1968. "Game for Learning." In *Simulation Games in Learning*, ed. S. Boocock and E. Schild, 65–84. Beverly Hills, Calif.: Sage.

———. 1970. *Serious Games*. New York: Viking Press.

Amory, Alan. 2007. "Game Object Model Version II: A Theoretical Framework for Educational Game Development." *Educational Technology Research and Development* 55:55–77.

Ang, Chee-Siang, Panayiotis Zaphiris, and Shumaila Mahmood. 2007. "A Model of Cognitive Loads in Massively Multiplayer Online Role Playing Games." *Interacting with Computers* 19:167–79.

Asgari, Mahboubeh. 2005. "A Three-Factor Model of Motivation and Game Design." Vancouver: Digital Games Research Conference (DIGRA).

Avedon, Elliott M., and Brian Sutton-Smith. 1971. *The Study of Games*. New York: Wiley.

Baranauskas, Cecilia C., Nelson G. G. Neto, and Marcos A. F. Borges. 2001. "Learning at Work through a Multi-user Synchronous Simulation Game." *International Journal of Continuing Engineering Education and Life-Long Learning* 11:251–60.

Belanich, James, Daragh E. Sibley, and Kara L. Orvis. 2004. *Instructional Characteristics and Motivational Features of a PC-Based Game*. Arlington, Va.: U.S. Army Research Institute for the Behavioral and Social Sciences.

Bennett, Justin, and Mary Warnock. 2007. "Instructional Game Characteristics." In *E-learning Concepts and Techniques*, a collaborative e-book project by Bloomsburg University of Pennsylvania. Available at http://iit.bloomu.edu/Spring2006_eBook_files/ebook_spring2006.pdf (accessed January 5, 2007).

Björk, Staffan, and Jussi Holopainen. 2003. "Describing Games: An Interaction-Centric Structural Framework." Utrecht: Digital Games Research Conference (DIGRA).

Caillois, Roger. 1962. *Man, Play, and Games*. London: Thames and Hudson.

Crawford, Chris. 1982. *The Art of Computer Game Design*. Available at http://www.vancouver.wsu.edu/fac/peabody/game-book/Coverpage.html (accessed October 5, 2007).

Csikszentmihalyi, Mihaly. 1990. *Finding Flow: The Psychology of Optical Experience*. New York: Harper Perennial.

de Felix, Judith W., and Richard T. Johnson. 1993. "Learning from Video Games." *Computers in the Schools* 9(2–3): 119–34.

Federation of American Scientists. 2006. "Harnessing the Power of Video Games for Learning." Washington, D.C.: Federation of American Scientists, Summit on Educational Games.

Gagné, Robert M., and Marcy Driscoll. 1988. *Essentials of Learning for Instruction.* Englewood Cliffs, N.J.: Prentice-Hall.

Garris, Rosemary, Robert Ahlers, and James E. Driskell. 2002. *Games, Motivation, and Learning: A Research and Practice Model.* East Lansing, Mich.: National Center for Research on Teacher Learning.

Gredler, Margaret. 1994. *Designing and Evaluating Games and Simulations: A Process Approach.* Houston: Gulf Publishing.

———. 1996. "Educational Games and Simulations: A Technology in Search of a Research Paradigm." In *Handbook of Research on Educational Communications and Technology,* ed. D. H. Jonassen, 521–40. New York: Macmillan.

Hays, Robert T. 2005. *The Effectiveness of Instructional Games: A Literature Review and Discussion.* Orlando, Fla.: Naval Air Warfare Center Training Systems Division.

Irlbeck, Sonja, Elena Kays, Deborah Jones, and Rod Sims. 2006. "The Phoenix Rising: Emergent Models of Instructional Design." *Distance Education* 27:171–85.

Johnson, Steven. 2001. *Emergence: The Connected Lives of Ants, Brains, and Software.* New York: Simon and Schuster.

Kasvi, Jyrki J. J. 2000. "Not Just Fun and Games—Internet Games as a Training Medium." In *Cosiga—Learning with Computerised Simulation Games,* ed. P. Kymäläinen and L. Seppänen, 23–34. Espoo, Finland: Helsinki University of Technology.

Kirriemuir, John, and Angela McFarlane. 2006. *Literature Review in Games and Learning.* Report 8, Futurelab Series, Futurelab, http://www.futurelab.org.uk/resources/documents/lit_reviews/Games_Review.pdf (accessed February 23, 2009).

Malone, Thomas W. 1980. *What Makes Things Fun to Learn? A Study of Intrinsically Motivating Computer Games.* Palo Alto, Calif., Xerox Palo Alto Research Center.

———. 1981. "Toward a Theory of Intrinsically Motivating Instruction." *Cognitive Science* 4:333–69.

Malone, Thomas W., and Mark Lepper. 1987. "Making Learning Fun: A Taxonomy of Intrinsic Motivations for Learning." In *Aptitude, Learning, and Instruction,* ed. R. E. Snow and M. J. Farr, 3:223–53. Hillsdale, N.J.: Lawrence Erlbaum Associates.

McGrenere, Joanna. 1996. *Design: Educational Electronic Multi-Player Games—A Literature Review.* Vancouver: University of the British Columbia.

Miller, Joe. 2007. "Wii Speeds Up the Rehab Process." *USA Today,* http://www.usatoday.com/tech/gaming/2007-07-24-wii therapy_N.htm?csp=34 (accessed February 19, 2008).

O'Neil, Harold F., Richard Wainess, and Eva L. Baker. 2005. "Classification of Learning Outcomes: Evidence from the Computer Games Literature." *Curriculum Journal* 16(4): 455–74.

Rieber, Lloyd P., and Michael J. Matzko. 2001. "Serious Design of Serious Play in Physics." *Educational Technology Research and Development,* 41:14–24.

Serious Games Initiative. 2007. Web site, http://www.seriousgames.org/about2.html (accessed October 1, 2007).

Suits, Bernard H. 1990. *Grasshopper: Games, Life, and Utopia.* Boston: David R. Godine.

van Merriënboer, Jeroen J. G., Richard Clark, and Marcel B. M. de Croock. 2002. "Blueprints for Complex Learning: The 4C/ID-Model." *Educational Technology Research and Development* 50(2): 39–64.

14

Access Grid Technology

An Exploration in Educators' Dialogue

SHARON TETTEGAH, CHERYL MCFADDEN,
EDEE NORMAN WIZIECKI, HANNA ZHONG,
JOYCELYN LANDRUM-BROWN, MEI-LI SHIH,
KONA TAYLOR, AND TIMOTHY CASH

Human–computer interaction and networking technologies such as video conferencing tools have prompted many research studies in multiple fields (computer science, communication, psychology, and education) to investigate the use of media technology as collaborative tools. Most literature in the area focuses on either point-to-point video collaboration tools or e-mail and e-mail list software as communication tools, with little attention paid to multipoint collaboration tools. Recent "research in education suggests there are many advantages in using multipoint collaborative tools and Web-based technologies" (Tettegah 2005, 273), especially in the realm of ubiquitous learning. Multipoint collaborative tools combine oral, auditory, and visual stimuli to create an apparatus that transmits learning throughout multiple locations and in multiple modes at the same time, and they have the ability to reach different types of learners with diverse pedagogical needs. In this chapter we provide a brief overview of multipoint collaboration systems, challenges, and opportunities to use a specific multipoint collaborative tool (the Access Grid) to view animated narrative vignettes (ANVs) and to engage educators in critical dialogue (Tettegah 2007; Tettegah and Anderson 2007).

Synchronous Tools and Video Conferences Tools

Several interesting projects on multipoint collaboration learning in the past decade are described in the literature (Clark 1992; Fox et al. 2002; Gong 1994;

Lopez-Gulliver et al. 2004; Patterson et al. 1990; Sonnenwald, Whitton, and Maglaughlin 2003; Watabe et al. 1990; Zhu, Kerofsky, and Garrison 1999). However, most of these studies describe group collaboration using Polycom teleconferencing, videoconferencing systems, and Web conferencing tools. Multipoint videoconferencing means that three or more participants are involved in a teleconference. There are several outstanding multipoint collaboration tools available for both business and educational purposes, but one of the most powerful ones on the market is the Access Grid. While many point-to-point systems are available, we focus on a few, with a specific emphasis on Access Grid technology, because not only is it powerful, it seems to provide the most opportunity for ubiquitous learning.

Multipoint Video Collaboration and Conferencing Tools

Multipoint collaboration technologies provide real-time transmission between three or more locations. Since multipoint collaborations involve participants in at least two, and usually three or more sites, there are usually some basic requirements, such as technical supports, audio/video control, network service, and a conference environment. Thus, while ubiquitous in nature, multipoint video collaboration and conferencing tools are not designed to be used "anytime" or "anywhere" like a cell phone, yet they do have the ability to connect people from all over the world in a manner that transcends physical location and the ability to provide a full-body display of multiple individuals. In addition, these requirements are all important for conducting successful multipoint conferences and collaborations, because in order to effectively share the experiences with others using digital multimedia data, a multiuser interaction environment is necessary. In addition, multipoint mode users can work in parallel or synchronously to interchange opinions. Multipoint collaborative systems afford interaction across time and space and allow all users to participate, while at the same time permitting them to receive direct scaffolding from peers and experts, mediated by supercomputing machines. In the next sections, we describe several multipoint collaboration systems, including Access Grid technology.

SENSEWEB

The SenseWeb system is an example of a multiuser interactive information environment (Lopez-Gulliver et al. 2004). Equipment includes several multimedia technologies, including cameras, common halogen lamps as an infrared light source, and a piece of software to make a rear projection screen interactive and multiuser capable. The purpose of the SenseWeb system is to support shared experiences and collaboration among multiple users. It allows users to simultaneously interact with digital multimedia elements by using their bare hands.

A multiuser system like SenseWeb also means that multiple users can directly interact with the data simultaneously.

Lopez-Gulliver and colleagues (2004) looked at the effectiveness of SenseWeb's multipoint capabilities. Results from this study indicated that nineteen out of twenty users found the SenseWeb system easy to use. Most of the users appreciated the dual capabilities of the multipoint mode because it allowed them to work in parallel or in a synchronous way.

MERMAID

Other systems, such as MERMAID (Multimedia Environment for Remote Multiple Attendee Interactive Decision-making), engage users through a specialized architecture. MERMAID's design is based on group collaboration system architecture, which provides an environment for widely distributed participants, seated at their desks, to hold real-time conferences by interchanging information through video, voice, and multimedia documents (Watabe et al. 1990).

While multipoint systems such as MERMAID focus on specialized architecture for real-time conferences, other systems like XGSP (XML-based General Session Protocol) are based on Web services technology for creating and controlling videoconferences. Using a Web-services framework, researchers developed the prototype system, Global Multimedia Collaboration System (Global-MMCS) (Watabe et al. 1990). The Global MMCS integrates various services, including videoconferencing and instant messaging and streaming, and it supports multiple videoconferencing technologies and heterogeneous collaboration environments.

MULTIPOINT CONTROL UNITS

The next system, Multipoint Control Units, is a central server used to coordinate and distribute video and audio streams among multiple participants in a video conference (Willebeek-LeMair, Kandlur, and Shae 1994). There are three methods for video bit-rate reduction. In the most straightforward method, the input video bitstream is decoded to the pixel domain, and the decoded video signal is reencoded at the desired output bit rate. In addition, the picture quality is improved by processing skipped macro blocks and applying frequency-weighted thresholding.

INTEGRATED SERVICE DIGITAL NETWORK

The Integrated Service Digital Network (ISDN) is part of the work carried out by the European collaborative project Multipoint Interactive Audiovisual Communication (MIAC) and Multipoint Interactive Audiovisual System (MIAS) (Clark 1992). In the late 1960s, the audioconference used the telephone network to bring audio together. In the 1980s, the new system allowed users to draw interactively on the face of a television screen by means of a light pen (Clark 1992). Videoconferencing, which is the newest technology, has been available for business and education for the past twenty years.

ACCESS GRID

Access Grid (AG) technology was developed by the Futures Laboratory at Argonne National Laboratory and is deployed by the National Center for Supercomputing Applications (NCSA) PACI Alliance (Cyberinfrastructure Tutor n.d.). The AG is a cutting-edge virtual audio/video videoconferencing and audio/video collaboration system that aims to create a real-time communication among multiple people from geographically separate locations as if they are engaged in the same room (Refka 2003).

> The Access Grid (AG) is the ensemble of resources that can be used to support human interaction across the grid. It consists of multimedia display, presentation and interactions environments, interfaces to grid middleware, interfaces to visualization environments. The Access Grid will support large-scale distributed meetings, collaborative work sessions, seminars, lectures, tutorials and training. The Access Grid design point is group to group communication (thus differentiating it from desktop to desktop based tools that focus on individual communication). The Access Grid environment must enable both formal and informal group interactions. Large-format displays integrated with intelligent or active meeting rooms are a central feature of the Access Grid nodes. Access Grid nodes are "designed spaces" that explicitly contain the high-end audio and visual technology needed to provide a high-quality compelling user experience. (Cyberinfrastructure Tutor n.d., para. 1)

In other words, the AG environment is very interactive and can possibly improve the participants' experiences by providing an increased sense of social presence, supporting natural human interactions, eliminating distance problems, and allowing for complex multisite visualization environments (Argonne National Laboratory et al. 2002).

Systems such as the Access Grid allow the building of collaborative knowledge through virtual computing; interactive, just-in-time teaching; and visualization affordances. It provides the environments for engaging collaborations in places often hard to reach and navigate, such as remote locations in Australia and Alaska.

Purpose of This Research

While others have researched user effectiveness of multipoint systems, the evaluation of AG technology has lagged behind in this area, which is vital when considering continuing and future use of this type of ubiquitous technology.

There are so few studies conducted on the use of the AG that basic questions have yet to be answered. The remainder of this chapter explores several ways AG technologies can be used for educational purposes and ubiquitous learning. In our research we explored the efficacy of AG technologies for collaborations and dialogue. This assessment was composed of two applications related to AG use: evaluation as a tool for ANVs and as a tool for engaging educators in dialogue. This chapter does not discuss details related to the dialogue data but rather describes the technical aspects of using the AG as a collaborative ubiquitous technology for education.

General Use of the Access Grid

To fully appreciate the AG and its use, it is first important to understand all of the technical aspects that constitute the AG. The AG is made up of connected "nodes" throughout the United States and the world, which as of 2005 numbered more than five hundred (Wikipedia 2007, para 3). In addition, an interactive map of worldwide AG nodes is available at http://www.accessgrid.org/map. Within each node are audio and video systems, as well as hardware, essential software, and a high-performance network. The following sections highlight each of these technological aspects and how they fit together to become the AG. We will then discuss the different applications of the AG in regard to ubiquitous learning, and finally our research results using the AG.

AG TECHNOLOGY

AG NODE

An AG Node (AGN) is a collection of hardware and software located in a room that uses AG technology and permits electronic communications to other AGNs (Access Grid n.d., "What Is the Access Grid?"). While in use, each AGN has staff present to assist with set-up and any technical difficulties. The number of staff varies and depends on the size of the events. Usually, the number of staff is larger at a formal event than an informal one. Specifically, "the staffs are responsible for making audio adjustments, monitoring the network, adjusting camera angles, monitoring and adjusting display windows, managing microphones, and running collaborative tools" (Disz 2001, para 1).

AUDIO AND VIDEO SYSTEM

The audio system for each node needs to be high in quality, so participants in any size meetings can be heard and seen by all participants in the event. Since the AG is on a high-speed network, the video quality is good as well, and jerky motion is reduced (Refka 2003). What this means is that people at different locations can still interact with each other as if they are meeting each other face to face.

Unlike other commercial videoconferencing tools, the AG screen display is the size of a wall. This allows local and remote participants in an AG event to view each other simultaneously as well as to view and manipulate other visuals. Also, because the screen display is so large, it improves communication by transmitting important nonverbal information, such as participants' facial expressions and gestures, more easily. As a result, participants appear to be engaged as if they were face-to-face, and the event is much more interactive. For example, scientists and engineers at multiple sites can share their scientific findings, conduct experiments, and manipulate the same data sets and visual simulations, while interacting between sites.

HIGH-PERFORMANCE NETWORKS

An AGN must have multicast-enabled networks. "Multicast-enabled networks allow one single output stream to branch off to multiple locations and to be sent only to the locations requesting the service" (Disz 2001, para. 1). As a consequence, multicasting reduces bandwidth and ensures that all participants receive the same information at relatively the same time. The minimum bandwidth is about 100 Mbit (Access Grid n.d., "Access Grid Installation Guide").

HARDWARE

The hardware for an AGN is readily available at a reasonable cost, which allows participants (or educators) to set up their own AGN. The hardware includes four computers, cameras, projectors, speakers, and echo cancellation equipment (Elliot 1993). The echo cancellation equipment is an important feature in producing high audio quality. The computers are run on Windows and Linux and are used for video and audio capture, camera control, speaker volume control, and displays.

SOFTWARE

The AGN also requires open source software such as Videoconferencing Tool (Vic), Robust Audio Tool (RAT), Distributed PowerPoint (DPPT), Virtual Network Computing (VNC), and Chromium-vic (VTK/VIC). The Vic is multicast-based. The display computer runs on this, along with virtual venues software and DPPT. The virtual venues software provides a virtual space for participants in an AG event, which means that they have space on the Web where they meet, the equivalent of a physical room for a meeting. RAT has high audio quality.

DPPT allows a presenter to control a PowerPoint slide show on multiple sites from a single machine. Thus, each participant in the same AG event has a copy of the presenter's PowerPoint slides. The VNC is a system for application sharing—a participant can view an application not only on the machine from which it is running, but also from anywhere on the Internet. The use of VTK/VIC improves visualization when using the AG (Argonne National Laboratory n.d.).

PUTTING IT ALL TOGETHER

Figure 14.1 illustrates how the different technological parts of the AGN work together. It shows how the display computer is responsible for the projectors; the video capture computer is responsible for the cameras; the audio capture computer and control computer are both responsible for the echo cancellation equipment, speakers, and microphones.

APPLICATIONS OF THE AG

The AG can be used for formal and informal events, collaborative work sessions, seminars and conferences, lectures, and training sessions. An AG event can be as simple as two people meeting at two different locations or as complex as a large conference with multiple participants from as many as ninety or more different sites. "Other than spoken and written words, other means of communication also include visualizations, computer-aided searching, shared software, image processing, virtual reality experiences, telepresence experiments, and remote instrument operation" (Welcome to the Access Grid at NCSA n.d., 1). As stated earlier, the AG supports all of these forms of communication.

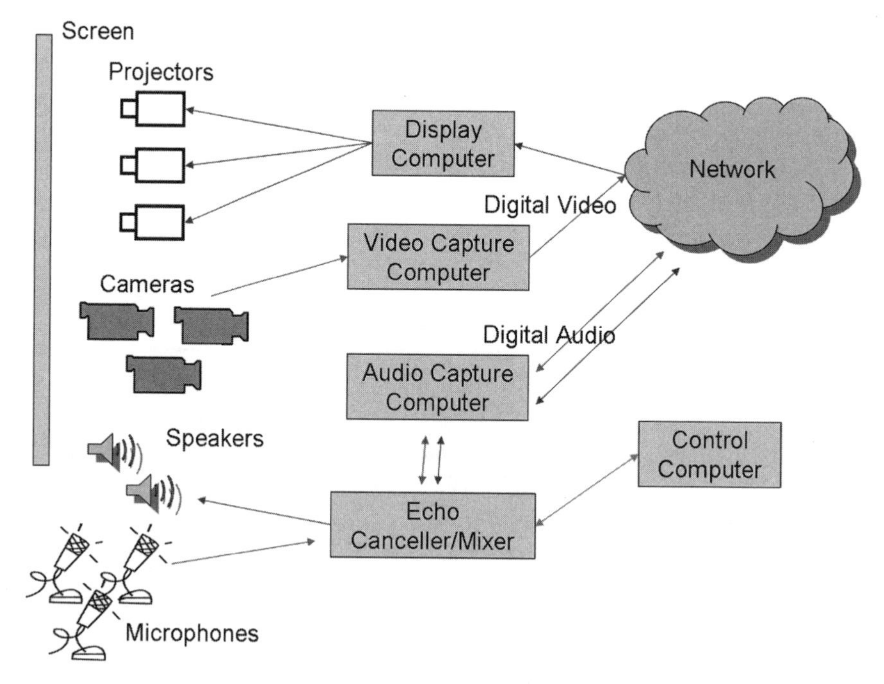

Figure 14.1. Access Grid Node (AGN) Flow Chart, October, 2004. (Courtesy of Hanna Zhong.)

Figure 14.2 depicts people participating in remote meetings. The screen display is very large, so participants can view other participants at multiple sites. Figure 14.3 illustrates how AG enables participants to view multisite visualizations (i.e., screens). For events where some visuals are necessary to better understand a topic, not only is a large screen display indispensable, but so too is the quality of the audio/video systems. Small groups or individuals can access the AG using the "Personal Interface to the Access Grid (PIG)." The AG functionality is reduced with PIG, but so is the required equipment. As illustrated in figure 14.4, the display screen is much smaller than the normal AGN, and only one computer and three monitors are needed.

The AG plays an increasingly important role in the field of education. As mentioned before, the AG environment is interactive, and it encourages active teaching and active learning. This research utilized an ANV as the starting point for the participants' discussion. The focus of this chapter is the actual application of the AG and the students' reactions to using it.

METHODS

PARTICIPANTS

Two universities participated in this project: University of Illinois at Urbana-Champaign (UIUC) and East Carolina University (ECU). Each university provided two groups of students for the project. UIUC had a total of eight participants: five participants in group 1 and three participants in group 2. ECU had a total of twelve participants: six participants in each group.

The eight students at UIUC were all Caucasian females and comprised seven undergraduates and one master's degree candidate. Table 14.1 shows information about the participants at UIUC. For each UIUC group there were also additional participants: Sharon Tettegah (ST, facilitator), Edee (Ed, AG coordinator), George (Ge, technical assistance), Joycelyn (JL, dialogue facilitator), and Grant (Gr, research assistant).

The twelve students at ECU included five males and seven females who were first- to third-year doctoral candidates employed in postsecondary institutions in entry-level positions. No other demographics were available. Table 14.2 provides information about the ECU participants. For each ECU group, Cheryl, a facilitator, was also present during each session.

MATERIALS

The materials for this project included laptops with Internet access for each of the participants, an AGN at UIUC and ECU, and the ANV. An example of how the AGN was set up is shown in figure 14.5. The typical room has a capacity of about thirty participants and has a large-scale display with three projectors. The

Figure 14.2. An image of an Access Grid meeting, June 2008. (Courtesy of the National Center for Supercomputing Applications and the Board of Trustees of the University of Illinois.)

Figure 14.3. A view of multisite visualization at NCSA, June 2008. (Courtesy of the National Center for Supercomputing Applications and the Board of Trustees of the University of Illinois.)

Figure 14.4. Personal interface to the Access Grid (PIG) is represented in this image, October 2004. (Courtesy of Sharon Tettegah.)

Table 14.1. Characteristics of UIUC Participants

Group 1	Group 2
Caucasian female, junior, music major	Caucasian female, junior, agricultural education major
Caucasian female, junior, elementary education major	Caucasian female, senior, finance major
Caucasian female, junior, psychology major	Caucasian female, junior, human development and family studies major
Caucasian female, freshman, accounting major	
Caucasian female, graduate student in special education	

Table 14.2. Characteristics of ECU Participants

Group 1	Group 2
Male, works in the college of education	Male, works as an assistant analyst at ECU
Female, works in the Agape center and teaches in the education department	Male, works for student services at ECU
Female, works for student services and with the business education students	Female, works in the medical education department at the school of medicine
Male, works for student professional development at ECU	Female, works in the judicial affairs office at ECU
Female, works at a community college	Female, works for recreational services at ECU
Female, works at the college of education in a scholarship program	Male, works in the office of international affairs at ECU

Figure 14.5. An example of the participation setup, using the AG at NCSA, June 2008. (Courtesy of the National Center for Supercomputing Applications and the Board of Trustees of the University of Illinois.)

ANV used for this research focused on student–teacher interactions within an educational context.

PROCEDURES

The primary investigator, Sharon Tettegah, discussed the Access Grid project with a codirector at the National Center for Supercomputing Applications, Edee Norman Wiziecki, who suggested a couple of possibilities about how to find other university sites willing to participate. From this conversation, the primary investigator decided to distribute the research plan to several universities and asked if any were interested in participating. East Carolina University, in collaboration with Cheryl McFadden, agreed to join the project.

In January 2004, the primary investigator sent an e-mail message describing the study to all the doctoral students in the educational leadership–higher education concentration at East Carolina University. The participants had a chance to win a laptop computer and two gift certificates as incentives for being part of this project. Twelve students contacted the primary investigator and agreed to participate in the study. They were divided into two groups of six each. The primary investigator also posted the project on the bulletin board of the human subject pool at UIUC. Eight students signed up for participation in the project.

They were also divided into two groups. There were five participants in group 1 and three participants in group 2.

The primary investigator set up the Access Grid technology and met UIUC participants at the South Research Park (SRP) on the University of Illinois-Urbana-Champaign campus. Each group (groups 1 and 2) from UIUC and ECU met at the same time (i.e., the UIUC students and ECU students were hundreds of miles apart, but they were able to engage in virtual conversations as though they were face to face in real time using Access Grid technology).

Both groups (groups 1 and 2) from UIUC and ECU followed the same procedures even though they met at different times owing to time zone differences. When the students sat down and were ready at both sites, the primary investigator introduced the project and explained the procedure to all the participants. The participants from both sites were also asked to briefly identify themselves at the beginning of the project. Since all the students had laptop computers in front of them, they had a chance to browse and explore the Inter-Cultural and Cross-Cultural Teaching Portal (ICCTP) Web site for a few minutes. The researcher also gave participants directions on how to find the ANV social simulation link and how to register for the vignette page. All participants were asked to use a pseudonym and password to log into the Web site to view the ANV. Using pseudonyms kept participants' identities confidential in this research.

The students observed the ANV simultaneously on both sites. There were a few technical difficulties that occurred during registration and the observation of the ANV. However, all students were able to see the ANV and responded to the ANV questions. Participants were also asked to complete a site survey and paper survey after responding to the ANV questions.

When all participants finished the surveys, the researcher and the participants discussed their thoughts and perspectives about the vignette story, as well as what they thought about the use of the AG (data discussed in this chapter). The participants from each site were able to see each other with a wall-size screen and were able to engage in a dialogue simultaneously by using the video conference system.

RESULTS

PARTICIPANT REACTIONS

Overall, the participants seemed to split pretty evenly between those who enjoyed using the AG and those who did not, with two participants expressing both their enjoyment and frustrations with the AG technology. One UIUC student said: "I thought it was pretty cool, uh, I don't know it, it was a little hard to, at some points to uh, understand what you guys [ECU participants] were saying, but I thought it was neat that, you know, like, we can communicate with people in a totally different room and talk about this stuff." An ECU group member commented: "Except for the breaking up it has been great." These participants recognized both the benefits and shortcomings (technical difficulties) of using the ubiquitous technology of the AG.

A few of the participants did not enjoy the AG and preferred true face-to-face meetings with people because face-to-face meetings encourage more discussion. A UIUC participant remarked: "I've actually had a distance class in this kind of format and the only thing that's difficult about it is it's hard to be interactive with people on the other side. Limits what you can do." And one of the ECU students said: "I would rather be face to face. I prefer that. It is a unique technology advancement, but I would rather be face to face." One of the UIUC group members agreed: "I really didn't like it [smiled and laughed nervously]. I feel like, uh, if I was just like talking with a group of people here we might have gone a little further and it's really hard, you know, with people breaking up, and you know, I'm looking into a camera when I'm talking and it's just, and I didn't like it really!" Two of these participants noted a general dislike of the technology for this application, and another participant noted that it was not comfortable for her and the technical difficulties did not help to ease her discomfort.

On the other side, some participants indicated a lot of enthusiasm and enjoyment with using the AG. Three of the UIUC students had entirely positive reactions. One observed: "Yeah, I think it's a very interesting way to discuss something different. I've never done it before, so I think that, yeah, it was really cool." Another noted: "I wasn't expecting it at all, so it was something, something new and interesting." One more exclaimed: "I really enjoyed it! I think it's neat that you can see people from like, how, I don't know how far away, like half the United States away." All of the participants who had positive reactions to the AG seemed to find "the technology to be important and intriguing," as did some who also preferred face-to-face meetings. Most thought the AG provided an advantage of being able to see and speak with people from across the United States and the world.

TECHNICAL ISSUES

The AG collaboration was a successful project; however, we found several problems associated with using the tool. During the study, the dialogue had to be adapted for the setting. The participants were not able to sit facing each other in a circle, and they often had to raise their hands and be addressed before beginning to speak, rather than just being able to chime in when they wanted. A time-delay occurred that inhibited each group's communication. For example, sometimes when participants spoke to each other there had to be a sufficient amount of space between them so that the video could capture their faces. It was very distracting for the participants when they sat in a circle because one participant could block the view of another owing to the location of the cameras. Participants were spaced apart, facing forward, and not sitting directly behind or in front of someone else so that everyone could be seen. In addition, there were multiple problems hearing the speakers (as mentioned by some of the participants above), and participants often had to wave their hands while speaking so people on the other side could identify who was talking.

When playing the ANV over the Access Grid for both groups to hear simultaneously, there were extended pauses between vignette characters, and the study facilitators commented that the speech seemed to be delayed. Several participants also had trouble turning up the volume on their computers to hear the vignettes. Once the volume was up, however, and all vignettes were playing, it was difficult for participants to hear them because of the noise of the other computers. In addition, the microphones had to be muted in order to reduce the sound coming through to the other side (i.e., UIUC's microphones had to be muted so that ECU could hear their vignettes and vice versa). Once the second group of participants finished listening to the vignettes, they were instructed to shut down their computers. Several computers from both sides could be heard shutting down while other participants were working on their surveys, which appeared to be distracting.

Technical problems unrelated to the AG also cropped up. Required computer software (Quick Time) was not available, so the "ask the professional" portion of the ICCTP Web site could not be viewed. Two ECU participants had difficulty registering on the computer because they did not include their full e-mail addresses (including the @ symbol), and one site experienced other technical difficulties unrelated to the AG. Edee (the AG coordinator)'s computer froze up as she was trying to register. In addition, ECU's AG was located in a very large room with partitions dividing the space into several classrooms. Noise could be heard from the other classrooms and was very distracting to the participants.

Conclusion

The purpose of this chapter was to explore the use of the ubiquitous technology of the AG for a specific educational purpose. We tested the ability of the AG to stream ANVs. Exploring and examining an educational application of the AG provided us with a baseline for using the AG to stream video and engage a dialogue session across the AG for multiple viewers. After an ANV was shown, participants discussed and reflected on the event that took place in the vignette. In a situation like this, mere verbal communications could not capture participants' reactions adequately, yet with the AG technology, the participants could communicate using verbal and nonverbal forms, a hallmark of ubiquitous learning. In addition, not only was information shown and shared, but also facial expressions were transmitted and responded to in turn. In the context of social communication, this is especially vital and illustrates how well-suited AG technology is as a ubiquitous learning tool that affords temporal, spatial, and participatory modes of mixed representation. However, it will be important to address the technical and logistical issues identified in this study prior to using this technology for future research. For example, it will be important to make sure that all the participants at one site can hear and see the participants at the other site and are informed of the time-delay between sites. Also, the location of the AG should be considered.

In this study, ECU's AG was located in a large, open room with multiple classrooms. All of these technical and logistical issues could be minimized and possibly eliminated while making this technology appropriate for engaging in collaborations and dialogue. The appropriate space should be identified before attempting to engage any type of open discussion over the AG.

Further uses of the AG (and other multipoint collaboration technologies) include being able to quite literally bring the world to the classroom in the sense that anyone from across the world can connect with anyone else to share resources, network, or collaborate (von Hoffman, Wiziecki, and Arns 2006). The AG educators could easily bring experts to the classroom and provide live demonstrations and real-time interaction with other students as well as instructors and other "experts." In addition, the interconnectedness in this type of ubiquitous technology helps users to link other technologies they use daily to this AG technology. Yet, some problems persist with this technology, including the limited visual screen, which means participants may miss some things going on in the other location, such as facial cues, hand gestures, and other body language movements. Some of the biggest problems revolve around technical usability issues as well as the fact that AG technology is not portable like many ubiquitous technologies such as laptops, cell phones, and GPS devices. As technology advances, perhaps AG technology will become even more affordable so that AG becomes a household name.

Readings and References

For further reading on the topic of multipoint collaboration technologies and ubiquitous learning, see William J. Clark's multipoint multimedia conferencing article (Clark 1992), as well as Takeshi Utsumi's journal article on "Globally Collaborative Experiential Learning (http://tojde.anadolu.edu.tr/tojde19/pdf/article_3.pdf). For additional case studies on collaborative education using the AG, see the white paper by Jennifer von Hoffman, Edee Norman Wiziecki, and Laura Arns (http://www.accessgrid.org/files/EPIC-VI-case-studies3-8-07.pdf), Wenjun Liu and Rick Stevens's conference paper on the AG as knowledge technology (http://www-new.mcs.anl.gov/fl/flevents/wace/wace2004/papers/paper-liu.pdf), Hyunju Kim and colleagues' conference paper on the experience of using the AG for a distance education course (Kim et al. 2006), and the Wikipedia article listed below (Wikipedia 2007).

Access Grid. n.d. "Access Grid Installation Guide for Fedora 10." Access Grid, http://www.accessgrid.org/node/1133 (accessed February 22, 2009).

———. n.d. "What Is the Access Grid?" Access Grid, http://www.accessgrid.org/faq/show/51#q_1742 (accessed February 22, 2009).

Argonne National Laboratory, BAE Systems, California Institute of Technology (Caltech), inSORS Communications, Rutherford Appleton Laboratory, UKERNA, and the Universities of Cambridge, Edinburgh, Glasgow, Manchester, and Southampton. 2002. "Multi-site Videoconferencing for the UK e-Science Programme." UK e-Science Technical Report Series, http://www.dspace.cam.ac.uk/bitstream/1810/197088/1/VCReport_FINAL_Oct2.pdf (accessed February 22, 2009).

Childers, Lisa. 2000. "The Access Grid Node: The Operator's Manual." AG Tutorial, March '00, http://www-fp.mcs.anl.gov/ag/events/tutorial-mar00–presentations/ag-tutorial-mar00.htm (accessed June 19, 2004).

Clark, William J. 1992. "Multipoint Multimedia Conferencing." *IEEE Communications Magazine* 30(5) (May): 44–50.

Cyberinfrastructure Tutor. n.d. "AG01: How to Build and Install an Access Grid Node (AGN)." Cyberinfrastructure Tutor, http://ci-tutor.ncsa.uiuc.edu/index.php (accessed February 22, 2009).

Disz, Terry. 2001. "The Access Grid Collaboration Environment." *Campus Technology,* April 3, available at http://campustechnology.com/articles/2001/04/the-access-grid-collaboration-environment.aspx (accessed February 22, 2009).

Elliot, Chip. 1993. "High-Quality Multimedia Conferencing through Long-Haul Packet Network," 91–98. *Proceedings of the First ACM International Conference on Multimedia.* Anaheim, Calif.: ACM Press.

Fox, Geoffrey, Wenjun Wu, Ahmet Uyar, and Hasan Bulut. 2002. "A Web Services Framework for Collaboration and Audio/Videoconferencing." *Proceedings of the 2002 International Conference on Internet Computing,* 1–6. Las Vegas, Nev. Available at http://grids.ucs.indiana.edu/ptliupages/publications/avwebserviceapril02.pdf (accessed February 28, 2009).

Gong, Fengmin. 1994. "Multipoint Audio and Video Control for Packet-Based Multimedia Conferencing." In *Proceedings of the Second ACM International Conference on Multimedia,* 425–32. New York: ACM Press.

Kim, Hyunju, Loretta A. Moore, Geoffrey Fox, and Robert W. Whalin. 2006. "An Experience on a Distance Education Course over the Access Grid Nodes." In *Proceedings of the 4th International Conference on Education and Information Systems, Technologies, and Applications.* Orlando, Fla., July 20–23. Available at http://grids.ucs.indiana.edu/ptliupages/publications/eista06.pdf.

Liu, Wenjun, and Rick Stevens. 2004. "The Access Grid as Knowledge Technology." *Proceedings from the Workshop on Advanced Collaborative Environments.* Nice, France. Available at http://www-new.mcs.anl.gov/fl/flevents/wace/wace2004/papers/paper-liu.pdf.

Lopez-Gulliver, Roberto, Hiroko Tochigi, Tomashiro Sato, Masami Suzuki, and Norihiro Hagita. 2004. "SenseWeb: Collaborative Image Classification in a Multi-user Interaction Environment." In *Proceedings of the 12th Annual ACM International Conference on Multimedia,* 456–59. New York: ACM Press.

Patterson, John, Ralph D. Hill, Steven L. Rohall, and Scott W. Meeks. 1990. "Rendezvous: An Architecture for Synchronous Multi-user Applications." In *Proceedings of the 1990 ACM Conference on Computer-Supported Cooperative Work,* 317–28. New York: ACM Press.

Refka, Gary. 2001. "Building an Access Grid Node: From Room Construction to Equipment Configuration." Version 2.4.1. Access Grid Documentation Project, http://www.accessgrid.org/agdp/guide/building-an-access-grid-node.html.

———. 2003. "Building an Access Grid Node: From Room Construction to Equipment Configuration." Version 2.4.6. Access Grid Documentation Project, http://www.accessgrid.org/agdp/guide/building-an-access-grid-node/2.4.6/html/book1.html (accessed February 22, 2009).

Sonnenwald, D., M. Whitton, and K. Maglaughlin. 2003. "Evaluating a Scientific Collaborator: Results of a Controlled Experiment." *ACM Transactions on Computer–Human Interaction* 10(2): 150–76.

Tettegah, Sharon. 2005. "Technology, Narratives, Vignettes, and the Intercultural and Cross-Cultural Teaching Portal." *Urban Education* 40(4): 268–93.

———. 2007. "Pre-service Teachers, Victim Empathy, and Problem Solving Using Animated Narrative Vignettes." *Technology, Instruction, Cognition and Learning* 5:41–68.

Tettegah, Sharon, and C. Anderson. 2007. "Pre-service Teachers' Empathy and Cognitions: Statistical Analysis of Text Data by Graphical Models." *Contemporary Educational Psychology* 32:48–82.

von Hoffman, Jennifer T., Edee Norman Wiziecki, and Laura Arns. 2006. "Access Grid in Collaborative Education: Case Studies." Available at http://www.accessgrid.org/files/EPIC-VI-case-studies3-8-07.pdf (accessed February 13, 2008).

Watabe Kuzuo, Shiro Sakata, Kagutoshi Maeno, Hideyuke Fukuoka, and Royoko Ohmori. 1990. "Distributed Multiparty Desktop Conferencing System: MERMAID." In *Proceedings of the 1990 ACM Conference on Computer-Supported Cooperative Work,* 27–38. New York: ACM Press.

Wikipedia. 2007. "Access Grid." Wikipedia, http://en.wikipedia.org/wiki/Access_Grid (accessed September 5, 2007).

Willebeek-LeMair, Marc, Dilip Dinker Kandlur, and Zon-Yin Shae. 1994. "On Multipoint Control Units for Videoconferencing." In *IEEE Proceedings of the 19th Conference on Local Computer Networks,* 356–64. New York: IEEE Computer Society.

Zhu, Qin-Fan, Louis Kerofsky, and Marshall B. Garrison. 1999. "Low-Delay, Low-Complexity Rate Reduction and Continuous Presence for Multipoint Videoconferencing." *IEEE Transactions on Circuits and Systems for Video Technology* 9(4) (June): 666–76.

15

Physical Embodiment of Virtual Presence

KARRIE G. KARAHALIOS

Mark Weiser's seminal paper (1991) that introduces ubiquitous computing describes an environment where people collaborated and communicated using tabletlike interfaces of various scale. Large screens were used by groups of people, whereas smaller screens were used for more intimate or private work. These screens were scattered throughout the surroundings and were connected via a network. The form and rectilinear screens of these tablets dictated how they should be used—often as one would use a software application on a computer. Although their location might suggest function (a large screen in a public space could be used by a large group of people to collaborate), the remainder of the space was not incorporated into the experience.

This work presented in this chapter pushes the boundaries of the virtual and the physical. Weiser anticipated this in his explanation of the role of the library (Weiser 1994). He argues that putting all books and documents online is not a library. A library is also the space that provides the opportunity for interaction, socialization, and exploration of data and people. Chit Chat Club, described below, takes the first steps in moving away from the rectangular screen and melds into its environment—in this case, a café. By looking at how interaction evolves in such a setting, we gain insight to designing future ubiquitous spaces that combine the virtual and the physical.

Chit Chat Club

Cafés function very well as informal public gathering places. One can enjoy the company of others or be quite comfortable alone. And they are great places to sit and watch people. The online world also functions as a public gathering place. As in the café, conversation is one of the primary activities—but with some striking differences. Online, conversing with strangers is quite common, and there are few barriers to such interactions, while in the real world such encounters are less common and occur couched in complex social rituals. In the online world, one is fundamentally alone: although there are many others virtually present, one's sense of their presence is minimal. In the real-world café, the number of people is fewer, but their presence is far greater.

These two worlds come together in Chit Chat Club. It reproduces a real café, with real tables, coffee, and pastries. Yet the customers gathered round the tables may be present physically or virtually—some are real people, sitting in ordinary chairs; others are seated "telesculptures," equipped with monitors and network connections. While this is a ubiquitous computing environment, great care has been taken to make the interaction between the real and virtual seamless, and to mitigate the appearance of the traditional computer display and interface.

In this chapter, through an examination of the Chit Chat Club, I explore the physical embodiment of virtual presence.

THE CAFÉ SCENARIO

Chit Chat Club is an experiment in bringing people together in a mixed physical and virtual environment. Online chatrooms and real-world cafés are both venues for social interaction, but with significant differences—for example, the participants' knowledge of each other's expressions and identity and the traditional etiquette governing face-to-face introductions, turn-taking, and so forth. The goal is to create, through careful design of the physical environment and computer interface, a place that gracefully combines these two cultures (see figure 15.1); the analysis of how well this space actually functions will further our understanding of social interaction, both online and in person.

THE FIRST CHIT CHAT CLUB INSTALLATION

TELESCULPTURE

The telesculpture was designed to be of human scale. The idea was to communicate with an interface that has an embedded "face," as opposed to being a screen with a face on it. I and my collaborators, Judith Donath and Kelly Dobson, designed the telesculpture to be anthropomorphic to a degree, but not so anthropomorphic that one would expect human movement and human expression.

The body frame was meant resemble a relaxed figure of human proportion (see figure 15.2). The head resting on the frame has some curvature and is painted white so that it makes a good projection surface. A projector hangs in a wire basket beneath the crossed "hands" of the telesculpture, in this case named Slim. This projector is aligned to project moveable faces onto Slim's head. Above Slim's

Figure 15.1. *Top:* Artistic rendering of the Chit Chat Club. A café space is populated by people who have walked into the café, as well as by those who are remotely connected to it through the conduit of the telesculptures at the tables. (Kelly Dobson, artist.) *Bottom:* Early rendering of a telesculpture. (Karrie Karahalios, artist.)

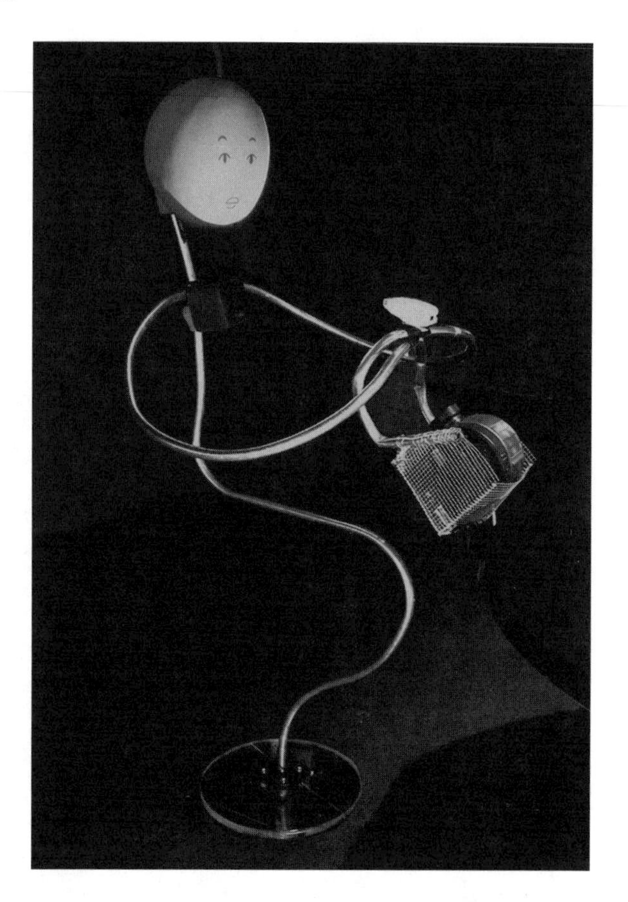

Figure 15.2. Slim, the first Chit Chat Club telesculpture. (Photo by Karrie Karahalios.)

crossed "hands" rests a camera facing away from Slim. This camera captures video of Slim's companions in the physical Chit Chat Club.

THE LOCAL SPACE

The local space of the Chit Chat Club is a café setting. The telesculpture "sits" at a table, and people entering the café may choose to sit near him or her. A rendering of the Chit Chat Club scenario can be seen in figure 15.3. Figure 15.4 shows a picture of one table in a Chit Chat Club.

THE REMOTE INTERFACE

The online site is a portal for the remote visitors to enter the Chit Chat Club. Using the Chit Chat Club Web site, the remote café attendees can create an appearance for their telesculpture's face, they can choose where to sit, and they can converse with the café's local participants by using either audio or text. While they

Figure 15.3. *Left:* The physical Chit Chat Club space. *Right:* Remote user environment. (Kelly Dobson, artist.)

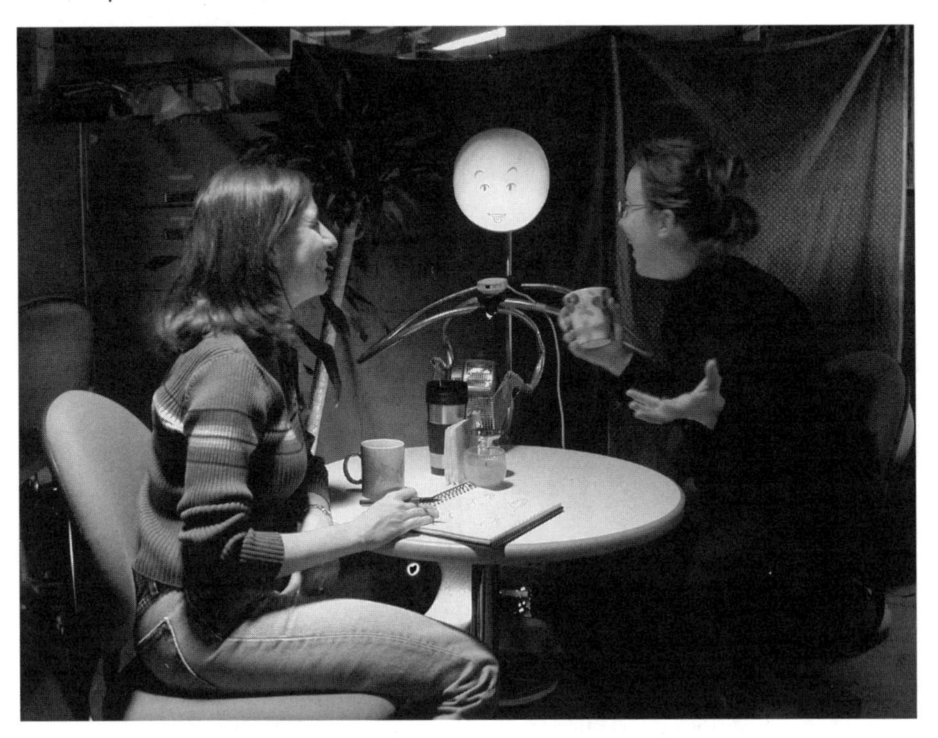

Figure 15.4. Two people sitting on each side of Slim, a telesculpture. (Photo courtesy of Karrie Karahalios and Kelly Dobson.)

are conversing with the visitors of the physical café, they see an abstracted video representation of their table companions from the point of view of the seat their telesculpture occupies. Although the remote visitors may type as well as speak to converse, they always hear what the café's physical participants are saying.

GETTING STARTED

When participants first enter the online Chit Chat Club, they are presented with an interface for creating a customized face for their respective telesculpture (see figure 15.5). They may choose face shape, eyes, and lips, as well as the color of each feature from a selection of hand-drawn, claymation, and cartoon facial components. The faces resemble cut-out animations.

After visitors create their appearance, they are ready to proceed to the Chit Chat Club entrance. Here they see a graphical bird's-eye view of the layout of the physical space (see figure 15.6). This representation shows the location of the tables, chairs, and telesculptures. It also shows which seats—regular and remote—are occupied. Participants use this image to select which telesculpture place to occupy.

THE COMMUNICATION INTERFACE

Once a seat is selected, a two-way audio and video connection is established. In the café, the remote participant's selected face appears on the telesculpture. At the remote location, the participant sees a live, processed image of the café as seen from that chair (see figures 15.7 and 15.8) and can hear, see, and participate in the conversation at that table.

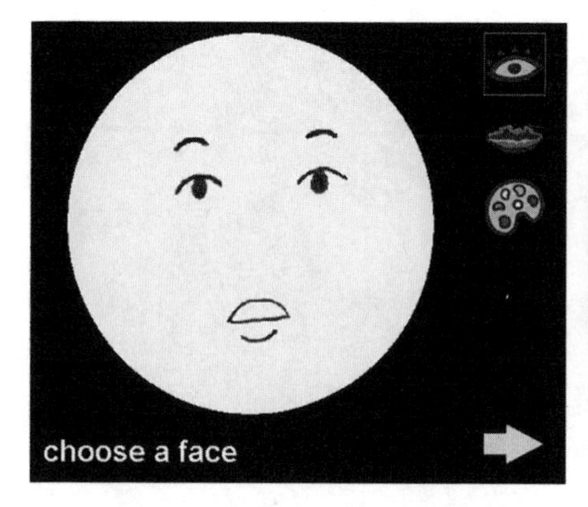

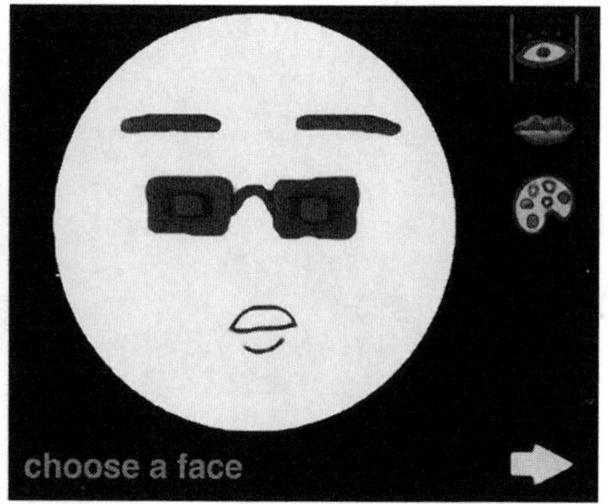

Figure 15.5. *Left:* The face selection interface. The user can cycle through different eyes, lips, and face color by clicking on the representative icons on the right. *Right:* A snapshot of a completed face.

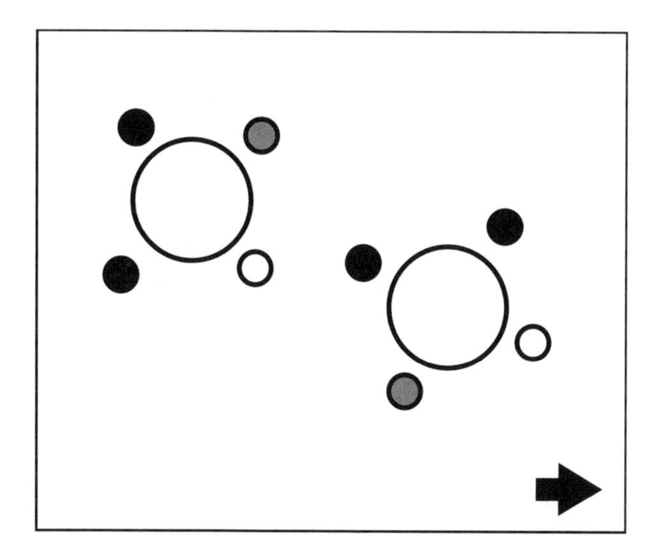

Figure 15.6. Bird's-eye view of the café. A vacant seat is depicted by a white circle; an occupied seat is depicted by a shaded circle. Black represents walk-in visitors and gray represents remote visitors.

While connected, remote visitors can communicate by talking or by typing and can momentarily change their telesculpture's expression to appear happy, bored, disgusted, sad, or angry. Conversation from the café to the online participant is still received in the form of audio and processed video.

This interface was ultimately flawed. The remote users would spend a large portion of their time selecting facial animations; this deterred them from joining the conversation. They also continued to click on the facial expressions so as not to appear inattentive. Users also wanted to direct the gaze of their telesculptures themselves as opposed to negotiating with the visitors to the physical café for rotation of gaze. We concluded that for these reasons, we had to make the selection of facial expressions easier and effort-free, and to allow the remote users to see how they appear at the physical café end.

THE SECOND CHIT CHAT CLUB INSTALLATION

TELESCULPTURE

We began to design a new telesculpture to complement the needs of our new proposed remote interface. Allowing the remote users to control their gaze into the space was a priority. The new telesculpture, therefore, would require a redesign with a motor. Sketches of our preliminary designs can be seen in figure 15.9.

The new telesculpture would also possess an anthropomorphic form, yet it would not be a human sculpture. The building of the telesculpture can be seen in figure 15.10; the final design and implementation of the second telesculpture, Orlando, is shown in figure 15.11.

Figure 15.7. Original prototype communication interface with vertical expression icons.

Figure 15.8. The remote interface. *Top:* A live video feed of the physical space. *Bottom:* The user can choose from five expressions. The telesculpture's face assumes that expression and then reverts to neutral.

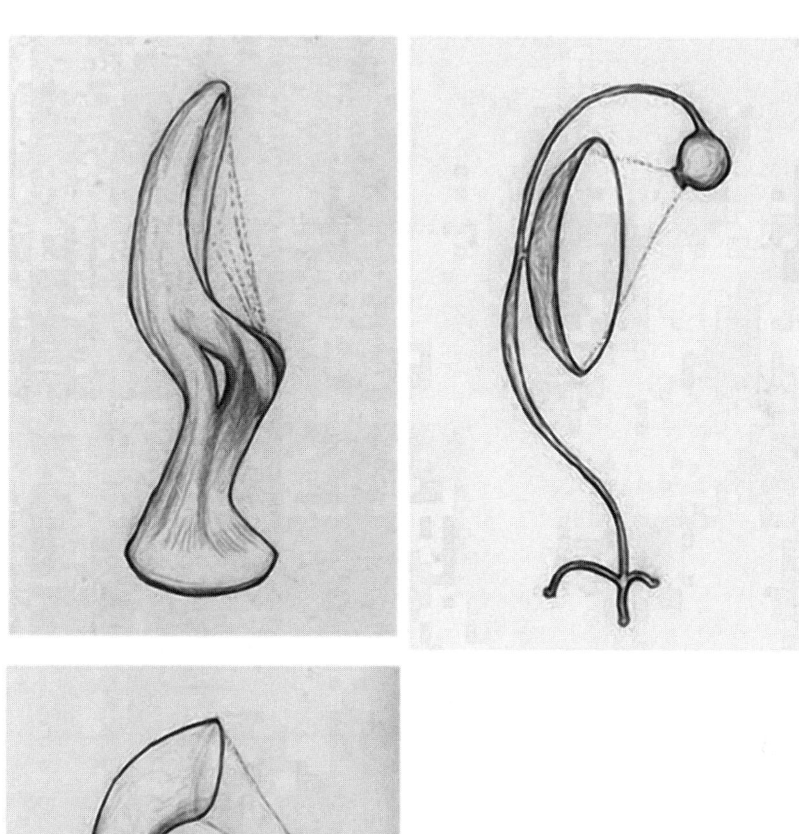

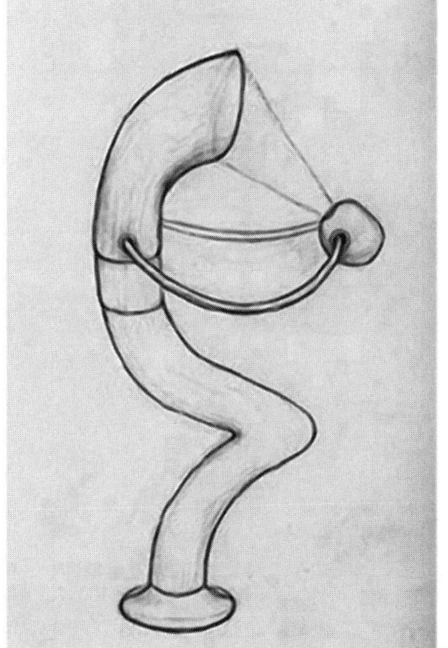

Figure 15.9. Design sketches for the second telesculpture. The top two designs were for experimentation with more abstract social cues. The bottom design housed a motor for controlling gaze. We chose this design.

Figure 15.10. Building the new chair.

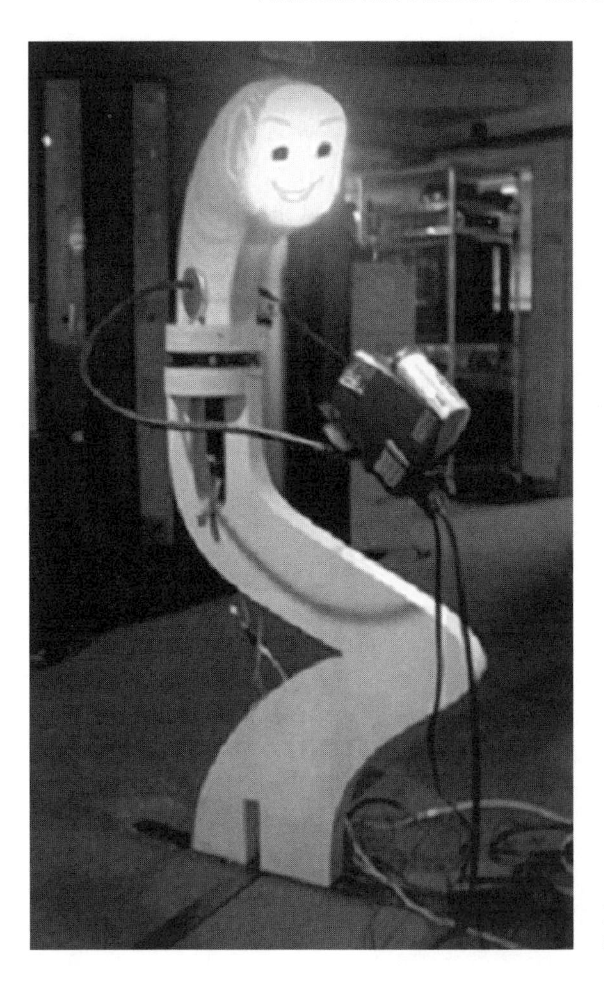

Figure 15.11. Orlando, the robotic telesculpture.

THE REMOTE INTERFACE

Entering the virtual component of the café is the same as in the previous version. What has changed in the second version is the addition of a set of facial components, the communication interface, and the telesculpture.

THE COMMUNICATION INTERFACE

In the new remote communication interface, the remote participants can view the expressions that are being projected onto their telesculptures' heads and can control the motorized gaze (see figure 15.12). Novel to this interface is a new, comprehensive expression palette in the form of a wheel.

EXPRESSION WHEEL

The expression wheel is designed to be a simple, intuitive interface for displaying facial expressions. Facial expressions composed of componential elements (Smith and Scott 1997), such as the lowering of eyebrows and the raising of lip corners, are mapped in smooth transitions around the circle, clockwise (see figure 15.12). Higher intensities of these expressions are at the perimeter of the circle and blend to more neutral expressions toward the center. To make it easier for the user, no clicking is involved. One simply has to move the mouse over the area of the expression.

Even with this new continuous wheel, users still focused on the expressions and not on the conversation. To shift their attention to the verbal interaction while maintaining expression cues during the conversation, we decided to abstract the representation of the expression wheel and make the expression selection somewhat autonomous. This new wheel can be seen in the interface in figure 15.14.

We do this by tracking the pitch of the remote user's voice in real-time and using simple heuristics to alter facial expression. One example of this is the correlation of rise in pitch to rise in eyebrows. Although the expression selection is semiautonomous, the users always have the ability to override the system and select their own expressions independently.

The abstracted expression wheel (see figure 15.13) allowed the remote users to focus more of their attention on the conversation and less on moving the

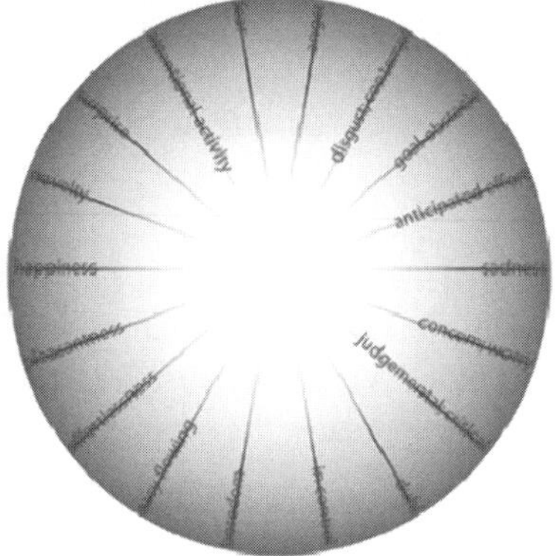

Figure 15.12. *Left:* Remote interface with visible remote expressions, gaze control, and new expression wheel. *Right:* Close-up of the continuous expression wheel. Counterclockwise from left horizontal: happiness, novelty, surprise, attentional activity, fear, anger, disgust/contempt, goal obstacle, anticipated effort, sadness, concern/worry, judgmental/critical, duh!, in control, boredom, easy flowing, effortlessness, pleasantness.

Figure 15.13. Abstracted continuous emotion wheel. This expression wheel, which shows warm colors in the top half and cool colors in the bottom half and duller colors to the left and more intense colors to the right, maintains the continuum of the previous wheel and also allows for a level of automation in expression selection.

Figure 15.14. The Chit Chat Club communication interface. This implementation incorporates the abstracted expression wheel while maintaining gaze control and remote expression visibility.

mouse. There was, however, a trade-off in the expressiveness of the faces (see figure 15.15). With the automated expression selection, we were cautious not to deduce a false expression. Hence, the arc of the expressions did not always reach the extremes. In retrospect, it seems that it was the extreme, cartoonlike animations that provided more of a catalyst for interaction than the subdued ones.

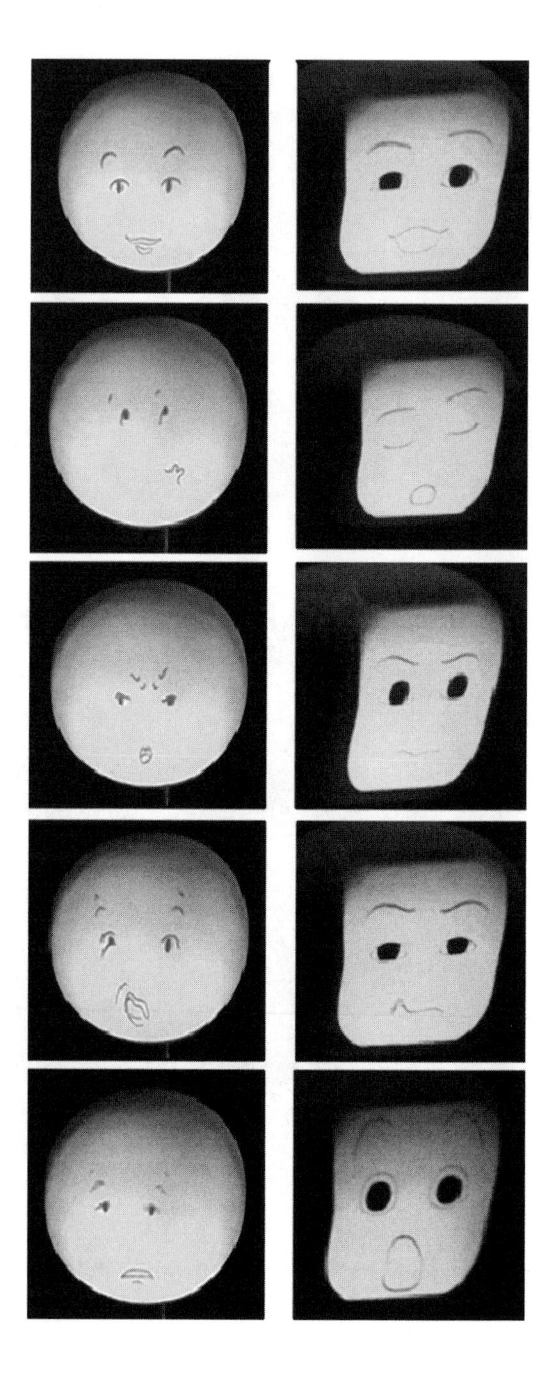

Figure 15.15. The telesculpture's projected expressions. *Left column:* Slim expressions (from top to bottom)—happy, bored, angry, "duh," sad. *Right column:* Selected Orlando expressions (from top to bottom)—happy, sleepy, angry, disgusted, surprised.

SCALE IN CHIT CHAT CLUB

Chit Chat Club was designed through several iterations. Care was taken to make the telesculptures human size. If they are bigger than life and look down on a person, they are intimidating; if they are much smaller, they are often ignored. This way, the remote participants occupied a space similar to that of the physical participants.

The telesculpture was made to look anthropomorphic. It had a head, a seated body, and arms. We did not want it to look so human that participants would expect human attributes, but we also wanted it to be accepted as an interesting seated visitor. The second telesculpture was motorized so that the remote user could direct its gaze. This offered more control to the remote user and a focus of attention for the local users at the physical Chit Chat Club.

Conclusions

Physicality and human scale are the central social catalysts of Chit Chat Club. The physicality makes for interaction far different from what happens while staring at a computer screen. In contrast to the small desktop units in the Hydra system (Buxton 1992), the human scale in Chit Chat Club provides gestural behaviors at eye-level rather than on several chess piece–like screens. The similarity in scale blends the physical and virtual worlds to accentuate togetherness over remoteness.

A final note on Chit Chat Club: although the installation emphasizes togetherness, there is an asymmetry in the public and the private venues (as can be seen in figure 15.3). The local, physical Chit Chat Club occupants perceive more of the social catalysts and the physicality, and they only see an abstracted representation of the remote café-goer. In contrast, the remote user sees a fuller view of the participants, albeit at a smaller scale and in a physically remote setting.

Readings and References

This work was inspired by the art pieces of Tony Oursler and interaction in online communication spaces. For examples of Oursler's work, see http://www.tonyoursler.com. Kit Galloway and Sherrie Rabinowitz created many installations that connected remote spaces. Their work can be seen at http://www.ecafe.org. Arnheim's work, in particular the book *Visual Thinking,* was very useful when designing the Chit Chat Club faces and interfaces. Papers on computer-mediated communication can be viewed at the *Journal of Computer-Mediated Communication* Web site (http://jcmc.indiana.edu). Early work combining the virtual and the physical can be found in Yuichi Ohta and Hideyuki Tamura's *Mixed Reality: Merging Real and Virtual Worlds* (New York:

Springer, 1999). For the latest implementation of Chit Chat Club, see http://social.cs.uiuc.edu/projects/Ginger.

Arnheim, Rudolf. 1969. *Visual Thinking.* Berkeley: University of California Press.

Bly, Sara A., Steve Harrison, and Susan Irwin. 1993. "Media Spaces: Bringing People Together in a Video, Audio and Computing Environment." *Communications of the ACM* 36(1): 28–47.

Buxton, William A. S. 1992. "Telepresence: Integrating Shared Task and Person Spaces." In *Proceedings of Graphics Interface 1992,* 123–29. San Francisco: Morgan Kaufmann Publishers.

Dourish, Paul, Annette Adler, Victoria Bellotti, and Austin Henderson. 1996. "Your Place or Mine? Learning from Long-Term Use of Audio-Video Communication." *Computer Supported Cooperative Work* 5(1): 33–62.

Reich, Vicky, and Mark Weiser. 1994. "Libraries Are More Than Information: Situational Aspects of Electronic Libraries." See also *Serials Review* 20 (3): 31–38. (Also CSL [Computer Science Laboratory] Technical Report 93-21, June.)

Scherer, Klaus R. 1986. "Vocal Affect Expression: A Review and a Model for Future Research." *Psychological Bulletin* 99:143–65.

Smith, Craig A., and Heather S. Scott. 1997. "A Componential Approach to the Meaning of Facial Expressions." In *The Psychology of Facial Expression,* ed. James A. Russell and José Miguel Fernández-Dols, 229–54. New York: Cambridge University Press.

Weiser, Mark. 1991. "The Computer for the Twenty-first Century." *Scientific American* (September): 66–75.

———. 1994. "The World Is Not a Desktop." *Interactions* (January): 7–8.

16

Administrative Implications of Ubiquitous Learning for Nonprofit Colleges and Universities

FAYE L. LESHT

This volume provides insights into the emerging field of ubiquitous learning. At the heart of the matter is how to best use the burgeoning number of technologies in meaningful ways to facilitate high-quality learning experiences throughout our lives. A critical aspect of nurturing the potential of ubiquitous learning is to take seriously the caution offered by Kalantzis and Cope in this book's introduction, that "it will be quite some time before the vision of ubiquitous learning is realized if we find progress blocked by forces of institutional inertia and heritage senses of what education should be like."

In this chapter, I argue that administrative practices in nonprofit colleges and universities have and will continue to influence our ability to respond well to the challenges and opportunities inherent in ubiquitous learning. It is through these practices that we as a society constructively address the implications of ubiquitous learning, including the question: What happens when anyone can learn anything, anytime, and anywhere 24/7 just in time and on demand?

Just as Nicholas Burbules notes in his chapter, "Meanings of 'Ubiquitous Learning,'" the opportunity for schools to serve as a "hub" for learners with "spokes" stemming from the hub enabling learners to make full use of ubiquitous learning opportunities, I suggest that the administration (working with others to achieve organizational goals) serves as the "axle" in facilitating order and continuity of the educational experience. In the best of academic worlds, that "axle" encourages creativity, innovation, and learning; in the worst, it squelches or limits these very tendencies.

As noted by L. C. Smith, professor and associate dean responsible for coordinating online graduate education in library and information science at the University of Illinois at Urbana-Champaign (personal communication, May 15, 2007), "those wishing to facilitate ubiquitous learning need to consider barriers that students may encounter and how to reduce or eliminate them. Many of those relate to administrative factors and require active involvement of administrative units providing services for faculty and students."

What are these barriers? The following are four examples.

First, on many college campuses today, debate continues as to whether online education, let alone ubiquitous learning, is a viable way to educate. Historical attitudes about how students learn best can present significant barriers to administrators attempting to keep their institutions viable, as well as to faculty and to students. Note, for example, the rise of the private, for-profit higher education sector (Tierney and Hentschke 2007).

In their chapter, Cope and Kalantzis point to seven different modes of ubiquitous computing. Each of these has implications for learning and in turn for administrative processes in support of learners. Each also points to current barriers in the educational process. For example, "participatory computing" encourages faculty to incorporate multimedia in their courses. Today's students expect to be "engaged" in meaningful ways. They will incorporate digital media in their assignments even if instructors do not use it in their instruction. Are those faculty who are interested in using media afforded the necessary time and resources to reshape their courses to make the best use of tools that can enhance student learning? Without administrative support for release time of this nature, students' experience of technology-enhanced offerings in the classroom tends to be disappointing (Young 2004).

To fully benefit from "temporal computing" or "anyplace/anytime" learning in substantive ways, more faculty should incorporate appropriate uses of educational technologies into their curricula. Technologies should be incorporated both as a means to enhance learning and to further engage those students who grew up with computing—so much so that it is intuitive for them, as suggested by Evangeline Pianfetti in her chapter. We want to adopt what is best about traditions of the past, while working for a future that recognizes the realities of the digital age. Administrative leadership is required to engage in fruitful discussions.

Second, and related to the first barrier to more effective uses of ubiquitous learning, is the faculty reward system. It was only recently that colleges and universities began to formally recognize distance education, including online offerings, in the promotion and tenure process. To participate in any educational enterprise, faculty must know that their efforts are viewed favorably and that they will not be covertly punished for participating in these types of educational endeavors. This includes but is not limited to financial recognition.

Critical administrative factors facilitating faculty participation in online education include formal recognition in the promotion and tenure process; commitment on the part of the entire faculty toward the effort; access to academic, administrative, and technological support; technology training; opportunities to explore ways to best use technologies that enhance the educational experiences of learners; release time for revising coursework; adjustments for teaching online courses as well as teaching students in campus courses and for using technologies in new ways; and time for related research (Haythornthwaite and Kazmer 2004; Meyer 2001).

These are significant factors in the mix of variables to facilitate the educational process of the future. They require an investment of resources many institutions lack. Consequently, administrators will play an increasingly important decision-making role, along with learners and faculty, in determining directions and priorities for scarce resources.

Third, there is a tendency for traditional colleges and universities to resist change. It can be difficult to change long-standing policies and procedures that have worked well in the past. We are in the midst of a "sea change" in education, particularly in higher education. What led to the rise of the private, for-profit sector in education? One clear factor has been the resistance on the part of American higher education to adapt more quickly to learners' needs (Tierney and Hentschke 2007). That is a policy issue.

A recent story illustrates this point. At the February 2008 meeting of the American Association of Collegiate Registrars and Admissions Officers, a topic high on the agenda was "credit transfer" (Lederman 2008). While concerns pertaining to the transfer of credit between institutions, and especially between unlike institutions (private, for-profit as compared with nonprofit) remain, that is not the issue that captivated the audience. Rather, registrars are grappling with a new kind of credit transfer issue—a type that reflects the students of today: more students are transferring and "having to repeat coursework because of lack of coordination and alignment between previous and current institutions" (Lederman 2008).

Let us extend the impact of ubiquitous learning to campus registrars. Students are enrolling in online courses at institutions other than their "home" campus, and they expect those credits to transfer and meet their degree requirements. Lederman (2008) continues, "And most of the work that is occupying college and state higher education officials is trying to knock down the barriers and smooth connections within state systems or between individual colleges, to ease students' transition from one institution to another."

It is important to keep in mind that most administrative policies governing students were written in the 1940s and 1950s as a result of the dramatic increase in enrollments following World War II. A number of policies have evolved over time; however, most policymakers at the time could not envision the emergence of an information age that would warrant an entirely new way of thinking about the dynamics between students, teachers, and learning environments.

For example, one state institution recently revised its definition of "residency" so that students taking classes online, students needing to interrupt their educations briefly, and students taking summer courses elsewhere would not have to petition for their work to be recognized and applied toward their degree requirements. Policies in student codebooks of traditional institutions make assumptions that need to be reviewed and modified for today's learners.

Furthermore, barriers pertaining to policies and procedures especially affect off-campus students—particularly, adult students who are unable to relocate to a traditional campus owing to family and career responsibilities, and students that live near a campus but who are unable to leave home or work to attend classes because of other obligations. I mention these two groups because it is important to keep sight of the importance of ubiquitous learning for all students. Programmatic options abound as a result of educational technologies, and they need to be used to connect residential and nonresidential students as well as to enhance each group's opportunities for learning.

The current higher education environment requires faculty, administrators, and institutions to work together to revise curricula, policies, and procedures to meet the needs of today's students. For example, a growing number of interinstitutional consortia have created their own unique agreements among member institutions that specify how each campus should offer its online courses to students at the other campuses.

For higher education to prosper, colleges and universities must develop collaborative relationships with other institutions; professional organizations; corporations; local, state, national, and international governmental agencies; and other stakeholders interested in providing their students, members, employees, and citizens with a quality education. Institutions today also have an increased awareness of the importance of providing international experiences for their diverse and multicultural students. In today's dynamic, interconnected world, current and prospective students need to be able to collaborate with each other through the use of handheld devices and Web 2.0 technologies.

Fourth, colleges and universities are routinely asked by state and national agencies to provide reports of their continuing education course offerings, delivery methods, and enrollment trends. The lack of standardized definitions and templates inhibits the ability of campuses to submit reports on their ubiquitous learning activities, particularly in the area of distance education. For example, the Illinois Board of Higher Education's definition of "off-campus" courses includes online offerings, while national surveys (such as *U.S. News and World Report*) request online data without providing clear definitions of what information needs to be submitted. For the data to be meaningful, institutional reporting itself needs to be examined nationally. Colleges and universities need agreed-upon definitions and templates to facilitate reporting and to enhance the usefulness of the information they provide about organizational goals.

What happens when anyone can learn anything, anytime and anywhere? While many students already have this ability, most do not, particularly in developing countries. Certain disciplines, such as science and technology, are making it their business to make 24/7 learning opportunities available to their members. We continue to live in a society where formal education and advanced degrees tend to dictate the standards of living. Consequently, while one might be able to learn 24/7, what one does with that learning still rests largely on socioeconomic and political factors (Rossman 2007). Furthermore, knowledge acquisition is a process. Implementing knowledge and skills so they can be applied in society takes effort and experience.

At the same time, ubiquitous learning has changed the terrain of education. For example, students can surf the Internet while sitting in class. Is this always advisable? Generally, it is best to focus fully on one thing at a time (Hallowell 2006). As noted by Bomsdorf (2005), reflecting on Fischer (2001), "the challenge is not only to make information available to people at any time, at any place, and in any form, but specifically to say the right thing at the right time in the right way."

Let's consider the metaphor introduced by Nick Burbules in chapter 2, the notion of school as "hub" with "spokes" for helping learners make appropriate connections, and this essay's suggestion that administration serves as the "axle" or support structure. Colleges and universities can use their existing infrastructures, including faculty senates as well as other decision-making bodies, to take a more holistic approach toward reshaping curricula, programs, and policies affecting students and faculty to best incorporate ubiquitous learning. The stakeholders in this endeavor include students, teachers, parents, professionals, government officials, and the companies that create the tools that make "anytime/anyplace" learning possible. Administrative practices in traditional colleges and universities (nonprofit sector) need to be reviewed and modified. In this way, there is a better chance that opportunities to integrate digital technologies will result in constructive educational reforms for the benefit of society.

Readings and References

For further reading on the intersection of administration, higher education, and ubiquitous learning, see Donald E. Hanna and Michael J. Johnson, "The Challenges and Opportunities of Technology in Higher Education," *Effective Practices for Academic Leaders* 1(6) (2001): 1–16; Rossman 2007; and *A Test of Leadership: Charting the Future of U.S. Higher*

Education; A Report of the Commission Appointed by Secretary of Education Margaret Spellings (Washington, D.C.: U.S. Department of Education, 2006). For more information on adapting ubiquitous learning to e-learning opportunities and more on the "plasticity of digital learning spaces," see Bomsdorf 2005.

Bomsdorf, Birgit. 2005. "Adaptation of Learning Spaces: Supporting Ubiquitous Learning in Higher Distance Education." Available at http://drops.dagstuhl.de/opus/volltexte/2005/371/pdf/05181.BomsdorfBirgit.Paper.371.pdf (accessed February 24, 2008).

Fischer, Gerhard. 2001. "User Modeling in Human–Computer Interaction." *Journal of User Modelling and User-Adapted Interaction* 11(1): 65–86.

Hallowell, Edward M. 2006. *CrazyBusy: Overstretched, Overbooked, and about to Snap! Strategies for Coping in a World Gone ADD.* New York: Ballantine Books.

Haythornthwaite, Caroline, and Michelle M. Kazmer, eds. 2004. *Learning, Culture and Community in Online Education: Research and Practice.* New York: Peter Lang.

Lederman, Doug. 2008. "The 'Other' Transfer of Credit Problem." *Inside Higher Education,* electronic version, http://insidehighered.com/news/2008/02/19/transfer (accessed February 22, 2008).

Meyer, Joyce D. 2001. "24/7/365: Implications of Anytime, Anywhere." In TCC 2001 Online Conference: What Have We Discovered and Where Are We Headed? http://kolea.kcc.hawaii.edu/tcc/tcon01/papers/meyer.html (accessed June 24, 2007).

Rossman, G. Parker. 2007. "The Future of Higher (Lifelong) Education: For All Worldwide, a Holistic View." Available at http://ecolecon.missouri.edu/globalresearch/chapters/index.html (accessed February 24, 2008).

Tierney, William G., and Guilbert C. Hentschke. 2007. *New Players, Different Game: Understanding the Rise of For-Profit Colleges and Universities.* Baltimore: Johns Hopkins University Press.

Young, Jeffrey R. 2004. "When Good Technology Means Bad Teaching." *Chronicle of Higher Education* 51(12): A31–A32.

PART C

Practices

17

History

The Role of Technology in the Democratization of Learning

ORVILLE VERNON BURTON,
JAMES ONDERDONK,
AND SIMON J. APPLEFORD

The twenty-first century is witnessing a blurring of traditional divisions between the domains of learning, teaching, and research. This change has been spurred, to a large extent, by advances in information technology, which have had far-reaching implications for hardware, software, new pedagogy, access, accessibility, and the collection, application, and distribution of data. The collaborative promise of new technologies and the so-called Semantic Web are uniquely positioned to liberate information, making it available to all citizens and creating a culture of what is coming to be known as ubiquitous learning.

Underpinning this emerging culture are the huge challenges and the enormous potential posed by the availability of information, which is impelling a major step forward in the evolution of education—namely, how knowledge is weighed and imparted to succeeding generations. Web-sourced information varies enormously in its character and reliability, from pornography and unapologetically racist blogs to archives of rare materials and course resources made freely available online by such giants of higher education as MIT and Yale. The emergence of the online collectivized databases known as learning commons and the ongoing, fascinating struggle of Wikipedia to create a credible and continually updated "people's" reference speak to the nature of learning as a universal, self-organizing process. The consonant demand, huge and growing, for information online poses exceptional opportunities for institutions of higher education to emerge as leaders in promoting the public good by providing vetted, detailed, state-of-the-art information from research and scholarship across a range of disciplines and in an array of formats and media. With such powerful tools for transmission of knowledge and values at hand, the humanities and the arts are positioned to help develop and nurture the informed citizenry essential to democracy in ways that pure computer science could never do.

The Emergence of Ubiquitous Learning

At the close of the agrarian age, it became obvious to a broad spectrum of the public that the American educational system, which had served that age well, was inadequate for a dawning industrial era that demanded a well-trained workforce. Led by states with large rural populations, educational systems were transformed to meet this demand—the chief enduring result being mandated, universal secondary education. Unfortunately, America's schools have evolved into an excellent example of an autocratic rather than a democratic organization, where a rule-bound culture is vetted by standardized testing that unreflectively—and all too often punitively—enforces its requirements. Today, with a new world information order evolving, the educational structures of the industrial age are proving inadequate and inappropriate for the demands of the information age. Data—that is, information—are the rich raw materials for this age, much as iron ore and coal were to an earlier one. The transformation of that data into knowledge, experience, and responsible action is a primary function of the learning processes and must be encouraged. It is imperative that the academy lead a sophisticated and complex response to the promise of information technology.

Ubiquitous learning is forcing education to come to terms with a reality that has long been known in the sciences but has been less acknowledged in the humanities—the mercurial nature of information. The abundant, quick, and changeable character of learning in today's data-intensive world demands capture and management through information technology. Information is, moreover, as at no other time in the history of civilization, available in an astonishing array of formats, from raw data and text right through to high-quality imagery and streaming audio and video. These realities have profound implications for much broader approaches to scholarship, teaching, and learning.

The social critic John Ralston Saul (1994, 116) observed, "Highly sophisticated elites are the easiest and least original thing a society can produce. The most difficult and the most valuable is a well-educated populace." The ubiquitous learning empowered by technology must not widen the gap between those who have access to new information and tools and those who do not. Technology has the potential to become a tool increasingly wielded by the elite, and our goal must be to ensure the democratization of knowledge and education. It is of particular importance that colleges and universities—and especially the land grant colleges, those public institutions labeled "Democracy's Colleges" in the nineteenth century—commit to expanding the community of learning.

The Humanities and Ubiquitous Learning

Why should we be particularly concerned with the application of ubiquitous learning in the humanities? As social critics often observe, good judgment comes from experience, and experience comes from bad judgment. We need humanities for an understanding of who we are and where we came from. Having that knowledge we can then presumably make better choices about where to go next. The humanities constitute our nation's very identity: who we are, how we understand ourselves, and how we tell others, as well as the generations to come, who we are. Diligence in the study of the humanities can reveal to us the judgments, both considered and poor, of our predecessors and help us profit from them. Humanists deal with interpretation and appreciation of human culture, and the humanities are about the creation and interpretation of meaning. Carefully constructed, meaning allows learners to see what they share in common with others and how they differ, in learning as well as outlook.

What we value as a society is an evolving social compact, not an algorithm. It is the task of information technology to maximize these values. That many humanists seem reluctant to incorporate information technology into their disciplines is a deep irony. As the largest portion of the human experience, the humanities is an area where critical achievements and endeavors in digital applications are already under way, and many more exciting developments are possible.

Ubiquitous learning, if one defines that as the use of technology to make information accessible anytime, anywhere, is pushing the classic textbook toward obsolescence; the lead time alone for the production of a bound text has made it a trailing-edge resource rather than a leading-edge one. The classic textbook, in form and substance, signals the permanence of its own information when it is likely in our best interest to educate to a standard that presumes the temporary nature of most learning. This single fact presents a monumental learning opportunity for anyone involved with education in any form. Ubiquitous learning may allow us to create resources for learning that are more temporary and less detailed and yet function at a higher conceptual level than is now possible, permitting material to be tailored to the aptitudes and preferences of the learner.

Ubiquitous learning encompasses the unvetted resources of the Web and the vetted ones of the multitude of libraries that are accessible via the Web. In the intersection of these two worlds lies the challenge to educators and learners. In this new, but not entirely unfamiliar juncture, there may be more emphasis on learning and a radically changed role for teachers.

RiverWeb

Given these observations, how can the humanities use information technology in its broadest application, to democratize learning? Here at the University of Illinois, the Institute for Computing in Humanities, Arts, and Social Science developed RiverWeb in an attempt to address the needs of undergraduate education in support of inquiry-based learning. A dynamic multimedia archive of Mississippi River history and information, RiverWeb was created to meet the challenge of integrating information technology into the classroom by providing an interactive, Web-based research and learning environment that engages the students and brings the humanities, arts, and social sciences to life. It is structured so that faculty can offer their students the assistance they need to identify a problem; create hypotheses; explore humanities, arts, and social science information from different sources; combine, classify, and analyze that data; work with others interactively; and present conclusions in a cogent and concise manner.

These skills, which structure all intellectual inquiry, are fundamental to transforming data to knowledge and knowledge to action, forming the capstone of research. RiverWeb integrates these critical data resources into cohesive narrative stories that follow individuals and cases over time and are linked to other sources in a coherent manner. The hands-on, inquiry-based approach to teaching and learning is supported by giving students access to original documents and artifacts, enabling them to "do" research instead of simply reading about it, thereby contributing to their own sense of genuine discovery. By providing access to interesting, concise, and relevant primary materials for research projects, RiverWeb also provides a learning environment that can help prepare students to handle life in a society that is increasingly dependent on science and technology. And because RiverWeb is Web-based, it is accessible at any time.

Modern computer networks allow access to an incredible amount of data, yet very few portals or Web sites have been explicitly structured for dissemination of relevant and distilled data for use in a teaching or research context. One of the problems with using general-purpose search engines to hunt for this data is the sheer amount of potentially relevant information available. This growth of information makes it increasingly harder for learners to identify and make use of the most appropriate and highest quality educational resources. While digital libraries and some existing portals help address these problems, RiverWeb already offers access and opportunity to explore such learning resources within developed and tested curriculum modules. It provides a multimedia, multidimensional information workbench with a self-sustaining framework that facilitates access to and collaborative use of knowledge, tools, and data.

RiverWeb has a working prototype with a wealth of accumulated Web-based knowledge, plus an effective delivery system. Project members have worked extensively in formal educational environments as well as with real-world interface design problems and Web-based learning environment applications to determine the best possible methods of creating sites with appealing design, easy navigation, advanced data retrieval, online discussion forums, and effective use of search engines. A flexible and extensive Web-based architecture provides anywhere, anytime access to engaging, high quality, on-line, multimedia resources. RiverWeb interfaces empower students and others to "time-travel" through humanities, arts, and social science data while hyperlinks lead them to a wealth of information banks, including spatial data, video clips, sound clips, maps, photographs, and paintings, along with text. RiverWeb provides a systematic framework for integrating fragmented and scattered data mined from archives, museums, libraries, and courthouses; scientific journals, newspapers, photographs, city directories, statistical data, tax records, marriage licenses, military rosters, church records, maps, audio recordings, and other textual information provide students with a unique and exciting window into discovery. Natural curiosity drives student inquiry through computer searches, while RiverWeb provides multiple pathways to exploring and understanding complex concepts and relationships between ideas in humanities, arts, social sciences, mathematics, and core content sciences.

RiverWeb's goals are clearly in line with national benchmarks for student learning goals, as outlined by Project 2061. This initiative, begun by the American Association for the Advancement of Science in 1985, promotes literacy in science, technology, and mathematics. It focuses on research and on developing pedagogical tools for educators, teachers, and community leaders to use not only in instruction but also in informing decisions about science education. It also emphasizes curriculum diversity and the interrelatedness of knowledge, both points germane to the conceptualization behind RiverWeb. (Its name derives from the period of Halley's comet—visible from Earth in 1985 and scheduled to return in 2061. See http://www.project2061.org/default.htm for a description of this project.) RiverWeb's aims focus on the need to enhance chronological thinking and comprehension, analysis, data interpretation, research, and decision making—precisely those skills critical to public participation in a civil society. RiverWeb provides a scaffold for the cognitive development of these capabilities. Moreover, the resources assembled are especially sensitive to and inclusive of the influences of race, gender, class, and regionalism—influences that have been both divisive and enriching. The resources are designed for use by a large community, including undergraduate students, faculty, scientists, and other interested people, local citizens among them.

RiverWeb also aligns with the often overlooked SCANS (the Secretary's Commission on Achieving Necessary Skills) report of 1991. This report, prepared for the Secretary of Labor, focused on skills that the workforce, as well as higher education, needed from secondary school graduates. Among these were "thinking creatively, making decisions, solving problems, seeing things in the mind's eye, knowing how to learn, and reasoning" (SCANS 1991, iii). These seem skills worth transmitting in the interests of an educated citizenry.

The prototype of RiverWeb focuses on one stretch of the Mississippi River, the American Bottom Region of East St. Louis. Specific regional information is rich and locally relevant. Among RiverWeb archival materials, for instance, are vivid archaeological additions from Illinois State Museum scientists, including their work on the Cahokia Mounds. Designated a World Heritage Site by the United Nations, Cahokia was the preeminent Native American community in the region between A.D. 800 and 1300. Its population, actively engaged in a far-flung trading network through which ideas and goods were exchanged in all directions, had its most profound effects on the area immediately surrounding the city and its mounds. Communities altered the physical landscape—often to its detriment—through farming, deforestation, and development. The Illinois State Museum used a geomorphic analysis of Quaternary deposits, topographic features, and soil surveys to reconstruct the floodplain and its environment circa A.D. 1100, and then deployed contemporary measurements and historical and archaeological data to document existing mounds and reconstruct those destroyed long ago. All this information is available through RiverWeb.

The architecture of RiverWeb is built to be fully modular and extensible, allowing faculty to integrate new content in a timely, cost-effective manner. A set of interfaces designed with the needs of faculty in mind allows the instructor to explore, navigate, add, and design flexible new areas of the site without requiring any in-depth familiarity with the foundational technologies that make RiverWeb possible. A suite of easy "wizard software" provides both guidance and back-end support. The technologies that drive RiverWeb are made transparent to the end user, which enables it to be used by people in a variety of formal and informal educational settings.

RiverWeb is very much a work in progress, reflecting the nature of ubiquitous learning itself. Its structure has undergone regular reorganization and continual design modifications as different thematic overviews, navigational techniques, site hierarchies, and technological applications have been tested. It now has two principal modes of navigation: nonlinear and thematic. While some learners use RiverWeb in a nonlinear fashion, others desire more structure. The nonlinear mode of navigation allows multiple paths based on specific needs rather than an imposed structure. The thematic mode revolves around the interrelated core themes of Environment, Society, Economy, Technology, and Art. The interconnection of these themes is obvious, but as separate means of exploration and pedagogy, they serve as organizational tools and as hotspots for further investigation. Interpretive navigation also lends itself to integrating RiverWeb materials in educational environments through the development of related activities, lectures, and projects.

In an unanticipated development, RiverWeb has become a site for informal learning. Recently, RiverWeb received an e-mail message from an individual who came across the site on the Web. The encounter triggered his own memories of the East St. Louis area, and he unearthed a series of seventy-five photographs he took in the mid-1970s of the old National Stock Yards in St. Louis. He contacted RiverWeb to see if we would be interested in them and then sent them to the university for scanning and posting on the site. He also forwarded a reminiscence of his time working there, which will also be posted.

In a similar vein, a local amateur historian and community activist in East St. Louis retrieved historical documents relating to the city—literally rescuing them from a dumpster. The materials proved to be city directories and other documents relating to the development of East St. Louis, some dating from the late nineteenth century. He contacted the university to inquire if we would be interested in preserving the materials. East St. Louis figures prominently in RiverWeb, and the city directories can be invaluable in showing population migrations, particularly as they relate to historical events in the city, such as the infamous race riots of 1917. It also developed that there are at least a dozen residents who are more than one hundred years old, and a related project may be to collect oral histories from them about their experiences in East St. Louis.

A question that arises in the teaching of the humanities in general and in history in particular is the question of the value of teaching localized subjects. How, for instance, in this day of transnationalism and globalism, can one justify teaching about, for example, Illinois history—let alone East St. Louis—and why should we emphasize local community studies? The answer seems obvious. In the realm of ubiquitous learning, people everywhere around the globe are part of a linked community. There is a sense in which (as Charles Joyner [1984] has reminded us) all history is local history—someplace. All too often, scholars address history at what we think of as the national or transnational level without realizing that these "higher, broader" levels are in fact intellectual constructs rather than concrete realities. No history, properly understood, is merely local nor is it merely transnational. Moreover, the difference between history as opposed to antiquarianism is that either explicitly or implicitly, history must be comparative. Tools such as RiverWeb allow students to work individually and as a class from our nation's documentary record and determine for themselves where various forces of history interact. As John Dewey (1958, 324) observed in a slightly different context, "The individual who has an enlarged and quickened experience is one who should make for himself his own appraisal." Ubiquitous learning is certainly one mechanism to enlarge and quicken experience.

In teaching any course, one effective strategy is to insist that students seek some agreement on definitions. History courses, for example, deal with meanings of freedom and liberty in the United States, so it is important for students to see how definitions vary and how differences affect an argument. This leads to an awareness of how historians think, what historians do, what tools they use to interpret the past, and how interpretations change. In the basic survey course, especially if this is the only history course students will ever take, it is all the more important that students know that historians disagree over facts as well as interpretations. We are not doing students in the surveys of American history a service to assume that historiography is too complicated and that they need to know the facts before they understand differing interpretations. It is important to emphasize that all historians, including the authors of their textbooks, select facts to include and exclude others. How someone chose his or her facts tells us something. An easy assignment to get students thinking critically is to have them ask themselves if other groups (Native Americans, Hispanics, African Americans, Asian Americans, non-Europeans) would have used the same facts or interpreted them the same ways. In other words, students should be challenged to imagine different voices telling the story. The promise of ubiquitous learning, with its access to diverse sources, can greatly enrich this process, and sites such as RiverWeb can provide easily accessible venues for this enrichment.

A final thought on ubiquitous learning must include the caveat that we do not really know when learning takes place. What we can do in a digital environment such as RiverWeb is to show users how others constructed their research or investigations. Thus, students can graph the arc of their own investigation or research project and compare it to others who used RiverWeb. The best that we can say for certainty about learning in the classroom is that while we hope it does occur there, we remain unsure. Certainly the growth of online programs of all types and the relatively recent development of lifelong learning and the myriad venues employed by those programs strongly implies that learning takes place in many different ways and in a multitude of places. Howard Gardner (1983) challenges us to consider multiple intelligences when designing curriculum, and technology may make it possible for the learner to self-develop such curriculum. The marvelous tools that make ubiquitous learning possible seem to follow Toyota's "just in time" supply chain management techniques for manufacturing. But we must be careful not to mistake data retrieval for real learning, and on this score it may be helpful to recall William James's observation of 1890: "Thus, we notice after exercising our muscles or our brain in a new way, that we can do so no longer at that time; but after a day or two of rest, when we resume the discipline, our increase in skill not seldom surprises us. I have often noticed this in learning a tune; and it has led a German author to say that we learn to swim during the winter and to skate during the summer." So, in somewhat whimsical fashion, James reminds us that the occurrence of true learning can rarely be fixed and that learning, while once potentially ubiquitous in time now appears to be potentially ubiquitous in both time and space.

Readings and References

Dewey, John. 1958. *Art as Experience.* New York: Capricorn Books.

Gardener, Howard. 1983. *Frames of Mind: The Theory of Multiple Intelligences.* New York: Basic Books.

James, William. 1890. *The Principles of Psychology.* Classics in the History of Psychology, http://psychclassics.yorku.ca/James/Principles/prin4.htm#f1 para 9.

Joyner, Charles. 1984. *Down by the Riverside: A South Carolina Slave Community.* Urbana: University of Illinois Press.

Saul, John R. 1994. *The Doubter's Companion.* New York: Free Press.

The Secretary's Commission on Achieving Necessary Skills (SCANS). 1991. *What Work Requires of Schools: A SCANS Report for America 2000.* Washington, D.C.: U.S. Government Printing Office.

18

Computer Science

Pen-Enabled Computers for the "Ubiquitous Teacher"

SAMUEL KAMIN

What Ubiquity Means

The deepest and most difficult kinds of learning require a teacher who understands the student's struggle to learn. The teacher engages with the student in a beneficial feedback loop, continually probing the student's progress and adjusting her teaching to the student's needs. While computers and the Internet make information ubiquitous, they cannot do the same for teachers—there are not enough of them to go around. Making learning truly ubiquitous requires that we *make teachers ubiquitous.* The research of my student, Chad Peiper, and I is aimed at using two technologies—pen-enabled computers (specifically, tablet PCs) and computer networks—to restore the essential feedback loop that is at the heart of the best teaching—not only for online courses, but for large in-person classes as well.

To understand this odd phrase—"making teachers ubiquitous"—consider why one-on-one teaching is so effective (Cohen, Kulik, and Kulik 1982). In this mode, the teacher develops a keen sense of the student: what he knows, what he is capable of absorbing at any moment, how fast he can absorb it, and how best to present it. From the student's point of view, the individual tutor is "ubiquitous" in the sense that the student never feels her absence: no sooner does a question come to the student's mind than it is answered; no sooner does he learn one concept than he is presented with another.

By contrast, a teacher in a large class—such as one commonly finds in a university—is barely present to the student, even during a lecture. And her absence is keenly felt: questions go unasked; misconceptions go uncorrected;

new subjects are introduced before old ones are mastered. A teacher in an online course, even a synchronous one, is at an even greater disadvantage, as are, accordingly, her students.

Being ubiquitous in a class—online or in-person—means the teacher knows each student, not just in general, but *right now*. She can sense the student's confusion, misunderstandings, lack of confidence, and disengagement, and counteract them. It is essential to the learning process that the student experience confusion and uncertainty, tries solving problems at the edge of his knowledge and abilities, and formulates questions based on these efforts. The importance of the teacher is in not letting these periods of uncertainty last longer than is helpful. Teaching is a dialectical process: the teacher explores the student's understanding and provides instruction of a kind and at a pace appropriate to that student; the student attempts to perform as the teacher wishes, expressing, in word or deed, how well the teacher is succeeding; these expressions in turn inform the teacher's next interaction with the student. Over the course of a lesson, the student becomes a better student, and the teacher becomes a better teacher.

The employment of educational technology—more specifically, networked computers—is an attempt to raise the effective "ubiquity" of the teacher. I provide several examples below. But to set the stage a bit more, consider how teachers in noncomputerized classrooms enhance their presence to the students.

In traditional classrooms, many techniques have been developed to, in effect, emulate the dialectical process between student and tutor described above. The simplest and most common is the in-class exercise, which can range from a simple question put to the class with a request for a show of hands (a "poll") to a written problem to be handed in and graded. With in-class exercises, the teacher is attempting to give the students a task they can do, or can *almost* do, and is hoping in turn to gauge what the students are learning. It is, then, an attempt to recover "ubiquity" in the classroom. However, it falls short of reaching this goal in several ways. The exercises will not be appropriate for all students; this is inevitable as long as there is more than one student present. More fundamentally, in this procedure, the loop is rarely closed: the teacher gets only a rough idea of whether students were able to do the exercise, and if not, why not. If the exercise is a simple multiple-choice poll, the responses probably do not carry very much information (even if a majority of students "vote"); if it is more complicated, it is impractical to tally the answers in class. The exercise is worthwhile in giving the students practice, keeping them engaged, and possibly helping boost their confidence. However, the teacher is left largely in the dark.

In our research, we have explored how tablet PCs connected by a network can increase the teacher's sense of a class (what Chen [2003] calls the "pulse of the classroom"), and the class's sense of the teacher's presence. Here "class" is conceived of in the sense of a synchronous, though possibly geographically distributed, group of students, with a human teacher. The following cases give some idea of how computers can do this. The first two represent older or less powerful technology than tablet PCs, but still offer interesting lessons concerning this notion of ubiquity. The third is representative of our own recent work with tablet PCs. Our research also has implications for more conventional notions of spatial and temporal ubiquity.

Case 1: PLATO

The notion that computers might be helpful in education goes back many years (Alessi and Trollip 1985). Its first major incarnation was the PLATO system, developed on the University of Illinois at Urbana-Champaign campus (Woolley 1994). Its intended use was as an "intelligent tutor," giving routine drill-type instruction. It also developed into a substantial social network, a precursor to the modern Internet. The system was not "networked" in the technical sense, but there were many terminals around campus connected to a mainframe computer, thereby giving the same effect. The community of users was large enough to develop "newsgroups" on various topics, an instant messaging system, and early versions of multiplayer online games. PLATO was eventually used in many courses on the campus. It was purchased by Control Data Corporation in 1974 but continued to be used at the university and many other locations; running on a large mainframe computer, it was gradually displaced by the newer technologies of PCs and the Internet.

When using the PLATO system, the student had no live teacher to consult. But the system itself was very much an attempt to personalize instruction—that is, to give the student the feeling of having an ever-present teacher. Lessons were designed so that the student could not stray far from the correct path, as every question was instantaneously graded. For each question, lesson writers attempted to anticipate misconceptions and build in answers that would reveal them, so as to guide students down the most helpful instructional paths. The dream of the PLATO developers was to provide the kind of teaching that normally comes only with a personal tutor, but both geographically and temporally ubiquitous, and at much lower cost.

PLATO-type programmed instruction now has many incarnations in a variety of fields. It is, however, little used on this campus. It is hardly surprising that it is very difficult to replace a live teacher with a machine. But some interesting lessons were learned:

Developing lessons for a computerized tutoring system is very difficult and time-consuming. For this reason, these systems are only usable in high-volume learning situations, and, more important, in situations in which the subject matter is very stable. At least at the college level, courses are remarkably unstable: even when the content of the subject does not change, teaching approaches do, and lessons designed to fit into a specific course structure may become useless when that structure changes. In short, it is not clear that, when the cost of lesson development and maintenance is taken into account, there is actually any cost savings to be had.

The keyboard was a limitation on the students' interaction with PLATO. The developers ended up inventing a new technology to overcome this: the computer touch screen. Input modalities are extremely important. The tablet PC is the logical conclusion of the development of computers with natural input modalities.

Research on "intelligent tutoring systems" continues (Graesser et al. 2005). Interestingly, some of this work is attempting to make the computer better emulate a human teacher by using various observations (including biometric measurements) to deduce the pupil's state of mind (D'Mello et al. 2005; Kapoor and Picard 2005). Tablet PCs are a far richer input device than keyboards or touch screens; it is reasonable to surmise that the characteristics of a student's writing might better reveal such information.

Case 2: "Clickers"

Classroom "clickers" have recently become quite popular (Caldwell 2007), in part owing to their being promoted by textbook publishers. These are devices that resemble TV remote controls and can be used in class to allow students to respond to teachers' poll questions (in-class exercises with multiple-choice answers). Recall our earlier discussion about the disadvantages of in-class exercises in which students answer by raising their hands. Because the answers provided by clickers are recorded, students tend to participate (the choice of whether to count these responses in the students' final grades is, of course, the teacher's); and because the teacher gets quantifiable results, coming from nearly all the students, she can form a clearer picture of the students' knowledge.

Though it is impossible to provide personalized instruction in the classroom, this technology does provide a better emulation of the "ubiquitous teacher" to more students than can be obtained without it.

Case 3: An Introductory Programming Class

Introductory programming classes in college suffer from a peculiar problem: students come into them with very different preexisting skill levels. It is not simply that they have different abilities; many of them already know how to program. Especially in the first half of the course, it has proven extremely difficult to find a balance between the needs of the less experienced and more experienced students. A large proportion of the class inevitably feels that it, in effect, has no teacher, in that the things the teacher is saying and doing are far removed from the students' needs.

In the spring 2007 semester, we tried an experiment. We hosted an introductory programming class in our laboratory classroom, equipped with about thirty-five tablet PCs, wirelessly networked. We employed a class structure that could not be implemented without computers (Peiper 2009, chap. 6). It was a partially self-paced class, with occasional "synchronization" points. The teacher planned the class as a sequence of objectives, each with the same structure: preflight (a brief introduction), content presentation, self-assessment, and postflight (brief recap). The class went through the objectives together, but they moved at different rates within an objective; in practice, most students remained in synchrony with the teacher, while some went more quickly and others lagged. This structure helped keep the more advanced students from getting bored too quickly, and at the same time allowed them to contribute to the learning of the other students. (Since the computer prevented them from moving on to the next objective, they spent the time helping their classmates through the current one.)

This class also incorporated a window on the teacher's computer—which we call the "teacher's dashboard"—indicating how many students were at each point in the current objective. This is an example of "passive monitoring," which is discussed further below. The class alternated between lecture time and periods when the students were working on exercises, during which the teacher could consult the dashboard.

This experiment points the way toward new kinds of class structures. In these structures, students and teachers are engaged in a variety of concurrent activities, with part or all of the class synchronizing at specified points. These classes fall somewhere between pure self-paced, "programmed" instruction and traditional teacher-led instruction. In terms of "ubiquity," the teacher has an excellent picture of the class, as the dashboard tells her where each student is. The geographically remote students participate fully, with the teacher being almost as current with those students' progress as she is with the on-site students.

Research Agenda

Two technologies that are now widely available can change the way learning is done: pen-enabled computers (of which the tablet PC is the most popular, but not the only, example) and computer networks (especially wireless networks). They can help make learning ubiquitous in the usual sense of making it possible for students to engage in learning experiences at any time and in any place. They can also move us closer to the ideal of the "ubiquitous teacher."

It seems likely that, in the future, classrooms equipped with pen-enabled computers will be so common that an observer entering a classroom *not* so equipped will be moved to ask, "How does the teacher know what the students are doing?" For the online class, they will be, if anything, even more essential, as there are fewer other clues for the teacher to rely on. In terms of the teacher's ability to assess the state of the class, pen and paper offer little. Computers—specifically, computers that students use in place of paper—offer a great deal.

The relative scarcity of fully computer-equipped classrooms, the difficulty of writing software for these devices, and technical issues associated with wireless networking have made it difficult to explore the many possibilities offered by these technologies. All of these are temporary problems that will probably be overcome within the next decade. Listed here are some of the possible uses of the technologies, as reported by various researchers (Anderson et al. 2004; Anderson et al. 2007; Mock 2004; Peiper et al. 2005; Willis and Miertschin 2004):

Pen-enabled computers allow the user to write on the screen with "digital ink." Being digital, it automatically offers some advantages over pen and paper: it can be erased cleanly; colors can be changed quickly; portions can be selected and copied; and the document can be saved and shared.

In a lecture class, the professor may choose to send her ink annotations to students' tablets, ensuring that they have an accurate copy of the notes. The professor may, on the other hand, decline to do so, because of reported pedagogical benefits of note-taking. Some combination of the two—such as broadcasting skeletal slides—is also possible.

The professor can send a poll to the students, requesting their answers on a question. This is, in effect, a formalized version of hand-raising, but is better in a number of ways, including the ability to easily count who voted and how.

Ink on a tablet can be replayed, providing a simple recording of the class.

Students can submit questions anonymously. To keep the instructor from being overwhelmed by questions, various mechanisms could be employed: a teaching assistant could respond to questions; each student could have a quota of questions in each class; or students might "vote up" other students' questions.

When exams are taken on the computer, it can assist in grading, including providing grade averages on individual questions, information that is extremely useful but rarely calculated.

The classroom structure can be changed to accommodate a certain amount of freedom for the students to pace themselves, as discussed previously in case 3.

An especially exciting possibility is "passive monitoring." The record created by students writing on their computers can be transmitted in real time to the teacher and displayed in various ways. One use is for the teacher to quickly review the students' notes, although there is rarely time for this in class. (The technology makes it simple for the teacher to obtain the notes of all students for review after class.) Another use is to provide a summary picture of the class's writing behavior (who is writing, and how much), but this may not be very useful in itself. Perhaps the computer can find unusual or anomalous behaviors and highlight those for the teacher. In the long run, we are interested to see if the computer can analyze the data in a deeper way, using the ink to determine, for example, which students are engaged with the material and which are bored or tired.

The technology described can be applied to any synchronous class, but remote classes, by increasing the potential number of students, can offer even more fertile ground for innovation and investigation. In large classes, two things happen. First, it becomes much more difficult for the teacher to know what the class is thinking, and that makes the role of passive monitoring that much more important. Chen (2003) monitored relatively small online classes using video cameras on each student, with some automated visual analysis, and that technology might also be useful here. Second, large-scale social forces within the class begin to have an effect. Students can share their notes in real time—during the class—and answer each other's questions. A voting mechanism, such as is used on Web sites like Slashdot (http://www.slashdot.com) might be established whereby the students choose what questions are "popular" enough to get the attention of the teacher. Davis et al. (2007) describe an in-person class where a small number of students were designated as live bloggers; using tablet PCs, they wrote annotations on the lecturer's notes that the other students could view on ordinary laptops. In short, the students can form an online community *during the class.*

The asynchronous case—providing temporal ubiquity—is more challenging. It is difficult to see how a teacher can be ubiquitous if she is not even present. Yet a certain kind of ubiquity might be obtained via post hoc analysis of the student's writing. (Recall that the teacher can *play back* the student's writing, not just view the final result.) The student would not feel the teacher's presence immediately but might feel afterward as if the teacher must have been there to have the insights the computer has helped provide.

With all these possibilities to explore, we are currently engaged in software development and data analysis. Finding ways to create software quickly for educational uses would be a boon to teachers and researchers alike. Given the ability to develop this software, these are the research questions that seem most interesting:

How, and how much, can the technology increase the teacher's "presence" in the class—her sense of the class, and the class's sense of her?

What kind of information about the students' state of mind can be extracted from the student's ink?

What class structures and teaching methods work best when using this technology?

How can the technology help education *researchers?* For example, the passive monitoring data that can be provided to the teacher might prove very useful to researchers.

What differences arise between in-class learning, synchronous online learning, and asynchronous learning?

What device/form factor/user interface is best for exploiting the technology?

How do teachers and students use the computer, and how does it affect the student–teacher relationship?

How are educational outcomes affected by this technology?

What kind of social processes will be created in a large-scale, geographically distributed class where hundreds or thousands of students are taking notes, and how can these processes yield educational value?

Acknowledgments

Besides Chad Peiper, students Boris Capitanu, Matthew Marquissee, and Michael Hines have worked in the Slice group and contributed to my thinking on ubiquity. I have also benefited from working with Michael Twidale of the Department of Library and Information Science and Tim Wentling of the National Center for Supercomputing Applications.

Readings and References

There is now an annual meeting, Workshop on the Impact of Pen-Enabled Technology on Education (WIPTE, http://www.wipte.org), devoted to the use of tablet PCs in education; proceedings of the 2006, 2007, and 2008 workshops are available from Perdue University Press. Papers on this topic also appear in the annual SIGCSE (Special Interest Group on Computer Science Education) and ITiCSE (Innovation and Technology in Computer Science Education) conferences; both can be obtained at the Association for Computing

Machinery, http://www.acm.org. The reader may also want to investigate the Tablet PC Education Blog (http://tabletpceducation.blogspot.com), a Web log devoted to tablet PCs in education. The annual Eurographics Workshop on Sketch-Based Interfaces and Modeling (http://www.eg.org/sbm) focuses on technical issues in the use of pen-enabled computers, but often with a strong education component. More details on the work described here can be found at the Slice (Students Learn in Collaborative Environments) Web site (http://slice.cs.uiuc.edu).

Alessi, Stephen M., and Stanley R. Trollip. 1985. *Computer-Based Instruction: Methods and Development.* Englewood Cliffs, N.J.: Prentice-Hall.

Anderson, Richard J., Ruth Anderson, Beth Simon, Steven A. Wolfman, Tammy VanDeGrift, and Ken Yashuhara. 2004. "Experiences with a Tablet PC Based Lecture Presentation System in Computer Science Courses." In *Proceedings of the 35th SIGCSE Technical Symposium on Computer Science Education,* 56–60. New York: Association for Computing Machinery.

Anderson, Richard J., Ruth Anderson, Krista M. Davis, Natalie Linnell, Craig Prince, and Valentin Razmov. 2007. "Supporting Active Learning and Example Based Instruction with Classroom Technology." In *Proceedings of the 38th SIGCSE Technical Symposium on Computer Science Education,* 69–73. New York: Association for Computing Machinery.

Caldwell, Jane E. 2007. "Clickers in the Large Classroom: Current Research and Best-Practice Tips." *CBE Life Sciences Education* 6(1): 9–20.

Chen, Milton. 2003. "Visualizing the Pulse of a Classroom." In *Proceedings of the Eleventh ACM International Conference on Multimedia,* 555–60. New York: Association for Computing Machinery.

Cohen, Peter A., James A. Kulik, and Chen-lin C. Kulik. 1982. "Educational Outcomes of Tutoring: A Metaanalysis of Findings." *American Educational Research Journal* 19:237–48.

Davis, Krista M., Michael Kelly, Roshni Malani, William G. Griswold, and Beth Simon. 2007. "Preliminary Evaluation of NoteBlogger: Public Note-Taking in the Classroom." In *Proceedings of the Workshop on the Impact of Tablet PCs and Pen-Based Technology on Education (WIPTE),* 33–42. West Lafayette, Ind.: Purdue University.

D'Mello, Sidney K., Scotty D. Craig, Barry Gholson, Stan Franklin, Rosalind W. Picard, and Arthur C. Graesser. 2005. "Integrating Affect Sensors in an Intelligent Tutoring System." In *Affective Interactions: The Computer in the Affective Loop Workshop at 2005 International Conference on Intelligent User Interfaces,* 7–13. New York: Association for Computing Machinery.

Graesser, Arthur C., Patrick Chipman, Mattie Haynes, and Andrew Olney. 2005. "AutoTutor: An Intelligent Tutoring System with Mixed-Initiative Dialogue." *IEEE Transactions in Education* 48:612–18.

Kapoor, Ashish, and Rosalind W. Picard. 2005. "Multimodal Affect Recognition in Learning Environments." In *Proceedings of the 13th Annual ACM International Conference on Multimedia,* 677–82. New York: Association for Computing Machinery.

Mock, Kenrick. 2004. "Teaching with Tablet PC's." *Journal of Computer Sciences in Colleges* 20(2): 17–27.

Peiper, Chad E. 2009. "A Teacher's Dashboard: Monitoring Students in Tablet PC Classroom Settings." Ph.D. diss., University of Illinois at Urbana-Champaign. Available at http://slice.cs.uiuc.edu.

Peiper, Chad E., David Warden, Ellick Chan, Boris Capitanu, and Sam Kamin. 2005. "E-Fuzion: The Development of a Pervasive Educational System." In *Proceedings of the Tenth International Conference on Innovation and Technology in Computer Science Education,* 237–40. New York: Association for Computing Machinery.

Willis, Cheryl L., and Susan L. Miertschin. 2004. "Tablet PC's as Instructional Tools, or the Pen Is Mightier Than the 'Board!" In *Proceedings of the 5th Conference on Information Technology Education,* 153–59. New York: Association for Computing Machinery.

Woolley, David R. 1994. "PLATO: The Emergence of On-line Community." In *Computer-Mediated Communication Magazine* 1(3): 5.

19

Biology

Using a Ubiquitous Knowledge Environment to Integrate Teaching, Learning, and Research in Biology and Chemistry

ERIC JAKOBSSON

An Evolutionary Context for Ubiquitous Learning

Many people wear emblems signifying a belief or set of beliefs, such as a flag lapel pin or a cross on a necklace. For most of my life I have not done so. Like many academics, I felt that things were too complex to be captured in a symbol that encompassed the essence of how I viewed life. Lately however, I have taken to wearing a pin that looks like the one in figure 19.1.

The fish with limbs, of course, expresses the relatedness, through the evolutionary process, of organisms that live in water and on land. The crescent wrench in the forelimb captures beautifully the fact that evolution as it plays out in life on earth functions much like a backyard mechanic, keeping an old car on the road. Evolution does not optimize. Rather it makes do, using the parts and tools that have accumulated over the years and reconfiguring and reshaping those parts to adapt to change.

Biological evolution has shown an overall trend toward increasing complexity at the level of both the genome (Adami, Ofira, and Collier 2000) and the gene and gene product (Fong et al. 2007). Woese (2000) summarizes the directions of evolution as "horizontal" (horizontal gene transfer at the genome level, domain recombination at the gene level) and "vertical" (variation from generation to generation). Horizontal processes drive innovation, while vertical processes drive evolution toward complexity.

Acquisition of the ability to learn—and the corollary enormous plasticity of behavior—is consistent with the trend to complexity and is perhaps the most

Figure 19.1. "Evolve" fish. (Courtesy of Ian Wrigley.)

distinctive evolutionary adaptation of *Homo sapiens.* This incredibly exaggerated ability of human beings to learn presumably stems from a successful initial evolutionary adaptation by our hunter-gatherer hominid ancestors to the savannah environment of eastern Africa (Diamond 2006), followed by an autocatalytic ("virtual cycle" positive feedback) growth in intelligence driven by competition among conspecifics (Flinn, Geary, and Ward 2004). The development of powerful technologies for information transmission and storage are having a similar autocatalytic effect on the rate of human social evolution (Wright 2007). Innovation in communication technology drives social evolution, which in turn drives innovation in communication technology, all tending to make human interactions more complex. Humans have always had ubiquitous learning, in the sense that all of our experiences modify our synaptic connections in ways that modify our future behavior, which is the neuroscientist's definition of "learning" (Fanselow and Poulos 2005). However, we now have the capability for ubiquitous learning in the sense that is the topic of this book, which means specifically being able to disseminate and access the fruits of research and scholarship anywhere at any time, in a form that people of any level of prior knowledge can utilize.

Information Technology in Biology

In biology, Web-based access to information and computational tools has become central to research. A survey in 2007 reported 968 publically accessible molecular biology databases on the Web, 110 more than the year before (Galperin 2007). Furthermore, the size of the databases is growing rapidly. The comprehensive nucleotide sequence database GenBank has approximately doubled in size every eighteen months since its inception (Benson et al. 2007). As the tools of computational biology have become accessible to experimentalists as well as computational specialists, they have also become available for education. Within education, these tools not only provide elucidation of biological principles but also enable students to engage in new explorations, since the sum total of accumulated data on biological systems is in many respects unexplored territory.

In spite of the potential of these approaches, most education in biology is still in traditional form, owing to some combination of institutional inertia and a lack of computational orientation of previous generations of students, who are today's faculty. However, the new campus of the University of California at Merced (opened 2005), given the chance to start a new university biology curriculum from scratch, is putting computation at the center of undergraduate biology education. Other campuses, not having the luxury/challenge of starting a brand new curriculum, are facing a different challenge—namely, changing course to account for the new role of computation and Web-based access to information and computational tools in biological research, teaching, and learning.

Where We Are Today

Enormous and rapidly growing amounts of molecular biology data are freely available, together with tools for analysis, to anybody with a networked computing device. The ubiquity of access has grown with the amount of information. Initially access depended on paying for it. Then it increasingly was freely available to an individual, if that person belonged to an institution that would pay for it. Now a growing amount of archival information is available literally for free, to anybody in the world. This includes the major textbooks in molecular and cellular biology (Corsi 2006), the major databases of molecular and cellular biology (Galperin 2007), a large and increasing fraction of the primary scientific literature, and a significant amount of the course content offered in universities (Downes 2007). In addition, many biological data analysis and simulation programs are available for free and in many cases are open sources on the Internet. Unlike the famously wrong prediction about nuclear-generated electrical energy, the flow of molecular and cellular biology information of many kinds has indeed become "too cheap to meter." At the same time, technological advances have made computers more portable. Many knowledge workers (including myself) no longer have a desktop computer. My office is wherever I can connect my laptop to the Internet; I do not need the same physical space that I used to. But I do need connectivity to the Internet, even though my hard drive contains far more information than my filing cabinets ever did, bulging with paper as they were. I now find it so frustrating to do any work without continual reference to information sources that I no longer try to work on my laptop if I am in a place without connectivity.

This chapter considers the implications of this situation for the future development and utilization of a ubiquitous, integrated learning and research environment for biology and chemistry. In a sense this chapter is a contradiction in terms. It is a chapter in a book—old technology—but is about a technology and a knowledge environment that is dramatically reducing the importance of printed matter. The printing press was originally about democratizing knowledge, making knowledge accessible beyond the elite few. All of the issues surrounding the democratization of knowledge that the Internet has led to, that we struggle with today, were issues initially raised by the printing press. How could one count on the validity of what was in print? In Europe before the printing press, only those who were vetted by the establishment (the Church) had access to the scriptures. What would happen to standards and rigor if everybody could read the scriptures and publish and disseminate his or her own interpretation, translation, or exegesis? Similarly today, those of us vetted by the establishment (universities, research institutions) worry about the quality and validity of the flood of material available on the Internet, material that may be beyond any institution's capability to control.

And yet the values that books and scholarly and scientific journals represent are as important as ever. A core body of knowledge that embodies intellectual rigor, integrity, and accountability is an essential foundation of civilization. A central question today for all of us who have been entrusted with the curation, protection, and dissemination of such a body of knowledge is: How can this body of knowledge be nurtured, disseminated, and passed on in the new knowledge environment? Biologists might pose the question as follows: How can this body of knowledge evolve so that it is optimally adapted to meet the needs of society? Which leads to a metaquestion: Do we need to worry about how this body of knowledge evolves, or will it happen in a sense automatically, like biological evolution? (The metaquestion has no answer. It is a societal version of the question of whether we have free will. Are we the drivers of how our bodies of knowledge evolve, or are we caught up in a tide that is beyond our ability to direct? The analogy I favor is that we are surfers on a wave of historical change in the knowledge enterprises. None of us can change the course of the wave very much, but we can try to ride the surfboards of our expertise and imagination to some place we would like to go.)

How can one properly annotate a book chapter about a topic that, by its definition, cannot be properly contained in a book? Some references to the printed literature are obligatory and useful, but they are static and may become obsolete over time. Universal resource locators (URLs), on the other hand, are the opposite of static—they may cease to exist at any time. At this time, the best combination of persistent archival knowledge and up-to-dateness is provided by the search engine. Therefore, sprinkled throughout this chapter are italicized words or phrases that I judge to be potentially useful or interesting to pursue on the Internet as one reads.

The Pace of Change

The rate of growth in biology information and the rate of change in how we access it are staggering by any historical measure. The amount of information in the archival gene and protein sequence databases maintained by the *National Center for Biotechnology Information* has over the past two decades maintained a growth rate of doubling every eighteen months. By "partial coincidence" the doubling time is essentially exactly the same as the eighteen months doubling time for computing power in the world that is embodied in the famous Moore's Law (Lundstrom 2003). I use the phrase "partial coincidence" because high-speed sequencing depends on the ability to break an organism's DNA into short fragments, so that many sequencing machines can run in parallel on the same genome. The subsequent assembly of those fragment sequences into complete genes, gene products, and genomes is done computationally, and is very computationally demanding. The databases could not have grown at the rate that they have if the available computing power had not kept pace.

Fueled to a great extent by computing power, including special-purpose microprocessors for automated experimental instrumentation as well as general-purpose computers for analysis and simulation, there has been a stunning increase in organized and curated knowledge—but not as great an increase as in the growth of databases. Our data are growing far faster than our knowledge. The pathway from biological data to knowledge and understanding is at once a major bottleneck in understanding living systems and a major opportunity to move our understanding to a new and previously undreamed-of level, to create what Woese (2004) has termed "a new biology for a new century." A ubiquitous biology learning environment for teachers, students, and researchers will be essential to the creation of the new biology.

Ubiquitous Biology Research Using the Biology Workbench

The *Biology Workbench* (Subramaniam 1998) was invented at the National Center for Supercomputing Applications by a team led by *Shankar Subramaniam*, now at the University of California at San Diego. The invention of the Workbench followed the invention of the Web browser by just three years. It was not only a pioneering enterprise in bioinformatics, but also in Web-based computing, providing an integrated environment for simultaneous search of multiple biological databases and analysis of data by a variety of programs. As described in *United States Patent 5859972*, the Biology Workbench marks the invention of Web-based computing. (The rights to the invention fell into dispute with Subramaniam's move to California; the patent was not defended against encroachment; and the hopes of the inventors for perpetual funding of their research labs by invention royalties were sadly not realized.) The interface to the Workbench, and all the databases and analysis programs contained in it, is the user's Web browser. Thus, the Workbench makes bioinformatics research, and biology research using bioinformatics tools, truly ubiquitous. The overall structure of the Biology Workbench is diagrammed in figure 19.2. The diagram refers to the "Information Workbench" to indicate that the workbench software architecture is applicable to any information-rich enterprise. However, the workbench that was constructed by Subramaniam's team was specific to biology.

One day at a scientific meeting in Boston, one of my colleagues asked me if there were calcium channels in *prokaryotic* organisms (*bacteria* and *archaea*). I said that I did not know, but I would check and let him know the next day. That night in my hotel room, I fashioned a probe sequence from the selectivity filter region of a eukaryotic (plants, animals, fungi) calcium channel and compared that sequence (by chance a human calcium channel) to the sequences of all known proteins in prokaryotic organisms. I discovered just one, in the genome of a bacterium that lives as far as possible from where any human being could live, in the region of a *black smoker* (a region of superheated water where lava is being released through a fissure in the deep ocean floor).

In my hotel room, I discovered a deep relationship between humans and a single-celled organism that lives in such an alien environment that it might be

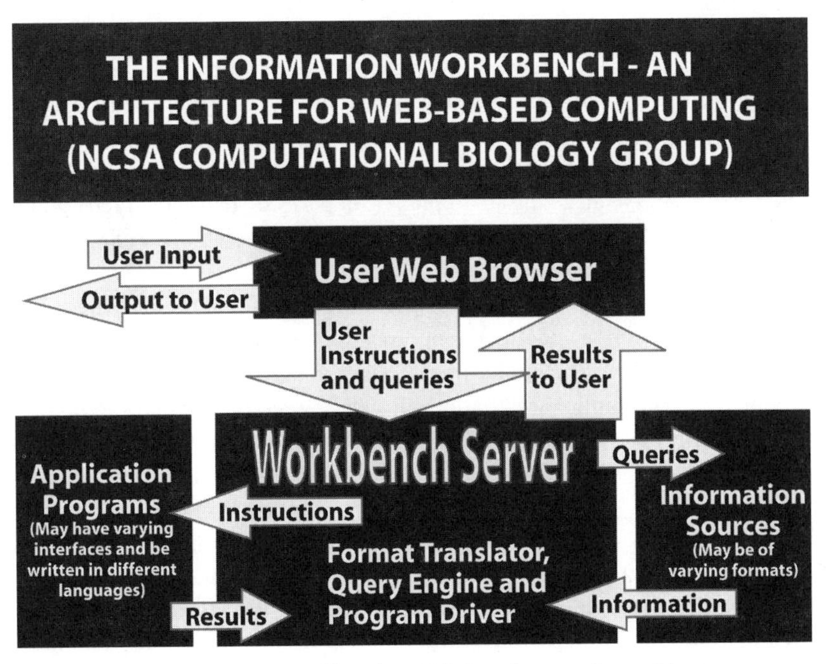

Figure 19.2. The Information Workbench, a Web-based computing architecture.

on another planet. It turns out, sadly by some measure, that I was not the first person to make this discovery. The laboratory of a colleague at the National Institutes of Health, Bob Guy, had made this discovery a few months earlier and his paper, unknown to me, was in press at the time that I made my version of the discovery (Durrell and Guy, 2001). But in a broader sense, this was nothing to be sad about. Because it meant that the discovery process in biology had broken out of being confined in books and journals and specialized laboratories and had become ubiquitously accessible to anybody with the requisite skills and a networked laptop.

I will describe in more detail another hotel room discovery that is perhaps of more general interest than a particular ion channel protein. One of the great joys of working in science education as well as scientific research is that one is moved to think of broad questions. One evening at dinner, at a science education meeting in North Carolina, after a couple of glasses of wine, the question came up as to whether modern humans might have interbred with *Neanderthals* during the period that they occupied the same geographic areas in Europe. Essentially, this is the basis for the series of prehistoric romance adventures by Jean Auell, the first volume of which is *The Clan of the Cave Bear.* As in Boston, I said I would check and report the next day. My ability to check depended on a bit of DNA that had been retrieved from a Neanderthal fossil and deposited at the Web site of the National Center for Biotechnology Information.

The next day I returned with the diagram shown in figure 19.3. This type of diagram is called an *unrooted tree.* At the end of each branch is the name of an organism. In this case the organism is represented by a particular sequence from the organism's *mitochondrial DNA.* The length of each branch on the tree is proportional to the degree of difference between the sequences representing each organism. We make the assumption (not perfect, but usually pretty good) that a tree constructed in such a fashion represents the evolutionary relationships among the organisms. The key to the validity of this assumption is whether the *homologs* (similar sequences from different organisms) are true *orthologs* (derived from a common ancestor) as opposed to *paralogs* (having separate roots that were created by gene duplication). So we are supposing that this particular tree represents evolutionary relationships among modern humans, Neanderthals, other primates such as *troglodytes* (the chimp), and three species of cattle that are biologically capable of *interbreeding.* The clustering on the tree indicates that humans and Neanderthals are closer to each other than the interbreeding cattle are close to each other, suggesting that the modern human–Neanderthal relationship might have been close enough to permit interbreeding.

The specific tasks that were done on the Biology Workbench to create this tree were as follows:

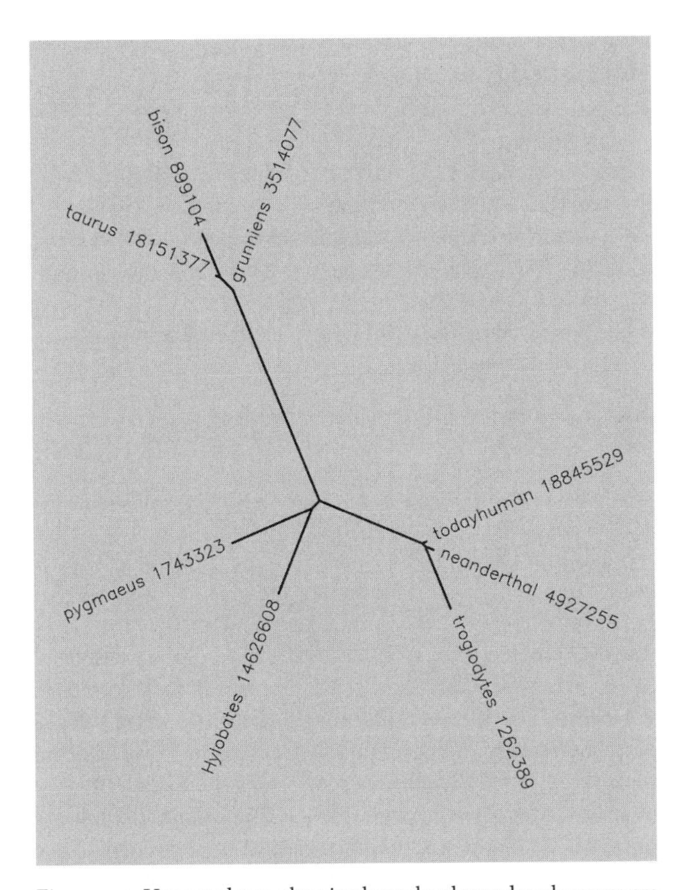

Figure 19.3. Unrooted tree, showing how closely modern humans are related to Neanderthals, as compared with how they both are related to other modern primates, and to varieties of cattle, which are often capable of interbreeding.

1. GenBank was searched with the keyword "Neanderthal," using the NDJINN tool provided within the Workbench.
2. A sequence of mitochondrial DNA, discovered by that search, was downloaded to the user workspace within the Workbench.
3. That sequence was used as a probe to find corresponding sequences for modern humans, other primates, and other species of vertebrates, using the BLAST tool provided within the Workbench.
4. The modern humans, primates, and cattle sequences were downloaded to the user workspace.

5. The sequences were aligned with each other, using the CLUSTALW tool provided within the Workbench.
6. The alignment was downloaded to the user workspace provided within the Workbench.
7. The tree above was drawn from the alignment using the tool DRAWTREE provided with the Workbench.
8. For display purposes, the scientific names and access numbers on the original tree were replaced with generic names for the organisms, using an editing tool provided within the Workbench.
9. The tree was saved in Postscript format, using a translator provided within the Workbench.

What are the lessons to be learned from the above experience? I would point out two:

1. Ubiquitous problem-based learning is technically possible. It is feasible to construct knowledge environments that are navigable, computable, and universally available via laptop, notebook, or even palm-size computers. These environments can enable finding and organizing existing knowledge, and even creating new knowledge by new analysis and synthesis.
2. Ubiquitous problem-based learning is inherently not easy. Solving problems is not easy. The Neanderthal problem above involved nine different steps. If you tried to read through the steps, and are still reading now—congratulations. There is hardly anything more soporific than reading through a list like that. In researching the Neanderthal relationship, I did not write out a task list ahead of time but rather followed a pathway marked by the relationships of different kinds of data to each other. So the question is: How can the ability to navigate a knowledge environment be taught? How can ubiquitous informational and computing capability such as is embodied in the Biology Workbench be used for teaching and learning as well as research?

The Biology Student Workbench: From Ubiquitous Research to Ubiquitous Teaching and Learning

The *Biology Student Workbench* is an attempt to start with the research-oriented Biology Workbench and create an environment for learning and teaching molecular and cellular biology (Gabric et al. 2005). Its organizing principle may be stated as follows: A teaching and learning environment should meet the student where he or she is and provide a scaffold for the student to (1) acquire knowledge and gain skills that the teacher has judged to be important, (2) explore new directions of the student's choice, and (3) go beyond the acquisition of knowledge and skills to enable the student to create new knowledge, that is, to join the research enterprise.

The Biology Student Workbench has now expanded its scope to include chemistry as well. The portal page into both chemistry and biology materials is shown in figure 19.4.

When the student elects a particular lesson from either the chemistry or biology choices, the "tutorial" tab comes to the front in the top frame, and the particular lesson is displayed, as in figure 19.5.

At several points in the lesson the students are guided through computations using the Biology Workbench at University of California San Diego. Figure 19.6 shows results of one such computation, a sequence alignment of hemoglobin from a human and from another species.

The Future

The Biology Student Workbench project has spent significant time and effort developing a Web portal that is optimally ergonomic to provide scaffolding for linking information technology and computing in the service of learning about biology and chemistry. Larger questions remain. How do we solve important problems, and how do we train young people to solve important problems, in a world that is becoming increasingly complex?

I think of the following: Jared Diamond, in an early section of his book *Guns, Germs, and Steel,* recounts a conversation with a member of a community of hunters and gatherers that has helped him survive in the wilderness while he pursued field biology research (Diamond 1997). Diamond has come to understand the enormous amount of specific knowledge about the environment that the members of such groups must have in order to survive—detailed knowledge of the properties of hundreds of plants and animals. The man asks Diamond why some of the people of the earth, such as Diamond and his countrypeople, have so much of the world's goods while others, such as himself, have so little. Seeing how helpless Diamond would be alone in the wilderness, he points out that it cannot be that those with all the goods are smarter. Diamond, thinking of the people he knows in Los Angeles, where he is on the UCLA faculty, agrees. And so the idea is born for *Guns, Germs, and Steel,* an exploration of how climate, geography, and ecology have influenced the development of human societies.

I think of a cliché that may well be true of us in modern societies, but possibly not of the hunter-gatherers—that we only use a small part of our brains—that we are potentially much smarter than we currently are. A large theme begins to take shape. Our enormous brain evolved in a hunting and gathering context, and we used all of it to thrive in that context. Then in a few places, because of favorable climate and domesticable plants and animals, we developed agriculture, the pro-

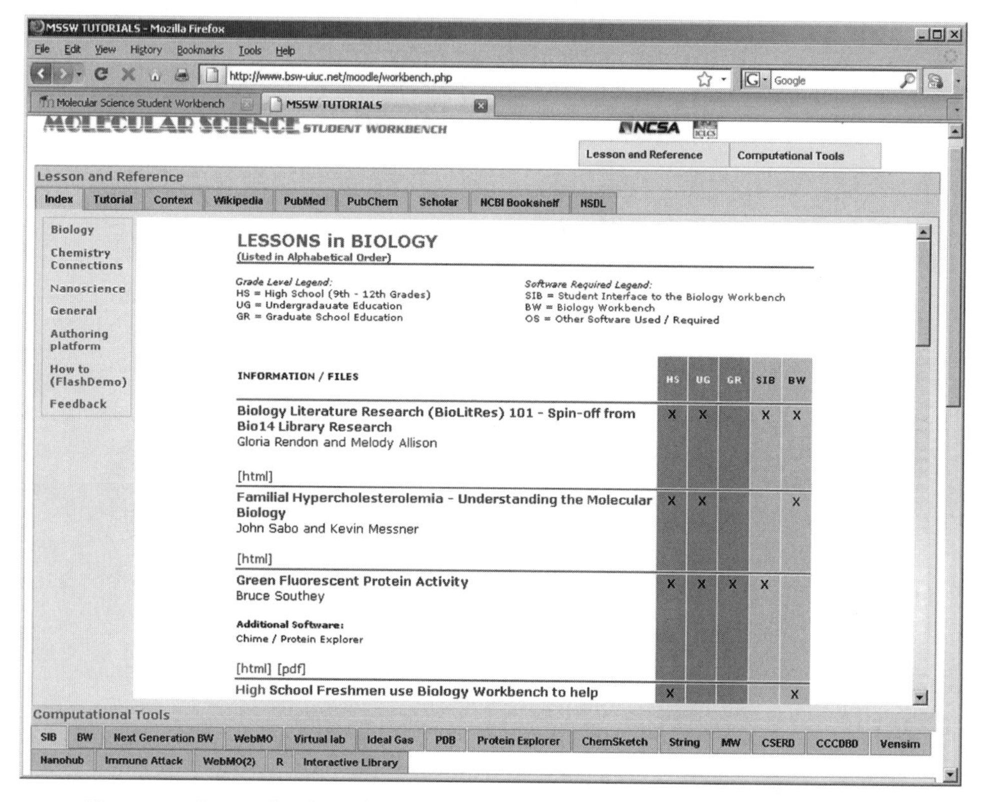

Figure 19.4. Screen shot from the Biology Student Workbench interface, implemented in frames and Java. The overall design and implementation were done by Gloria Rendon, Johnny Tenegra, and Chieh-Chun Chen. The Student Interface to the Biology Workbench was created by Bruce Southey. The top frame, with its tabs, is the information/tutorial frame, containing scaffolding material and access to multiple information sources for background and further exploration. In this image, the "Index" tab in the top frame is in front, which provides a list of either the biology or chemistry lessons available. The bottom frame (accessible by the bottom right scroll bar) is the computing frame. Transition between the information display and the computing interface is by the far right scroll bar. In this implementation of the Biology Student Workbench, all the components of figure 19.2 are accessible in the same window. The work was done at the National Center for Supercomputing Applications on the campus of the University of Illinois at Urbana-Champaign.

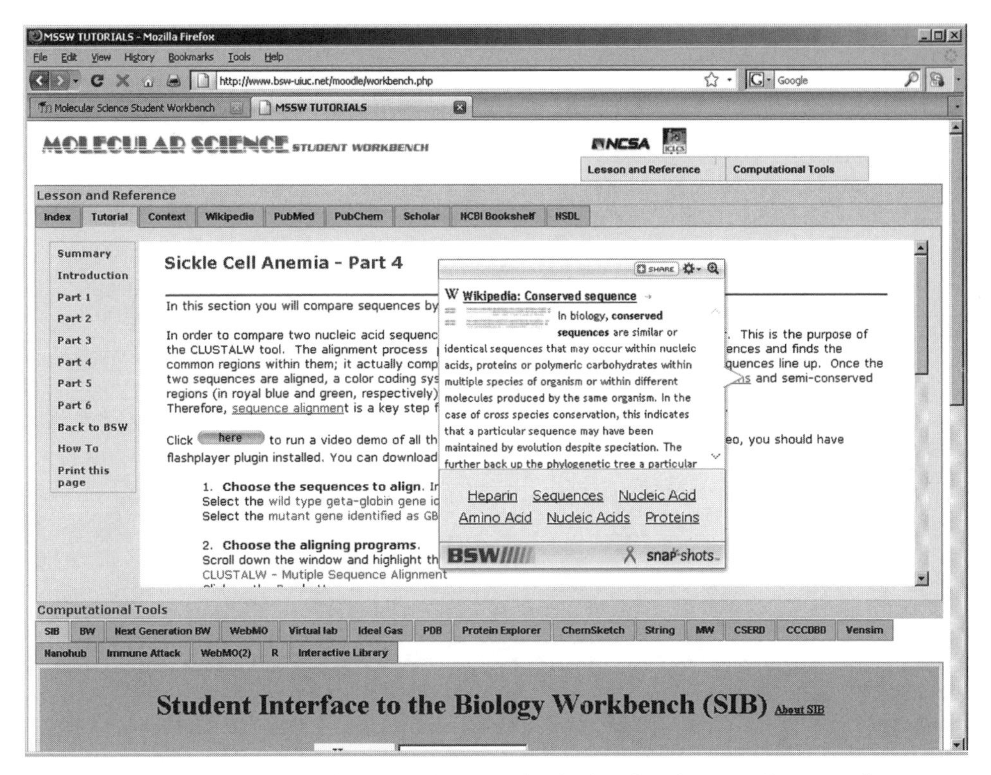

Figure 19.5. Here, a lesson has been chosen and is displayed in the upper frame, guiding the student in using computational biology tools to understand sickle cell anemia. Many phrases are in hypertext, so rolling the cursor over them will provide a link to further information. In addition, each word or phrase in the lesson text is linked to the online dictionary Answers.com, so that if the word(s) is double-clicked, a definition and links to introductory and/or deeper information appears. Thus, the student can either move straight through the text of the tutorial or follow a hyperlink as needed or desired. None of the hyperlinks go to a dead end, so the lesson is connected to an effectively infinite web of information.

ductivity of which enabled the growth of villages and then cities. On those farms and in those villages and cities we created simpler environments, in which less of our total intelligence was required to survive. Collectively we were as smart as ever—the sum total of human knowledge grew—but individually we became (is it too blunt to say?) stupider.

Enter the Web, which combined with portable computing, gives us the possibility of ubiquitous information-searching and problem-solving environments. Finally, for the first time since we started on the path to civilization, we have

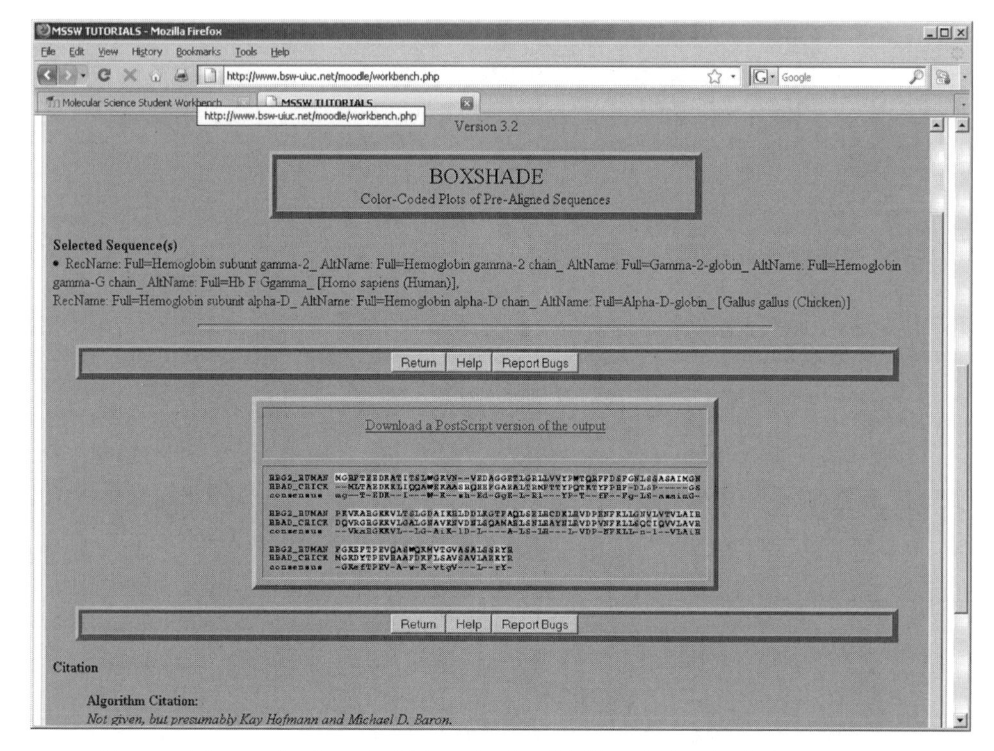

Figure 19.6. Screen shot from the Biology Student Workbench, showing in the computing frame a sequence alignment produced by the bioinformatics tools on the server at the San Diego Supercomputer Center.

the ability to experience an intellectually interactive environment rivaling in complexity the natural environment of the hunter-gatherer.

This should cause us to rethink one of the core assumptions underlying our academic and educational institutions: that academic excellence implies specialization in a discipline. We have taken it for granted, for example, that one can be either a first-rank physicist or a first-rank biologist, but not both. In fact, we have believed that within each of these areas one must find a subspecialty. But what if this belief is based on a level of inefficiency in gathering and processing information that is no longer valid? Perhaps needing to go to the library to follow up on advanced references in our textbooks or gathering and filing those paper journal articles to provide context for our research were fundamentally rate-limiting steps in our ability to cross disciplinary barriers and do excellent scholarship and research across a broad range of disciplines. What if ubiquitous computing and information technology removes that barrier and provides us with the capability to be truly multiple experts, so that deep interdisciplinary collaboration can take place within single brains—so that we can finally use our brains more completely in the pursuit of more knowledge about the world? In the terminology of computers, what if our intelligence has been bound not by our processing capability, but by input and output capability? Ubiquitous knowledge environments will enable us (indeed force us) to confront this question.

Readings and References

Adami, Christopher, Charles Ofira, and Travis C. Collier. 2000. "Evolution of Biological Complexity." *Proceedings of the National Academy of Sciences* 97:4,463–68.

Benson, Dennis A., Ilene Karsch-Mizrachi, David J. Lipman, James Ostell, and David L. Wheeler. 2007. "GenBank." *Nucleic Acids Research* 35:D21–D25.

Corsi, Ann K. 2006. "Books for Free? How Can This Be?—A PubMed Resource You May Be Overlooking." *Biology of the Cell* 98:439–43.

Diamond, Jared. 1997. *Guns, Germs, and Steel: The Fate of Human Societies.* New York: Norton.

———. 2006. *The Third Chimpanzee: The Evolution and Future of the Human Animal.* New York: Harper Perennial.

Downes, S. 2007. "Models for Sustainable Open Educational Resources." *Interdisciplinary Journal of E-learning and Learning Objects* 3:29–44.

Durrell, R., and H. R. Guy. 2001. "A Putative Prokaryote Voltage-Gated Ca(2+) Channel with Only One 6TM Motif per Subunit." *Biochemical and Biophysical Research Communications* 281:741–46.

Fanselow, Michael S., and Andrew M. Poulos. 2005. "The Neuroscience of Mammalian Associative Learning." *Annual Review of Psychology* 56:207–34.

Flinn, Mark V., David C. Geary, and Carol V. Ward. 2004. "Ecological Dominance, Social Competition, and Coalitionary Arms Races: Why Humans Evolved Extraordinary Intelligence." *Evolution and Human Behavior* 26(1): 10–46.

Fong, J. H., L. Y. Geera, A. R. Panchenkoa, and S. H. Bryant. 2007. "Modeling the Evolution of Protein Domain Architectures Using Maximum Parsimony." *Journal of Molecular Biology* 366(1)(February 9): 307–15.

Gabric, Kathleen M., Christina Z. Hovance, Sharon Comstock, and Delwyn Harnisch. 2005. "Scientists in Their Own Classroom: The Use of Type II Technology in the Science Classroom." *Computers in the Schools* 22(3–4): 77–91.

Galperin, Michael Y. 2007. "The Molecular Biology Database Collection: 2007 Update." *Nucleic Acids Research* 35:D3–D4.

Lundstrom, Mark. 2003. "Moore's Law Forever?" *Science* 299:210–11.

Subramaniam, Shankar. 1998. "The Biology Workbench—A Seamless Database and Analysis Environment for the Biologist." *Proteins* 32:1–2.

Woese, Carl R. 2000. "Interpreting the Universal Phylogenetic Tree." *Proceedings of the National Academy of Sciences* 97(8): 392–96.

———. 2004. "A New Biology for a New Century." *Microbiology and Molecular Biology Reviews* 68:173–86.

Wright, Alex. 2007. *Glut: Mastering Information through the Ages.* Washington, D.C.: Joseph Henry Press.

20

Visual Arts

Technology Pedagogy as Cultural Citizenship

ELIZABETH M. DELACRUZ

Art education in the twenty-first century is an eclectic profession composed of diverse and competing fields of inquiry, a hybridization of studio art practice, critical inquiry, and public engagement, layered with overlapping interests in aesthetic and media literacy; visual, material, and multi-culture; cognitive, emotional, and creative development; school and community relations; and technology. Of particular recent interest to K–12 visual arts educators are the ascent of electronic media in everyday life, the technology behaviors of young people, and questions about how to design visual arts programs of study in a technology-saturated world. Art educators well understand that for the youth of today, technology is ubiquitous, commonplace. Enthusiastic utilization by millions of young people worldwide of inexpensive computers, portable electronic media devices, desktop and Web publishing, digital video production and online video distribution, instant messaging, cell phones, roaming services, Internet cafés, electronic social networks, chat spaces, blogs, multiplayer role-playing games, virtual worlds, and other new technologies demonstrates the strength of their desire, unprompted by adults, to adapt new technologies to their own interests and purposes (Lenhart 2007; Rheingold 2007; Saveri 2004). Against this backdrop, the following discussion considers the aims of visual arts technology pedagogy and describes how one art educator, the writer of this chapter, attempts to engage the question, "What happens in art education when anyone can use technology for anything, anytime, anywhere, and for any purpose?"

Technology Ubiquity in the Professional Life of a Faculty Member

I fell into technology in 1996 at my university with an opportunity to apply for a university technology grant in which I proposed to make one of my courses more relevant to students through creation and utilization of a Web interface. I was interested at the time in new art forms, contemporary activist art, and multicultural art education. Inspired by an electronic asynchronous discussion software program that I saw demonstrated at a "Writing across the Curriculum" faculty workshop hosted by the University of Illinois Center for Writing Studies, I surmised at the time that I could engage my students in exciting new ways through this interactive new medium.

Numerous university-sponsored, technology-related course development opportunities followed, and I have come to greatly appreciate what it means to work in such a technology-rich place. I sought out university workshops, collaborated with innovative people on campus who knew considerably more than I did about new technologies, and found immense support in my efforts to bring these technologies into my teaching. I was one step ahead of my students, and my explanations were just right for our entry-level knowledge. I have come full circle in these past ten or more years, able to refocus my growing technology knowledge on things that matter greatly in my field—the connections between art, culture, and the education of young people.

Teaching technology courses both on campus to art education majors and off campus to practicing K–12 teachers has provided opportunities for me to observe firsthand some of the creative ways that students and teachers use electronic technologies. Employing software programs with imaging and hyperlinking capacities, pre- and post-service teachers in my classes have created original works of art, instructional materials, curriculum plans, interactive Web sites and digital slide presentations, digital video productions, and electronic portfolios for personal and professional purposes. We have dealt with the interface of technology with image construction and graphic design considerations; online inquiry and collaboration; online and electronic databases; search, retrieval, and evaluation of online information; interactive information design and new modes for instructional delivery; inquiry-based and cooperative learning strategies; authentic assessment; and technology working conditions in local school contexts, along with ethical, legal, and feasibility problems. Problems considered in my technology-infused courses for teachers have also included attention to disparities between national and local K–12 technology education standards and teachers' knowledge and ability to implement these standards; varied student interests, abilities, and needs; the digital divide; censorship, copyright, privacy, and safety issues; social networking; Internet predators; teachers' fear of litigation; and widely disparate school and community technology infrastructures (Delacruz 2004).

Our adaptations with technology have changed dramatically over time. In 1996, my students and I undertook the arduous tasks of teaching ourselves HTML code and using clunky digital cameras and flatbed scanners to create simple Web pages. We worked in computer labs with limited capacities and relied on floppy disks and cumbersome and unreliable server access for file storage. By 2006, we were creating sophisticated online multimedia and digital video portfolios with point-and-click ease and portability. In 1996, a graduate student asked me if she could type an assignment on her electric typewriter because she did not have a computer at home. Students now bring in personal wireless, networked, and fully loaded laptop computers, accompanied by a plethora of handheld digital devices: keychain-size flash drives, compact digital cameras, sophisticated calculators that talk to digital projectors, MP3 players, cell phones, compact digital audio recorders, and Blackberries. My college students today are plugged in, connected to their mobile digital networks, cued to the latest developments, and eager to adapt them to their own purposes.

My technology-enriched university experience is shared by colleagues in art education at other universities. Art education faculty in higher education institutions across North America extol how image making, reception, and consumption are both facilitated through and changed by computer technologies (Emme and Kirova 2005; Ettinger 1988; Freedman 1991); how technology-enhanced art programs facilitate constructivist, dialogical, and liberatory educational goals (Taylor and Carpenter 2002); and how they invite a social, semiotic, analytical approach to understanding digitally manipulated sites, spaces, and images (Emme and Kirova 2005). Utilization of computer technologies in K–12 art education programs of study is said to enrich artistic and aesthetic inquiry (Hubbard 1993; Kiefer-Boyd 1997); to increase interactivity between art teachers, between teachers and students, and among art students (Carpenter and Taylor 2003; Keifer-Boyd 1997); and to extend our reach beyond classrooms and into the cultural life of the communities we serve (Keifer-Boyd 2005; Knight 2005). My colleagues in higher education observe how a technology-facilitated vision of art education takes new forms: in the creation, consumption, and critique of digital images, Web-environments, and virtual galleries; zines, blogs, animation and time-based media; computer gaming, hyperlinked image, video, and audio text files; digital portfolios and online family and personal repositories; and a host of interactive cyberspaces (Congdon and Blandy 2003; Delacruz and Bales 2007; Freedman 2003; Garoian and Gaudelius 2001; Keifer-Boyd 1997; Krug 2002; Roland 2007; Stankiewicz and Garber 2000; Taylor and Carpenter 2003).

Given the rise of technology in the late twentieth century, academic discourse about the aims of art education now extends well beyond the realm of fine art or craft (Efland, Freedman, and Stuhr 1996) and shifts from a preoccupation with traditional notions of visual and aesthetic literacy to attempts to understand and foster multimedia, multimodal literacies in an image-laden, technology-infused age (Duncum 2004).

Startling Contrasts

One could conclude from this discussion that technology-facilitated learning is indeed ubiquitous in art education and that everyone is engaged in and benefited by the creative and educational potential brought about by the emergence of relatively inexpensive, accessible, user-friendly gadgets, virtual environments, and interactive multimedia. The fact is, however, most of this discourse comes from higher education, and very few scholarly studies of or writings by K–12 art teachers inform our current academic discourse about technology pedagogy. My own case studies reveal that K–12 teachers have integrated new technologies into their curricular and instructional practices but only to varying degrees, that student and teacher access to state-of-the-art digital media and communication networks is widely varied from school to school, and that content-rich models for technology utilization in the K–12 classroom are grossly lacking (Delacruz 2004). Currently, the idea of K–12 teachers seriously engaging the idea of ubiquitous (technology-facilitated) learning is little more than an academic construct for far too many teachers. In contrast to the impressive potential of technology suggested in the preceding section, K–12 teachers increasingly tell me that eleven-year-old kids know more about technology than they do and that their students have more and better equipment than they do. This coincides with the fact that many of my own students know more and have more than I do with regard to emerging technologies.

Recent studies confirm that young people use electronic technologies creatively and effortlessly, in widely varied ways, for widely varied ends. Conceptualizing these youth as "cyber-nomads," market analyst Andrea Saveri describes them as tech-savvy cultural creatives—digital age students, bloggers, gamers, consumers, designers, innovators, citizens, and activists. They have physical, digital, and social mobility; are opportunistic; and they simultaneously work across media (Saveri 2004), adopting distinct identities for each (Gross 2004). These are skills that young people learn in their teenage years (Lenhart 2007; Rheingold 2007), skills that they use creatively and freely on their own, but less so and less creatively in schools (Hitlin and Rainie 2005; Levin et al. 2002). In short, youth today are global and connected, but not so much in the K–12 educational institutions that are supposed to be preparing them for life in the twenty-first century. The stark contrasts between what contemporary students know and are able to do and what their teachers know and are able to do with technology is of high concern to me, but beyond the scope of this chapter other than to state the obvious: the current lack of technology support for K–12 teachers across the United States is an issue of national importance.

Visual Arts Technology Pedagogy in the Twenty-first Century

Despite technology gaps between teachers and students, the omnipresence of technology in the lives of the privileged, media-savvy youth of today has led many art educators like me to think differently about the roles of teachers in relation to the purpose and potential of technology-facilitated learning in the K–12 classroom. As our students have become more tech-savvy, I have begun to answer the "what happens" question posed at the beginning of this chapter, to focus on our need to distinguish technology training (learning procedures) from technology education (fulfilling aims), and to attempt to clarify my own vision of visual arts technology pedagogy for the twenty-first-century art teacher.

Appropriately, I have looked online for guidance, and writings about the digital knowledge commons and global civil society have been most useful. Media-savvy scholars observe that although highly capable, youth may not be self-inclined to participate in work for the common good without specific guidance from teachers. With this simple observation in mind, teacher-educators such as myself are able to resolve part of the problem of the disparity between what K–12 teachers know and what youth know about technology, and we are able to shift our concerns away from the questions of how to teach young people how to learn to use new technologies, and toward the questions of what to do with all these technologies. It is clear to me and many others that technology pedagogy must explicitly teach cultural citizenship and that it must engage notions of cultural citizenship as both a local and a global endeavor.

In this view technology education fuses with a form of moral education, in that cultural citizenship relies on development of two moral capacities: the capacity to pursue rationally a conception of the good and the capacity for an effective sense of justice (Bridges 2002). Both the concept of the good and the concept of social justice involve the development of empathy. Cultural citizenship also entails civic engagement, what civil rights leader Harry C. Boyte calls "public work," and which he defines as sustained, visible, serious effort by a diverse mix of ordinary people that creates things of lasting civic or public significance (Boyte 2002). It is here, within the realm of technology pedagogy in the K–12 art room, that connections between art education, technology pedagogy, and the notion of the common good are productively forged. In such a framework, new electronic media become the vehicle through which imagination and creative expression are added to the sphere of public opinion over matters of importance, and in which the Internet becomes a site for intercultural communication. The Internet, posed here as the realm in which civil society may come together to foster collective civic action both at the local level and in the global arena, creates new spheres for information exchange, debate, formation of public opinion, and fortification of plans for civic work (Fraser 2005; Habermas 1974, 1991; Kellner n.d.).

Public work is also full of tensions and conflicts, as individuals and groups from diverse backgrounds and different parts of the world bring varying perspectives, agendas, and life experiences to problems of mutual concern (Boyte 2002). Citizen activists must both embrace and bridge divisions of ethnicity, religion, language, and nationality in the formation of global civil society (Fraser 2005). Paradoxically, civic friendships form between persons from differing communities to the degree that they are able to both go beyond distinguishing and separating themselves through identification with particular communities *while at the same time* maintaining their particularistic communitarian identities within those friendships (Bridges 2002). Civic partnerships require these kinds of complicated friendships.

The idea that education might foster intercultural understanding and civic friendships across ethnic boundaries has long been a goal in art education (Blandy and Congdon 1987; Chapman 1978; Delacruz 2005; McFee and Degge 1977; Stuhr 1994; Zimmerman 2002). Seeing the visual arts as a form of personal and communitarian storytelling, advocates of the instrumental view of art believe that the creation and study of art facilitates development of communal identity and compassion toward others (Lankford 2002). Understanding the stories of diverse peoples provides a means by which connections between individuals with differing needs and expectations may be fostered (Blandy and Kellman 2004). Coupled with cultivation of a sense of social justice, political know-how, and a disposition toward public engagement, art education in the connected classroom becomes a vehicle for social change (Delacruz 2005).

Procedures for developing public opinion in the classroom are well rehearsed in art education (Barrett 1997; Battin and Silver 1989; Delacruz 1997; Hamblen 1985). Classroom strategies engage forms of inquiry that build on principles of philosophical reasoning (Lipman, Sharp, and Oscanyan 1980), rational debate and consensus building (Oliver 1980), and critical pedagogy (Friere 1998). Development of the kind of public opinion in the connected classroom that leads to public engagement requires more than rationalization and analysis; it requires a classroom context that facilitates a culture of caring (Noddings 1984, 2005).

Creating caring classroom conditions facilitates the desire to form alliances across divisions of race, gender, class, ethnicity, and the many other differences that divide students from one another. Advocates of such a notion maintain that for such a classroom culture to flourish, educators must dismantle the authoritative, hierarchical, lockstep mindset that characterizes public schooling today (Apple 2004; Giroux 2001) and that classroom conversations and creative expressions must focus on things that matter to students (Anderson and Milbrandt 2005; Delacruz 1997, 2005), things that are deeply *felt,* and that they must be followed by collective plans of action in behalf of others (Banks and Banks 2007).

Concluding Comments

This chapter briefly highlights how the profession of visual arts education both engages and is impacted by the omnipresence, or *ubiquity,* of emerging technologies, noting the facility with which young people learn with and through their new media, online social networks, and portable electronic devices. The cultural and ethical significance of the amazing adoption of new technologies by young people is not lost on media guru Howard Rheingold: "The tools for cultural production and distribution are in the pockets of 14 year olds. This does not guarantee that they will do the hard work of democratic self-governance: the tools that enable the free circulation of information and communication of opinion are necessary but not sufficient for the formation of public opinion. Ask yourself this question: Which kind of population seems more likely to become actively engaged in civic affairs?" (2007, para 2).

My own experiences lead me to embrace new media as a cultural phenomena full of potential for teacher-educators who like me are committed to pedagogical practices that privilege individual imagination, intercultural friendship, and civic engagement. Building on the ideas of scholars, artists, and activists that I admire, I have considered how technology pedagogy for cultural and global citizenship is really about a kind of teaching that nurtures kindness, listening, sharing, and doing good things because we care about one another in an increasingly smaller, more volatile, and more fragile world.

Extending out over the Internet, classroom activities that foster imagination, creative expression, dialogue, empathy, and civic action have global significance. In a classroom so envisioned, the teacher shifts from being the sole source of knowledge, authority on all things educational, and dispenser of grades, to creator of opportunities for engaged learning, inquiry, action, and reflection. The teacher in such a classroom is a co-learner in the reconstruction of knowledge and values, a catalyst, an active listener, and an opportunist, able to facilitate meaningful learning encounters and ready to follow intriguing student leads and possibilities. Although in great classrooms across the United States and elsewhere these shifts are already taking place (Delacruz 1997), with and without the aid of new technologies, there can be no doubt that technology facilitates and enriches such endeavors. Referring more than ten years ago to this style of teaching as *reciprocal teaching* (Delacruz 1997), I now see added benefits of this approach in classrooms in which students know more about technology than their teachers. Some of my most interesting technology educational work has occurred when my students have assumed leadership roles for teaching both me and their peers what they are able do with new and emerging technologies.

I have also observed that the promise, hype, and mythic discourse promoting the potential of technology for education represent an *unrealized promise* for many teachers (Delacruz 2004). Teaching of the sort promoted in this chapter and elsewhere in this book appears to be limited to special individuals, special occasions, or special schools. What is not clear to me is how intractable and retrograde our corporatized, bureaucratic, accountability-driven U.S. K–12 schools will remain amidst the current wave of technological innovation. Nevertheless, I have great faith in the next generation of art teachers entering the profession, those youthful digital natives who currently live, learn, and think with and through new technologies. I am confident that these future art teachers will bring this technological frame of reference with them into the classrooms of tomorrow.

I close this chapter with optimistic speculations about why visual arts education and technology pedagogy fit so well together. Philosophers, anthropologists, psychologists, and educators have long wondered what makes art special. Works of art embody the feelings, values, stories, achievements, and aspirations of individuals, communities, and civilizations (Anderson 1990; Dissanayake 1999; Langer 1980). The creation and study of art provides a means through which we come to a deeper understanding of what it means to be human (Anderson and Milbrandt 2005; Chapman 1978; Feldman 1987). Now created and proliferated with greatest ease and by the widest array of practitioners (artists?) imaginable, contemporary art positions itself worldwide as a form of cultural and social reconstruction. Returning to the idea that the power of art resides in its specialness, the path ahead in the connected visual arts classroom requires curricular choices and instructional strategies that engage the creation, consumption, and critique of art with, in, and through technology, and to link these learnings to notions of participatory citizenship in a globalized world. These choices and strategies build from a belief that the stuff of art is about things that matter greatly to people and that our omnipresent new technologies promote inquiry and action on these matters in important and dramatic ways.

Readings and References

For further reading on the relationships between technology and the development of civil society, see David Bollier's 2008 essay "Commoners as an Emerging Political Force," at OnTheCommons.org, http://www.commonsdev.us/content.php?id=2162; the 2008 UNESCO Bureau of the Intergovernmental Council of the Information for All Programme "2008–2013 Strategic Plan" at UNESCO, http://unesdoc.unesco.org/images/0016/001618/161860e.pdf; Howard Rheingold's 2000 revised edition of *The Virtual Community: Homesteading Frontier,* at his Web site, http://www.rheingold.com/vc/book/index.html; and the writings of Charlotte Hess about the knowledge commons, at International Association for the Study of the Commons, http://www.iascp.org/articles.html. For relevant readings about public work and civil society, see "Theoretical Framework: The Concept and Philosophy of Public Work," at the University of Minnesota Center for Democracy and Citizenship, http://www.hhh.umn.edu/centers/cdc/theory.html; the report of the Conference of Non-governmental Organizations in Consultative Relationship with the United Nations, http://www.ngocongo.org; and Robert Conner's "The Idea of a Civil Society," at National Humanities Center, http://nationalhumanitiescenter.org/publications/civilsoc/intro.htm. For readings about art relevant to this chapter, see John Dewey's *Art as Experience* (1934); Jan Cohen-Cruz, "An Introduction to Community Art and Activism," at Community Arts Network Reading Room, http://www.communityarts.net/readingroom/archivefiles/2002/02/an_introduction.php; and Elizabeth Strom's 2002 issue paper created for the Center for the Arts and Culture, Culture and the National Agenda initiative, "Strengthening Communities through Culture," at Cultural Policy Listserv, http://www.creativecity.ca/resources/making-the-case/general/strengthening-communities-culture.html.

Anderson, Richard L. 1990. "Art as Culturally Significant Meaning." In *Calliope's Sisters: A Comparative Study of Philosophies of Art,* 238–61. Englewood Cliffs, N.J.: Prentice Hall.

Anderson, Tom, and Melody Milbrandt. 2005. "Individual Expression and Creativity." In *Art for Life: Authentic Instruction in Art,* 65–78. New York: McGraw-Hill.

Apple, Michael. 2004. *Ideology and Curriculum.* London: Routledge.

Banks, James A., and Cathy A. M. Banks, eds. 2007. *Multicultural Education: Issues and Perspectives.* New York: John Wiley.

Barrett, Terry. 1997. *Talking about Student Art.* Worcester, Mass.: Davis Publications.

Battin, Margaret, and Anita Silver. 1989. *Puzzles about Art: An Aesthetics Casebook.* New York: St. Martins Press.

Blandy, Doug, and Kristin G. Congdon. 1987. *Art in a Democracy.* New York: Teachers College Press.

Blandy, Doug, and Julia Kellman. 2004. "Editorial: A Special Issue on Diverse Populations." *Visual Arts Research* 58(1) (August): 1–2.

Boyte, Harry C. 2002. *A Different Kind of Politics: John Dewey and the Meaning of Citizenship in the 21st Century.* Dewey lecture, University of Michigan, November 1. Civic Practices Network, http://www.cpn.org/crm/contemporary/different.html (accessed August 15, 2006).

Bridges, Thomas. 2002. "Civic Friendship, Communitarian Solidarity, and the Story of

Liberty." The Nature of Civic Culture, http://web.archive.org/web/20050211091850/http://civsoc.com/nature/nature10.html (accessed February 2009).

Carpenter, B. Steven, and Pamela G. Taylor. 2003. "Racing Thoughts: Altering Our Ways of Knowing and Being in Art through Computer Hypertext." *Studies in Art Education* 45(1) (January): 40–55.

Chapman, Laura H. 1978. *Approaches to Art in Education.* San Diego: Harcourt.

Congdon, Kristin G., and Doug Blandy. 2003. "Zinesters in the Classroom: Using Zines to Teach about Postmodernism and the Communication of Ideas." *Art Education* 56(3) (May): 44–52.

Delacruz, Elizabeth M. 1997. *Design for Inquiry: Instructional Theory, Research, and Practice in Art Education.* Reston, Va.: National Art Education Association.

———. 2004. "Teachers' Technology Working Conditions and the Unmet Promise of Technology." *Studies in Art Education* 46(1) (September): 6–19.

———. 2005. "Commentary: Art Education in Civil Society." *Visual Arts Research* 31(2) (December): 3–9.

Delacruz, Elizabeth M., and S. Bales. 2007. "Digital Sketchbooks, Scrapbooks, Blogs, Scripts, and Storyboards: Social Networking, Story Telling, and History Making in the Digital Age." Paper delivered at the 45th Annual Convention of the National Art Education Association, New York, March.

Dissanayake, Ellen. 1995. *Homo Aestheticus: Where Art Comes from and Why.* Seattle: University of Washington Press.

———. 1999. "'Making Special': An Undescribed Human Universal and the Core of a Behavior of Art." In *Biopoetics: Evolutionary Explorations in the Arts,* ed. Brett Cooke and Frederick Turner, 27–46. Lexington, Ky.: ICUS.

Duncum, Paul A. 2004. "Visual Culture Isn't Just Visual: Multiliteracy, Multimodality, and Meaning." *Studies in Art Education* 45(3) (March): 252–64.

Efland, Arthur, Kerry Freedman, and Patricia Stuhr. 1996. *Postmodern Art Education.* Reston, Va.: National Art Education Association.

Emme, Michael J., and Anna Kirova. 2005. "PhotoShop Semiotics: Research in the Age of Digital Manipulation." *Visual Arts Research* 31(1) (August): 145–53.

Ettinger, Linda. 1988. "Art Education and Computing: Building a Perspective." *Studies in Art Education* 30(1) (January): 53–62.

Feldman, Edmund B. 1987. *Varieties of Visual Experience.* Englewood Cliffs, N.J.: Prentice Hall.

Fraser, Nancy. 2005. "Transnationalizing the Public Sphere." Republicart, http://www.republicart.net/disc/publicum/fraser01_en.htm (accessed February 21, 2007).

Freedman, Kerry. 1991. "Possibilities of Interactive Computer Graphics for Art Instruction." *Art Education* 44(3) (June): 41–47.

———. 2003. *Teaching Visual Culture.* New York: Teachers College Press.

Friere, Paolo. 1998. *Pedagogy of Freedom: Ethics, Democracy, and Civic Courage.* Lanham, Md.: Rowman and Littlefield.

Garoian, Charles R., and Yvonne M. Gaudelius. 2001. "Cyborg Pedagogy: Performing Resistance in the Digital Age." *Studies in Art Education* 42(4) (March): 333–47.

Giroux, Henry. 2001. *Theory and Resistance in Education: Towards a Pedagogy for the Opposition.* Portsmouth, N.H.: Greenwood Publishing.

Greh, Deborah. 1986. "Using Computers in Secondary Education." *Art Education* 39(6) (November): 4–9.

Gross, Elisheva F. 2004. "Adolescent Internet Use: What We Expect, What Teens Report." *Journal of Applied Developmental Psychology* 25(6): 633–49.

Habermas, Jurgen. 1974. "The Public Sphere: An Encyclopedia Article." Translated by S. Lenox and F. Lenox. *New German Critique* 3 (Autumn): 49–55.

———. 1991. *Structural Transformation of the Public Sphere.* Cambridge, Mass.: MIT Press.

Hamblen, Karen A. 1985. "Developing Aesthetic Literacy through Contested Concepts." *Art Education* 38(5) (September): 19–24.

———. 1990. "Beyond the Aesthetic of Cash Culture Literacy." *Studies in Art Education* 31(4) (March): 216–25.

Hicks, John. 1993. "Technology and Aesthetic Education: A Crucial Synthesis." *Art Education* 46(6) (November): 42–46.

Hitlin, Paul, and Lee Rainie. 2005. "Teens, Technology, and School." Pew Internet and American Life Project, http://www.pewinternet.org/pdfs/PIP_Internet_and_schools_05.pdf (accessed February 21, 2007).

Horrigan, John, and Lee Rainie. 2006. "The Internet's Growing Role in Life's Major Moments." Pew Internet and American Life Project, http://www.pewinternet.org (accessed February 21, 2007).

Hubbard, Guy. 1993. "Hypermedia: Cause for Optimism in Art Curriculum Design." *Art Education* 42(1) (January): 59–64.

Keifer-Boyd, Karen. 1996. "Interfacing Hypermedia and the Internet with Critical Inquiry in the Arts: Preservice Training." *Art Education* 49(6) (November): 33–41.

———. 1997. "Interactive Hyperdocuments: Implications for Art Criticism in a Postmodern Era." In *Art Education: Content and Practice in a Postmodern Era,* ed. James Hutchens and Marianne Suggs, 111–21. Reston, Va.: National Art Education Association.

———. 2005. "Technology Interfaces with Art Education." *Visual Arts Research* 31(1) (August): 1–3.

Kellner, Douglas. n.d. "Habermas, the Public Sphere, and Democracy: A Critical Intervention." Douglas Kellner Essays, http://www.gseis.ucla.edu/faculty/kellner/essays/habermaspublicspheredemocracy.pdf (accessed February 15, 2007).

Knight, Wanda B. 2005. "Reconnecting Youth at Risk through Technology-Based Instruction." *Visual Arts Research* 31(1) (August): 103–16.

Krug, Don. 2002. "Electronic Media and Everyday Aesthetics of Simulation." *Visual Arts Research* 28(2) (December): 27–36.

Langer, Suzanne. 1980. *Philosophy in a New Key: A Study in the Symbolism of Reason, Rite, and Art.* Cambridge, Mass.: Harvard University Press.

Lanier, Vincent. 1969. "The Teaching of Art as Social Revolution." *Phi Delta Kappan* 1(6): 314–19.

Lankford, E. Louis. 2002. "Nurturing Humaneness." *Journal of Cultural Research in Art Education* 19/20:47–52.

Lenhart, Amanda. 2007. "Social Networking Websites and Teens: An Overview." Pew Internet and American Life Project, http://www.pewinternet.org (accessed February 21, 2007).

Lenhart, Amanda, Lee Rainie, and Oliver Lewis. 2001. "Teenage Life On-Line: The rise of the Instant-Message Generation and the Internet's Impact on Friendships and Family Relationships." Pew Internet and American Life Project, http://www.pewinternet.org (accessed February 21, 2007).

Levin, Doug, Sousan Arafeh, Amanda Lenhart, and Lee Rainie. 2002. "The Digital Disconnect: The Widening Gap between Internet-Savvy Students and Their Schools." 2002. Pew Internet and American Life Project, http://www.pewinternet.org/ (accessed February 21, 2007).

Lipman, Matthew, Ann Margaret Sharp, and Frederick S. Oscanyan. 1980. *Philosophy in the Classroom.* Philadelphia: Temple University Press.

McFee, June K., and Rogena Degge. 1977. *Art, Culture, and Environment.* Belmont, Calif.: Wadsworth.

Neperud, Ron W. 1997. "Art and Ecology." *Art Education* 50(6) (November): 14–20.

Noddings, Nel. 1984. *Caring: A Feminine Approach to Ethics and Moral Education.* Berkeley: University of California Press.

———. 2005. "Caring in Education." Encyclopedia of Informal Education, http://www.infed.org/biblio/noddings_caring_in_education.htm (accessed January 2, 2008).

Oliver, David. 1980. "Jurisprudential Inquiry: Clarifying Public Issues." In *Models of Teaching,* ed. Bruce Joyce and M. Weil, 2nd ed., 260–76. Englewood Cliffs, N.J.: Prentice Hall.

Rheingold, Howard. 2007. "The Tools of Cultural Production Are in the Hands of Teens." Blog dated January 1, http://www.smartmobs.com/2007/01/01/the-tools-of-cultural-production-are-in-the-hands-of-teens (accessed August 15, 2007).

Roland, Craig. 2007. Art Junction. Web site and blog, http://artjunction.org.

Saveri, Andrea. 2004. *The Cybernomadic Framework.* Palo Alto, Calif.: Institute for the Future.

Stankiewicz, Maryanne, and Elizabeth Garber. 2000. "Cyberfaculty: An Experience in Distance Learning." *Art Education* 53(1) (January): 33–38.

Stuhr, Patricia. 1994. "Multicultural Art Education and Social Reconstruction." *Studies in Art Education* 35(3) (March): 171–78.

Taylor, Pamela G., and B. Steven Carpenter. 2002. "Inventively Linking: Teaching and Learning with Computer Hypertext." *Art Education* 55(4) (July): 6–12.

Zimmerman, Enid. 2002. "Intercultural Education Offers a Means to Promote Tolerance and Understanding." *Journal of Cultural Research in Art Education* 19/20:68–80.

21

Writing (1)

Writing with Video

MARIA LOVETT AND
JOSEPH SQUIER

Literacy, Readers, Authors

The printing press democratized print literacy and in the process gave rise to the modern university; it promoted an expanded universe of knowledge and discourse that could extend beyond medieval monasteries and into the secular world. The availability of printed texts drove the ascension of alphabetic literacy to the point that, until very recently, the common assumption was that to be literate meant the ability to read words on a page. Of course, by the end of the twentieth century it was evident that contemporary literacy was becoming increasingly multimodal and hybridized. Today's communication landscape is characterized by forms that frequently combine the printed word with images and sound. This is particularly omnipresent in the reception and production of video in our contemporary world—to such an extent that some envision it as becoming the dominant form for the transmission of ideas: "The new video, with the assistance of computers, should become the means by which our more sophisticated information, ideas and experiences are recorded, shared, explored and analyzed. And as writing and print once did, the new video should begin to transform the nature of our information, ideas and experiences" (Stephens 1998, 201).

However, this evolution of communication has created significant tension within modern institutions. Students have had to confront a growing disconnection between their lived experience and the norms of the academy. One obvious friction point has been the undergraduate composition requirement that is an almost universal aspect of completing any degree. Historically, composition has meant writing. It was assumed, at least within the academy, that the most legitimate and powerful rhetorical forms were attached to the technologies of ink and paper. The problem, however, is that this premise no longer maps onto the ubiquitous experience of today's student, who encounters a densely constructed communication landscape in which printed text is but one among many rhetorical forms, and where words often function in concert with other modes of persuasion and discourse.

As we move into an era of ubiquitous networks, it is also important to note an increasing breakdown in the division between author and audience. The printing press increased access to knowledge, but contemporary technologies such as camcorders also afford a powerful means of authorship. When this affordance is teamed with easy access to high-speed global networks, the result is the emergence of social networks on a scale never before seen. Sites such as MySpace and YouTube provide a glimpse of a future in which citizens will be constantly engaged, not just as readers but also as authors.

Emerging from this technocentric space, and acknowledging the lived experience of our students, we developed a pedagogical approach that strives to meet the needs of twenty-first-century citizens. The course Writing with Video was developed as a response to these tensions. Specifically, we wanted to promote an expanded definition of the term "composition," one that we saw as being both more inclusive of multiple communication media and also more reflective of the contemporary world. Writing with Video is intended to empower students by giving them a diverse package of rhetorical, analytic, and creative skills. Methodologically, the course, informed by the pedagogical praxis discussed here, is an applied example of ubiquitous learning that has been successful at the University of Illinois at Urbana-Champaign (UIUC). It meets general education requirements in three categories at the university—advanced composition, arts and humanities, and cultural studies.

Classrooms, Laptops, and Ubiquitous Access

Students enrolled in Writing with Video are loaned an Apple laptop computer for the duration of the semester. The machines are specially configured with software that allows students to write, produce video, and connect to the Internet. They are expected to bring the laptops to class, but most choose to carry them constantly. For the typical student, the laptop serves multiple functions: writing journal, research tool, video production studio, communication conduit, publishing platform, viewing screen, and media archive. Many students also use the laptop for purposes not directly related to their work in the course: storing music collections, surfing the Web, accessing their e-mail, instant messaging, or completing work for other classes. This is encouraged. The repetitive point we wish to make here is that learning should not be fragmented into disparate parts. Instead, our educational philosophy promotes a form of living pedagogy: we emphasize a process that connects knowledge acquisition within intuitional spaces, with those lived experiences performed beyond classroom walls.

Likewise, Writing with Video instructors are encouraged to meet with their students outside of their assigned classrooms. Meetings, sometimes consisting of an entire class but at other times of small working groups, have been convened at the library, in other campus "commons" areas, outdoors, and at local cafés. Our assumptions about classrooms—rectangular rooms with lapboard desks and lecterns—are under rapid revision, much of it driven by technological change. We believe that traditional notions of standardized classrooms will progressively give way to *learning spaces* that are flexible in their configurations and uses. Laptops are one way to promote a new type of classroom dynamic. In particular, we see them as an attempt to erase the division between classroom time, "homework," and real life—divisions that may make less sense to students, enabled as they are by cell phones and instant messaging, than to their professors.

Laptops give students the means to take advantage of the increasingly ubiquitous nature of contemporary media and communications networks. Rather than being forced to go to a traditional computer lab to conduct research or produce content, students can now engage in all aspects of media research, authorship, and analysis on a 24/7 basis. For most Writing with Video students, place has become less of a factor. They can complete coursework as easily in their apartment as they can on campus. Students can produce video when the computer lab is shut down and can research projects even when the library is closed.

Another important component in the laptop program is the utilization of a proprietary Apple software program called Pages. This software effectively combines a word processing program with a design layout program, complete with several design templates. Most significant for our purposes, Pages can seamlessly and easily incorporate nontext elements such as video, still images, and audio. In other words, Pages allows authors to create sophisticated and visually compelling hybrid documents that communicate across multiple modes: text, images, and sound.

Writing with Video students create Pages documents that capture and inscribe every aspect of their project. Typical Pages files include lists of brainstorming ideas, research topics and sources, storyboards, shot lists, scripts, video rough cuts, audio recordings, meditations on unexpected questions or problems encountered, unused video clips and outtakes, self-reflection, and analysis. Frequently, these documents are then shared with other students—electronically via the network, of course—who often provide further written analysis and feedback directly in the original document. Lastly, students then upload their finished video projects to iTunes, where they can be viewed, and even downloaded, by other students.

Course Assignments

Writing with Video redefines what traditional educational practices consider as evidence of learning—the products. Our method does this in two ways: first, by valuing process as well as product, and second by utilizing video and multimedia as a form of composition. This is best explained by thoroughly describing the assignments.

Assignments are designed to begin with self-inquiry and move toward community and social engagement as a form of agency. Keeping detailed journals, students pose questions and conduct research to investigate their topic. In the field, they are situated as visual anthropologists or ethnographers. Assignments incorporate reflective writing about the production process—shooting, editing, and sharing the video. In addition, students engage in peer reviews of work-in-progress and completed projects. When evaluating their final videos, their reflective process as documented in their journals is significant.

Because Writing with Video is designed for students with little or no prior experience producing video, early assignments are meant to help students begin building a visual vocabulary and create links between written language and visual language. Each assignment builds on previous work and becomes progressively more complex and ambitious.

PROJECT 1: ADJECTIVES AND MOTIFS

Early projects ask students to draw on aspects of identity and personal concerns while simultaneously becoming familiar with the cinematic vocabulary and tools required to compose in media. They must consider form in relation to content, as informed by principles of design and studio art practice. Emphasis is placed on encouraging students to "see" the world more self-consciously and reflectively, and to give those with limited experience in the visual realm a comfortable entry point for creating visual work. Students translate a series of adjectives into short twenty-second video vignettes and create one-minute video pieces that convey a simple visual or conceptual motif. They write self-reflections about their finished work, and the class also engages in a group critique–style evaluation of the projects. This provides the opportunity to begin a conversation about standards by which visual communication can be deconstructed, evaluated, and critically analyzed.

PROJECT 2: AESTHETIC WRITING

Next, students are asked to write an expository essay about an event that was significant to them—an evocative piece of aesthetic writing. This essay employs descriptive language to *show* rather than *explain* their experience. The assignment draws on performative, ethnographic writing techniques (Madison 2005). Students are asked to make use of this multisensory articulation when translating their essay to the screen. This project encourages them to compare and contrast writing and video as two descriptive modes and also serves to introduce them to the significant relationship between image and sound. At this point, students are focused on representing themselves, their own thoughts and viewpoints, which will then provide a useful counterpoint to the next project.

PROJECT 3: REPRESENTING OTHERS

For the third project, students produce a short documentary—an environmental portrait of a person and a place. Through this assignment they investigate issues of subjectivity and objectivity in art and media representations. First, students determine a subject. This process includes writing an intersectional essay to reflect on who "we are behind the camera" and how "who we are affects what we see." In addition, this assignment asks students to contemplate moral and ethical dilemmas associated with representing another person. Student projects have explored topics such as a middle school for girls, women in hip-hop, Asian Americans at UIUC, a single mother in college, a homeless man on Green Street, the housemother of a sorority, a waitress at a local diner, and the constructed reality of an Internet blogger, just to name a few.

PROJECT 4: VISUAL ARGUMENT

For the last assignment, students are asked to take a position, to share a point of view on a concept, issue, or idea that concerns them. Focus is placed on video as a rhetorical medium—with parallels drawn to rhetorical writing—and how video is used in contemporary culture to inform, persuade, or even indoctrinate. For this final video, students frequently take on timely topics being debated in the culture at large. Some have remixed popular culture to speak back to issues of racism and the commodification of culture. We encourage students to utilize the resources around them: many graduate students and faculty members are doing research that lends itself in a compelling way to video representation. For example, a group of students in the pilot course worked collectively to take advantage of innovative research being conducted at UIUC by Rasul Mowatt about postcards documenting lynching in the United States. Combining their own research and interviews with Mowatt and a curator from the Chicago Historical Society, the students produced a disturbing yet enlightening video titled *Lynching as Leisure: America's Forgotten Pastime.*

Other students have used the progression of assignments to explore a single theme—beginning with the personal and then creating a video to speak back to the bigger societal picture. For example, throughout the semester a student named Valerie explored her identity as a Philippine-American and issues of discrimination and oppression—both in a personal sense and in terms of confronting manifestations of media representations promoting ideological messages. In her "aesthetic writing" assignment, Valerie wrote an essay about an experience of having her hair cut—the hairdresser commented that her hair was coarse because she was Asian. Valerie used this racist experience in her life as a point of departure for her video. She produced a video composition using magazine images to critique the proliferation of the ideal definition of beauty as whiteness. In her "representing others" project, Valerie interviewed staff and students from the Asian American Cultural House. Finally, for her last project, Valerie collaged historical research, her own poetry, sound, text, and images, and drew from not only personal experience but her education as a creative writing and English major to create a video essay that resonated with postcolonial literature.

Many former Writing with Video students have gone on to implement media arts projects of their own. For example, one former student has developed a project with local girls in Champaign exploring black girlhood and another will soon be implementing a photo and video documentary project with children in South Africa. We make this point to address the need in education to advocate lifelong learning—a living pedagogy if you will—and empower our students as not only co-learners but as co-teachers.

Pedagogy as Method

The philosophy of Writing with Video is informed by critical pedagogy and by the theory and praxis of media production, design, and art making. As pedagogy and as intervention, the course departs from the analytical to include the participatory. By "intervention" we mean that Writing with Video intervenes in pervasive forces of representations by positioning students as cultural producers to author their own media from a critically informed perspective. The class combines critical literacy with hands-on production practice to problematize issues of representation. The methodology redefines what is deemed the learning environment, positions students as cultural authors/producers, and utilizes a problem-posing approach, as Freire (1970) advocates, to allocate spaces for students to decode and deideologize the symbolic.

Writing with Video challenges students to question how we negotiate, resist, and reauthor popular texts in all modalities. Through this course students confront the commodification of culture and the widening gap between the producers and consumers of such popular texts. To teach criticality without also providing our students the skills and tools to re-present their stories fails to intervene in oppressive cultural conditions. Writing with Video seeks to disrupt the separation between what students experience in and out of traditional learning environments. Such inconsistency has resulted in what Maxine Greene (in Goodman 2003) calls "the language gap" between the print-based preference within institutional spaces and the audiovisual and digital culture that is prevalent in our students' lives and their meaning-making processes. To initiate student-led inquiry on a variety of topics, the course utilizes a sincere appreciation for lived experience and what students already know. The interventionist pedagogy of the course situates students as researchers. Data are collected through written text, images, and sound. Students reflect on, share, and discuss this material. Intersecting pedagogy and research through video production situates students as media arts–based inquirers to investigate the world in which they live. It is through this approach to teaching and learning that Writing with Video addresses significant issues relevant to ubiquitous learning.

Three pedagogical themes inform the curriculum. First, the need to employ critical literacy with hands-on production practices to identify, isolate, and unpack problematic and oppressive issues of representation in mass-mediated contemporary culture. An overwhelming number of stories and images in the media *narrate* the experiences and characterizations of others, but they are rarely afforded the chance to *show* their own story back. As Elizabeth Ellsworth (1997, 76) explains, "The process of representation is not a process that reflects reality. Media are not mirrors of the world. They're not windows onto the world. Media re-present the world. Representation presents its subject again, in ways that mediated it through language, ideology, culture, power, convention, desire." When we acknowledge and become conscious of this alteration, "re-presentation becomes recognizable and available as a crucial site of social, political and educational struggles over what particular people, events and experiences will be made to mean." Writing with Video addresses this not only through textual analysis but also through affording students the opportunity to author and disseminate media productions to *re-present* what has been traditionally presented.

Students are situated as researchers, educators, and media authors. This disrupts the stereotype of the teacher/adult as expert model and dismantles what Freire (1970) calls the banking-model of education because it situates students as experts in their own experience. As a philosophical framework for the process of the class this also alleviates the educator from feeling responsible for keeping up with technology at every turn: students share what they know—technically and conceptually. Furthermore, with online distribution sites such as YouTube and others, students can share their knowledge and ideas with an audience beyond the classroom. This notion of sharing what they know and learn in the public sphere impacts how students engage in the learning process, revise material, consider their audiences, and offer up a unique video representation of what they have discovered.

Second, Writing with Video critically considers the relationship of form and content. Our pedagogical method specifically addresses not only the subject matter and content but also the form. Students investigate the relevance of composition, structure, and construction as a crucial aspect of the content itself and how this affects knowledge production. For example, when recording in the field with video, what is included in the frame is as relevant as what is left out. How the images are composed, what angles are used, the setting, and so forth, are relevant to understanding the content. Such consideration adopts principles of reflexivity in filmmaking as evident in the praxis of filmmaker and scholar Trinh T. Minh-Ha. Trinh explores morality and issues of representation to theorize with the camera, using cinema as "a form of reflexive body writing . . . with the understanding that no reality can be 'captured' without trans-forming" (1992, 115). All of these decisions made by our students are relevant to what the overall message means and how it may be interpreted. They write with text, but they also simultaneously write with the camera.

Third, Writing with Video redefines the learning environment through technology. This occurs on multiple levels and permeates every aspect of the course. Camcorders, audio decks, editing software, and a whole host of digital tools are harnessed as inscription technologies that foster new ways to explore, capture, synthesize, and represent the world. Laptop computers provide an intersection point for research and production—frequently fusing these activities into an integrated single activity—and also engender different understandings of classroom use. Electronic publishing venues and emergent social networks provide students with new and expanded audiences for their own work, giving them access to the work of other authors and making them a part of a much larger, sometimes global, discourse.

Conclusion: Student Voices

Writing with Video yields specific attention to the process of communicating with video as a rhetorical device. The pedagogical process seeks to have students recognize the multiple modes available to them in making meaning. The emphasis on process is fundamental to the pedagogy supporting the course because it makes the cognitive process of translating experiences, perspectives, and ideas into a product utterly explicit and conscious for students. When students become producers and authors, rather than simply consumers of new media texts, they gain a fuller understanding of the ways in which new media shape how information is structured, organized, understood, and evaluated. They learn to look at, rather than simply through, such texts (Lovett et al. forthcoming).

Because composition courses enroll students from across the university, Writing with Video has helped bring art and design expertise in visual communication to a wider cross-section of students. Enrollment includes students majoring in art and design, education, communications, computer science, media studies, cinema studies, English, psychology, business, and engineering. The interdisciplinary reach of the course allows students to revisit what they are learning in other classes and explore it in visual form. The diversity of academic backgrounds has made for a lively mixture of unique voices and agendas. Media and cinema studies students in particular have mentioned how grateful they are to put into practice some of the theoretical knowledge they have gained from their other courses. A psychology major recently produced video interpretations of theories she had been reading in another course about the cognitive awareness of mortality. This cross-disciplinary aspect of the course reinforces how important it is for students to continue to make use of what they know and to push themselves to further develop critical thinking skills.

The course encourages students to demonstrate new technologies they are using, such as podcasting or sound-editing techniques. These technology-enabled social spaces are aspects of our students' lived experiences, and this often makes them the resident experts. Consequently, Writing with Video instructors frequently find themselves being educated by their students. In a course like this, where multiple inscription technologies are merged into something altogether new, we have found that students and teachers can learn equally from one another. Too often learning environments are structured in the top-down, hierarchical model. By redefining and offering new theories and methods for communication, Writing with Video challenges this historical structure. If we "reveal the frame" of the pedagogy and research, the process and knowledge exchange can be empowering for all participants.

Often as researchers and scholars we summarize the work and actions of our subjects. Our goal is to privilege the insight and knowledge of our students. So we conclude this chapter with selected testimonials from recent students.

NATE, SOPHOMORE, MAJOR UNDECIDED

When you have the camera in your hands, you think to yourself what can I shoot that will make my movie better? . . . The composition of every shot you have creates text within the film. It could be because of the angle that you use or you decide to place the interviewer on the right side of the screen with the background dominating the frame. Everything you do creates a different feeling for the viewers. You also learn that through editing you can make someone look like a complete jerk or like the nicest person. You have to create the characters for the movies just as the author of a novel has to create the characters. I realized that making a video is no different than writing a paper. In every one of my films

I always wanted to have a beginning, middle, and end and most importantly I wanted it to flow.

ELISE, SENIOR, PHOTOGRAPHY MAJOR

I do not like writing, but this class presented such a different type of writing. [The journal] was so personal and helped me figure out my intentions for making my work and thinking through what I learned, liked and disliked, had problems with. . . . The amount of writing is necessary, being a Advanced Composition course. But really, I never felt like I was writing a ton. Fifteen pages seemed to go by quickly when doing the journal because it is *personal.* It is of *our* experiences as students. Nothing is more depressing than to write about something you have no interest in.

VICTOR, SENIOR, COMPUTER SCIENCE MAJOR

I think an empowering aspect of the class is its use of technology, and a powerful aspect is its confrontation with ethical values. . . . I like how through this class we became literate in how to "read" films through the process of making them. The idea of visual evidence was very helpful for me. It made me keep in mind my audience and to focus more on what was in the frame of the final cut. Since video can be so powerful, I'm glad we learned about representation and subjectivity. Being conscious of and acknowledging my own biases has helped me be more objective (ironically). . . . We were constantly encouraged to address these issues when making our own films.

VENETA, SENIOR, PSYCHOLOGY MAJOR

It's so important to consider every single part of it: the structure, form, composition, shots, angles, colors, sound, speed, music, etc. . . . Being conscious of how all of these structural things affect the message is so important. . . . I am now more aware of the types or reactions other media sources are trying to get out of me. I really believe that it is so important to be aware of how style affects us. . . . To understand that there is such a thing as different perspectives is so important. It helps us understand and communicate with each other. We could be looking at the exact same situation and interpret it differently.

EMILY, FRESHMAN, MAJOR UNDECIDED

I've always loved the worlds of books. Instead of relaxing in the comfort of the freedom of words, I wanted to work with something a little less in my head and more in reality. I wanted to use this class to explore the tangible world visually with new eyes. I found ways to make the tangible and the intangible collide, which is such an amazing thing to be able to do. I was able to tangibly express my intangible feelings and the process I went through as I explored death and life in my aesthetic video. With the proliferation of visual technology in our culture it was so useful to learn the basics of creating a video. I felt like I was learning how to write all over again.

Readings and References

A great introductory text to visual culture through a critical lens is *Practices of Looking* by Sturken and Cartwright. For further reading on documentary and film production, see *Film Art* by Bordell and Thompson and *Directing the Documentary* by Michael Rabiger. For examples of other youth media projects, see *Portraits and Dreams* by Wendy Ewald and the "Photovoice Methodology" developed by Caroline Wang. Writing with Video was also informed and inspired by classic texts such as *The Fire Next Time* by James Baldwin, *Ways of Seeing* by John Berger, *On Photography* by Susan Sontag, and *Framer Framed* by Trinh T. Minh-Ha.

Baldwin, James. 1963. *The Fire Next Time.* New York: Dial Press.

Berger, John. 1973. *Ways of Seeing.* New York: Penguin Books.

Bordell, David, and Kristin Thompson. 2004. *Film Art: An introduction.* New York: McGraw-Hill.

Buckingham, David, and Julian Sefton-Green. 1994. *Cultural Studies Goes to School.* Bristol, Pa.: Taylor and Francis.

Ellsworth, Elizabeth. 1997. *Teaching Positions: Difference, Pedagogy and the Power of Address.* New York: Teachers College Press.

Ewald, Wendy. 1985. *Portraits and Dreams.* New York: Writers and Readers Publishing.

———. n.d. "Literacy through Photography Overview." Center for Documentary Studies, CDS Projects, http://cds.aas.duke.edu/ltp.

Finely, Susan. 2005. "Arts-Based Inquiry: Performing Revolutionary Pedagogy." In *The SAGE Handbook of Qualitative Research,* ed. Norman Denzin and Yvonna Lincoln, 681–94. New York: Sage.

Freire, Paolo. 1970/2003. *Pedagogy of the Oppressed.* New York: Continuum International.

Goodman, Steven. 2003. *Teaching Youth Media: A Critical Guide to Literacy, Video Production and Social Change.* Foreword by Maxine Greene. New York: Teachers College Press.

Lovett, Maria, Katherine E. Gossett, Carrie A. Lamanna, James P. Purdy, and Joseph Squier. Forthcoming. "Writing with Video: What Happens When Composition Comes off the Page?" In *Reading and Writing in New Media,* ed. James Kalmbach and Cheryl E. Ball. Cresskill, N.J.: Hampton Press.

Madison, D. Soyini. 2005. *Critical Ethnography: Methods, Ethics, and Performance.* Thousand Oaks, Calif.: Sage.

Mitchell, W. J. T. 1994. *Picture Theory.* Chicago: University of Chicago Press.

Rabiger, Michael. 1992. *Directing the Documentary.* Boston: Focal Press.

Renov, Michael. 1993. "Toward a Poetics of Documentary." In *Theorizing Documentary,* ed. Michael Renov, 12–36. New York: Routledge.

Sontag, Susan. 1966. *Against Interpretation.* New York: Picador.

———. 1977. *On Photography.* New York: Picador.
Stephens, Mitchell. 1998. *The Rise of the Image, the Fall of the Word.* Oxford: Oxford University Press.
Sturken, Marita, and Lisa Cartwright. 2003. *Practices of Looking: An Introduction to Visual Culture.* New York: Oxford University Press.
Trinh T. Minh-Ha. 1992. *Framer Framed.* New York: Routledge.
———. 1993. "The Totalizing Quest of Meaning." In *Theorizing Documentary,* ed. Michael Renov, 90–107. New York: Routledge.
Wang, Caroline. "Photovoice Methodology." Village Works, http://www.wellesley.edu/DavisMuseum/VillageWorks/Background/photovoice.html.

22

Writing (2)

Ubiquitous Writing and Learning: Digital Media as Tools for Reflection and Research on Literate Activity

GAIL E. HAWISHER, PAUL PRIOR,
PATRICK BERRY, AMBER BUCK,
STEVEN E. GUMP, CORY HOLDING,
HANNAH LEE, CHRISTA OLSON,
AND JANINE SOLBERG

Ubiquity in Learning and Writing

Whether in sociocultural notions of mediated activity and agency (Scollon 2001; Wertsch 1991), the flat dynamic assemblages of actor-network theory (Latour 2005), Hutchins's (1995) notion of functional systems, or Lave and Wenger's (1991) account of situated learning, recent theory and research have foregrounded the ubiquitous character of social practice, that is, the ways situated activity inevitably spreads out across time and space. Independently and with colleagues, we have been involved in studying what Prior (1998, 138) termed "literate activity," that is, activity "not located in acts of reading and writing, but as cultural forms of life saturated with textuality." Examining this ubiquitous character of literate activity in the writing processes of undergraduates, graduate students, and professors (in part through asking them to draw visual representations of their processes), Prior and Shipka (2003) described the intricate ways writers' work is distributed across diverse contexts as well as how writers select and structure contexts (people, places, and tools) to support their thinking, textual production, and affective-motivational engagement. Selfe and Hawisher (2004) and Hawisher and Selfe (2006) have explored how people forge literate lives in this digital, information age and live their days in a variety of technological and cultural settings.

From our perspective, the ubiquity of literate activity is not new. Digital and new media technologies have not created ubiquity, just as they have not created multimodality. Multimodality and ubiquity have always been there: what is remarkable is how ideological framings and practices of selective attention have allowed them to be so widely ignored and denied. That said, digital media have altered—and continue to alter—the practices and potentials of ubiquitous writing and learning much as they have contributed to notions of multimodality. Spheres of life that were once thought to be distinct are reimagined as digital media pervade our everyday lives. Academic disciplines increasingly use digital technologies and writing in ways that reconstruct disciplinary spaces and artifacts, while also softening and shifting perceived borders between the disciplinary and the everyday.

In this chapter, we take up this notion of ubiquity and consider how video and sound, still and moving images might inform our understandings of literate activity when these tools are put in the hands of writers themselves. Specifically, we focus on video clips that academic writers have created of their own writing processes—videos that include such everyday objects as alarm clocks, coffee makers, city lights, subways, cornfields, and even an iguana named Caliban. We show how digital media can offer new images of the dispersed character of writing and learning, not as punctual events but as emergent flows. Overall, the chapter argues for the use of video and other digital media as tools for reflection, research, and the representation of ubiquitous writing and learning in this early twenty-first century.

For the past twelve years, in graduate seminars and Writing across the Curriculum workshops, Gail Hawisher and Paul Prior have been asking academic writers to draw images of their writing processes—drawings where writers feature texts, writing tools, clocks, food, people, pets, and various concrete scenes, activities, and tropes.

Two years ago, in connection with the Writing with Video initiative on campus (see Lovett and Squier's chapter), Gail began asking students in her seminar to produce digital videos that would represent their writing. The assignment read: "You should attempt to capture a representation of your writing processes on camera. You do not have to video yourself, but you do need to try to represent some of the thinking and processes you experience as you approach and carry out a writing task." What follows are five first-person accounts that suggest some of the ways this task was taken up and understood, along with our comments at the ends of these narratives.

Figure 22.1. Anonymous writing process drawings selected from the Writing Across the Curriculum seminars sponsored by the Center for Writing Studies, 1996–2008.

Private Space and Public Performance (Amber Buck)

Asked to represent my writing process through video, I first interpreted this idea literally. I thought about filming my typical paper-writing activities, sitting in front of the computer for hours. I grappled for weeks about the meaning of that self-representation. Should I show myself as I actually look when I write a paper? (My vanity told me that no, I probably shouldn't.) What meaning would my audience get out of this experience? How would I appear as a writer if I showed myself in front of the computer? I do a lot of research; how could I show that process in a way that looks authentic?

I was preoccupied with thoughts of who was going to watch my video. I always write alone, and the idea of having an audience that I would allow into my private space was unnerving. It was like inviting the entire class over to watch me write. There are elements of this process, like messy hair and pajamas on Saturday afternoons, that are best left unrecorded.

I decided in the end that it would be best to use a metaphor as a way of talking about my writing process. Instead of focusing on myself in the video, I decided to film my iguana. The more I tried to use Caliban's wanderings around the house in my video, the more it seemed like the perfect choice. Showing Caliban deciding whether or not to jump off the bed, for example, became a perfect representation of the way I often put off my first plunge into the text. Filming Caliban was my way of not showing my writing.

Looking back on the film later, though, I realized that I still portrayed my process pretty directly. As I write, everything within the space of my home becomes wrapped up in my acts of writing and thinking through the connections I need to make in a text. Not only do I sit in front of the computer to work, but in watching Caliban explore the corners and dark spaces of my house, I am working through my ideas as well. Since this video was made, Caliban has taken to sitting in my bookshelf as I write, which completes the circle of my writing process. She leads me from these other activities to record my wandering thoughts into text.

Figure 22.2. Screen shots culled from the writing process video of Amber Buck (2006).

Amber's vignette and the four that follow include still images from the videos. The stills miss much of what the videos convey. Some videos have voiceover narratives, whereas others use animated on-screen text. All use music, sound effects, and particular pacing to convey affect, atmosphere, and modes of engagement. All highlight how writing with digital media blurs the boundaries that separate personal, public, and disciplinary spaces.

Like an Inconsistent Heartbeat (Christa Olson)

I can't remember if a tripping heartbeat was part of my initial plan for my writing process video or if I added it after the fact, but when I think of that video now, it's the stumbling pulse of the soundtrack that I think of first. That ubiquitous, yet inconsistent pulsing increasingly seems an appropriate accompaniment to the fits and starts of my writing process: a constant heartbeat that refuses to keep its meter. In my video's alternation of image and black screen, writing and recreating, I tried to foreground the recursive, everyday nature of my writing process—happening in concentric circles of years, semesters, days. That rhythm of key-click, time-pass, heartbeat, and swallow all led, not surprisingly, to a soundtrack based on the idiosyncratic pulse of writing. As the process stumbles toward its peak, the heartbeat takes over and becomes steadier, propelling me forward with the tripping click of keys and the sharpness of disciplined breath, yet there is no conclusion. There is no final thud that ends the process. There is only the gradual fading out of the pulse with the clear implication of its continuation.

Because it is organized around contrapuntal rhythms of working and wandering, my video emphasizes the ways my writing expands beyond the actual action of putting down words. I do my best thinking, my best writing, when my hands are occupied with something other than the incessant rhythm of typing and my eyes focus on something other than a pulsing cursor. Walking, cooking, staring into the distance: these are the activities that reveal connections, spark synthesis, and send me rushing back to typing. In the video, whenever the camera faces my computer, the running narrative trails away from the task at hand as my attention invariably slides to other things. When the camera and I wander away from the keyboard, the narrative turns to topic exploration and theoretical connection. I had never really realized the extent of that contradictory, yet generative rhythm until I saw it played out scene after scene in my video.

Composing my video made me generally more aware of my writing as integrated into the rhythms of days. That awareness has, in turn, improved my ability to accommodate and alter the rhythms of writing. Mapping my writing process through video hasn't revolutionized my activity; it has, however, helped me see my writing as an everyday, ubiquitous practice.

The processes of inquiry, learning, and writing in each of the five vignettes are seen as ubiquitous, as spread through life, not contained in acts of inscription alone. The videos convey this ubiquity through concrete representations of acts of writing, but especially through film tropes (e.g., of journeys, of cooking, of ups and downs). They challenge, as Cope and Kalantzis remind us in chapter 1, apparently "unshakable spatial, institutional, and life boundaries."

Anatomy of a Writing Process (Video): Writing as Meditation (Steven Gump)

When challenged to portray a complex, creative, multilayered, multidimensional activity (writing) through an equally complex, creative, multilayered, multidimensional technology (video), I was initially caught up in a complicated, recursive web of meaning: How could I distill (simplify), translate (represent), and create (implement) a video of my writing process? Did I even have *a* writing process, in the singular? Ultimately, I embraced the ideas of inspiration and imagination. These two related engines of creativity would, I hoped, enable me to capture the essence of at least one particular writing event. The challenge was especially large for me, though, since I was new to both the technology (never before having held a digital video camera) and the software (never before having edited video).

Figure 22.3. Screen shots culled from the writing process video of Christa Olson (2005).

I crafted my video around the inherent complexities of mediated translation. Using unfamiliar technologies, I had to translate my idea of writing to (my idea of) video. Uncharted territory this was! In a deliberate attempt to place my classmates on unfamiliar terrain, I introduced a Japanese motif symbolic (in the West) of mystery and imagination. A three-minute segment of *shakuhachi* (a type of bamboo flute) music, performed by my Japanese flatmate, provided the soundtrack and thus set the mood; Morizou, a mascot of the 2005 World Expo in Aichi, Japan, was my co-star in the writing process. Yes, I am guilty of self-orientalizing—of "othering" myself as different and, on a certain level, enigmatic. But are not all writing processes, beyond the shared technicalities of the writing act, to some extent unique and context-dependent? As a tool for Zen meditation, the *shakuhachi* effectively emphasized the way I frequently write: alone but for the presence of my writing tools, my material accomplices in the writing act. To me, then, the idea of writing as meditation was not too far off the mark. Morizou became my muse as I attempted to mystify the idea of inspiration, a concept that is rarely straightforward (or, if straightforward, rarely believable) in narrative descriptions of the writing process. The result may have duplicitously suggested that I write with ease or confidence or an absence of stress—the ideal rather than the ordeal of writing. But so much of life in this age of ubiquitous learning is already frenetic, unfocused, overloaded, and fast-paced: I felt I could undermine those tendencies, even if momentarily, by portraying one writing process through a relaxing, meditative video.

Themes link these videos. Steve features Morizou, a stuffed being, represented as his muse. Amber uses Caliban, her iguana, as a stand-in for herself but also as a living being who is somehow integral to the process. Christa's dog, Ceisaf, makes several appearances, taking walks that become part of the shifting rhythms of her work. In the vignettes that follow, Hannah and Cory independently focus on night travels in cars and public transportation through rainy city streets.

Figure 22.4. Screen shots culled from the writing process video of Steven Gump (2005).

A Writer's Journey: Reflections (Hannah Lee)

The first thing that came to mind when I was assigned the writing process video was an image of Charlie Chaplin from *Modern Times,* as he gets caught in the cogs of a giant machine—a metaphor for the beginning of my writing process. As I held this image in my mind, other metaphors came into view: wheels turning, representing my mind at work; close-ups of eyes, representing the various sources that I turn to before writing; public transportation, representing the writer's journey. Images that are ever-present in my daily life; images that, when placed together, take on a deeper meaning.

My video camera went with me wherever I went—the bus, the airport, my apartment, my mother's house. I knew that I wanted to collect a montage of my daily activities, to translate these images, sounds, and words into something that would portray the mundane, yet mind-wrenching activity that is my writing process.

Notions of stretched and retracted time were invoked. Time seemed to pass by without my noticing as I worked on the video—which is nothing like the dread and procrastination that usually accompanies my typical writing assignments with their ever-present deadlines looming before me. The hours it took to get the various shots of myself typing at my computer amount to a few moments in the video. Yet the repetitive, insistent cuts evoke the feeling of stretched time. Quickly paced cuts of the activities that I engage in while not writing—checking my e-mail, going for a walk, getting a drink of water—push their way into my writing process and keep me from it, all the while engaging with it, briskly furthering the process along.

As I look back at the final video, the metaphors that I began with begin to resurface. That first image that I had of Charlie Chaplin has translated itself into out-of-focus city lights—both emblematic of the beginning of my writing process, in which things seem stalled and unclear. The initial image of turning wheels and public transportation has found its way in a more palpable form, through my (and ultimately the viewer's) point of view in a moving car and bus. The metaphor of eyes signifies the various perspectives and ideas that I've gleaned. And the metaphor of the writer's journey has weaved its way throughout—in a recursive loop that begins with uncertainty and ends in a moment of breakthrough.

Writing as a journey is a familiar metaphor. However, writing as a car ride through a rainy night, in a U.S. urban setting, with sad meditative music from the film *American Beauty* in the background, is not just an abstract journey. It is a specific trip through a landscape and with a particular texture of rhythms—rain on the windows, wipers screeching, the beat of the music. Digital video representation

Figure 22.5. Screen shots culled from the writing process video of Hannah Lee (2006).

foregrounds what print seems to easily elide, that writing is embodied-activity-in-the-world, that it is consciousness in action, that it is saturated with affect and identity, that it is social as writers interact with others (people, sometimes animals, and even things).

Writing for the Eye (Cory Holding)

Video moves metaphor fast as you can blink: two men descend to the subway. This night is New York. A spring breeze comes. But if you listen, I am talking about coffee. You (the viewer) are asked to attend with me this siren song of procrastination: "For those handful of seconds when you're in line, and then the sort of microseconds when you're sipping, you have a mini-distraction. You're not thinking in that half a second that you even can be typing." Follow the gentlemen around the corner and cut to black.

Sluggish to start, the train blurs to a steady clip, windows revealing in staccato motion the stare and gesture of people you will not see again. But this, with the gnashing hum of acceleration is meant to suggest the subterranean feel of thinking—the fleetingness and precipitation of ideas you must catch to pen. The train shoves into the tunnel. It quiets into voiceover: "Your heart beats a certain way. Sometimes you have an endorphin rush. But I think writing isn't *fun*. Um, which is why I'm so massively in need of distraction."

City lights from a car window fade from focus to dull-edged coins of orange, blue, white, and flicker with every quickly passing obstruction: "You just want time to kind of yawn. Between sit-downs to write, you just want time to stop. This translates to a certain amount of dread. And the funny thing is, the more you allow those interims between writing episodes to open up, the worse you feel." Here the city lights taper into long, even lines of suspension cables. I am asking you please to come across the bridge.

Finally, certain exasperation behind us, the mad dash comes. And here you have me running down the street a pace nothing short of hell-bent. My form is not pretty, but does in the heaviest-handed way what I ask of it: "Finishing makes me happy. It's like going through a full bottle of shampoo. You get to the end, and you may think 'wow, I lived through another whole bottle of shampoo.' You're going through life. It's a wonder. So you finish a paper, and you may think 'well, that's another sign of me on this earth!'"

It is asking a lot, this revelation, I know. But thank you for making the journey.

Toward an Agenda for Ubiquitous Literate Activity in a Digital Age

Whether aimed at narrative accounts or metaphoric representations, these digital video versions of literate tales feel intensely personal and yet are indexically anchored in the social and material ecologies of the day. They also produce recurring patterns and commonalities across vignettes—perhaps the product of common socialization and schooling, shared landscapes of representational conventions, the given tasks and available technologies, all further revealing the interconnecting web of ubiquitous literacies. Digital technologies afford new means of capturing the dispersed threads of literate activity that ultimately get woven together to form a particular text, event, object, or person. They open up a new space for learning, for reflecting on and trying to communicate such dispersed and situated literate activity and what it means to our lives and social relations. Working to represent (in words, images, and sound) our processes of inquiry and writing can reshape the way we experience and situate literate activity in our lives.

When compared with drawings (see Prior and Shipka 2003), the videos offer different representations of the textures of place and practice. They tend to provide a much sharper feel of affect, mood, and rhythm. They are visually denser than the drawn pictures, though we hasten to note that the drawings were usually mediated by talk and gesture as writers explained their visual representations, whereas the videos are composed to be stand-alone "performances." Taken together, these reflective, representational practices (penned drawings, situated

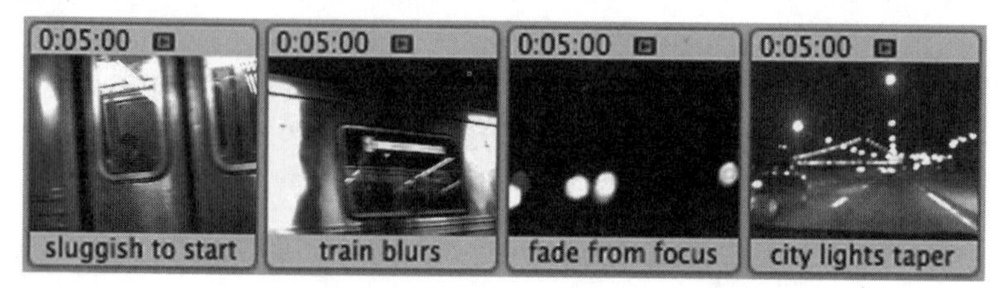

Figure 22.6. Screen shots culled from the writing process video of Cory Holding (2005).

talk and gesture, video) all work in particular ways to underscore the necessity for new learning paradigms that highlight the dispersed times and places in which knowledge is constructed. Ubiquitous computing has re-mediated and amplified these possibilities of ubiquitous learning, but there is no guarantee that old models of learning will not persist unless we vigilantly attend to the complexity of the literate encounters and ideologies that shape our disciplines and our lives.

These reflections on the ubiquity of writing and learning also begin to suggest how digital media tools can extend research into literate practices. Yet, when confined to print, they fall short of communicating the richness of these representations of writers' lived worlds. Although we have illustrated the reflections with still images culled from the videos, this print presentation suffers without a digital format. Until we have publishing venues that regularly feature digital texts alongside their print counterparts, researchers will have difficulty doing justice to the new meanings and identities that people continually assemble and reassemble through language, literate exchange, digital media, and the "things" of everyday living.

Readings and References

The texts we cited in the opening paragraph of this chapter all highlight key dimensions of the ubiquitous nature of literate activity and literate lives. We would also note similar perspectives in rhetoric (Nystrand and Duffy 2003), in Deweyan pragmatics (Bruce, forthcoming), and in Bazerman's (2007) expansive introduction to the field of writing studies. As in the work of the New London Group, we find especially valuable those who recognize the importance of connecting literate activity with an "active, willed human process" (Cope and Kalantzis 2000, 203). Other research intended to expand this line of thinking includes "Re-situating and Re-mediating the Canons: A Cultural-Historical Remapping of Rhetorical Activity" (Prior et al. 2007), "Re-designing Digital Literacies in the 21st Century" (Hawisher et al. 2007), as well as recent work in the journal *Computers and Composition.*

Bazerman, Charles, ed. 2007. *Handbook of Writing Research: History, Society, School, Individual, Text.* Mahwah, N.J.: Lawrence Erlbaum Associates.

Bruce, Bertram C. Forthcoming. "Coffee Cups, Frogs, and Lived Experience." In *Festschrift for Ken and Yetta Goodman,* ed. Patricia L. Anders. New York: Routledge.

Computers and Composition: An International Journal. Elsevier. http://www.elsevier.com/wps/find/journaldescription.cws_home/620371/description#description.

Cope, Bill, and Mary Kalantzis, eds. 2000. *Multiliteracies: Literacy Learning and the Design of Social Futures.* New York: Routledge.

Hawisher, Gail E., Patrick Berry, Maria Lovett, Shafinaz Ahmed, Sophie Dewayani, Yu Kyung Kang, and Vanessa Rouillon. 2007. "Re-designing Digital Literacies in the 21st Century." Paper presented at the Conference on College Composition and Communication, New York, March 21–24.

Hawisher, Gail E., and Cynthia L. Selfe, with Yi-Huey Guo and Lu Lui. 2006. "Globalization and Agency: Designing and Redesigning the Literacies of Cyberspace." *College English* 68(6): 619–36.

Hutchins, Edwin. 1995. *Cognition in the Wild.* Cambridge, Mass.: MIT Press.

Latour, Bruno. 2005. *Reassembling the Social: An Introduction to Actor-Network Theory.* Oxford: Oxford University Press.

Lave, Jean, and Etienne Wenger. 1991. *Situated Learning: Legitimate Peripheral Participation.* Cambridge: Cambridge University Press.

Nystrand, Martin, and John Duffy. 2003. *Towards a Rhetoric of Everyday Life: New Directions in Research on Writing, Text, and Discourse.* Madison: University of Wisconsin Press.

Prior, Paul. 1998. *Writing/Disciplinarity: A Sociohistoric Account of Literate Activity in the Academy.* Mahwah, N.J.: Lawrence Erlbaum.

Prior, Paul, and Jody Shipka. 2003. "Chronotopic Lamination: Tracing the Contours of Literate Activity." In *Writing Selves, Writing Societies,* ed. Charles Bazerman and David Russell, 180–238. Fort Collins, Colo.: WAC Clearinghouse. Available at http://wac.colostate.edu/books/selves_societies.

Prior, Paul, Janine Solberg, Patrick Berry, Hannah Bellwoar, Bill Chewning, Karen Lunsford, Liz Rohan, Kevin Roozen, Mary Sheridan-Rabideau, Jody Shipka, Derek Van Ittersum, and Joyce Walker. 2007. "Re-situating and Re-mediating the Canons: A Cultural-Historical Remapping of Rhetorical Activity." *Kairos* 11(3): http://kairos.technorhetoric.net/11.3/index.html.

Scollon, Ron. 2001. *Mediated Discourse: The Nexus of Practice.* London: Routledge.

Selfe, Cynthia L., and Gail E. Hawisher. 2004. *Literate Lives in the Information Age: Narratives of Literacy from the United States.* Mahwah, N.J.: Lawrence Erlbaum.

Wertsch, James. 1991. *Voices of the Mind: A Sociocultural Approach to Mediated Action.* Cambridge, Mass.: Harvard University Press.

About the Contributors

SIMON J. APPLEFORD works in the Illinois Center for Computing in Humanities, Arts, and Social Science at the University of Illinois at Urbana-Champaign. With Vernon Burton and James Onderdonk, he has worked on approaches to the development of cyberinfrastructure in the humanities.

PATRICK BERRY is a Ph.D. candidate in the Center for Writing Studies and the Department of English at the University of Illinois at Urbana-Champaign. His research concentrates on English teachers' literacy narratives as a family of genres, with an eye toward exploring intersections among literacy, personal experience, technology, and social class.

LISA BOUILLION DIAZ is an adjunct assistant professor in the College of Education and an extension specialist in technology and youth development at the University of Illinois at Urbana-Champaign. She is trained as a learning scientist and received her doctoral degree from Northwestern University. Her research interests include social equity and cultural relevance within distributed knowledge networks, the design of formal and nonformal learning environments, and youth–adult partnerships. She has been involved in K–12 school reform projects in Illinois, Minnesota, and Pennsylvania and currently oversees the science, engineering and technology mission mandate for the University of Illinois Extension 4-H program, which reaches nearly three hundred thousand young people. Her work is published in the *Journal of Curriculum Studies* and the *Journal of Research in Science Teaching*, among others.

JACK BRIGHTON is assistant director of broadcasting and director of Internet development at WILL Public Media, University of Illinois at Urbana-Champaign, where he manages Web site technology and content. For sixteen years he produced WILL's public affairs radio program Focus 580, and has also produced many news features, documentaries, and long-form broadcast and new media projects. He is a guest lecturer in online journalism at the Department of Journalism and presents workshops on Internet media, media preservation, and Web development at academic and media industry conferences. He chairs the News, Documentary, and Television Interest Group of the Association of Moving Image Archivists, and serves on the PBCore Resource Group established by the Corporation for Public Broadcasting. From 2002 to 2007, he chaired the University of Illinois Campus Webmasters, and in 2003 he cofounded the University of Illinois Educational Media Group to foster collaboration on best practices in Internet media for higher education.

BERTRAM C. (CHIP) BRUCE is a professor in library and information science, curriculum and instruction, bioengineering, the Center for Writing Studies, and the Center for East Asian and Pacific Studies at the University of Illinois at Urbana-Champaign. During 2007–8, he held a Fulbright Distinguished Chair at the National College of Ireland in Dublin. Professor Bruce's research goals include contributing to a conception of democratic education, meaning both the development of critical, socially engaged citizens and of learning environments (schools, universities, libraries, museums, community centers, workplaces), which are themselves democratic. Aspects of this work include research on community inquiry through collaborative community-based work; the theory of inquiry-based learning, drawing especially on scholarship of the American pragmatists and the history of progressive education; and research on the affordances and constraints of new media for learning, encapsulated by the term "technology-enhanced learning."

AMBER BUCK is a Ph.D. student in the Center for Writing Studies and the Department of English at the University of Illinois at Urbana-Champaign. Her research interests include computers and writing, new media, and the integration of technology in writing centers.

NICHOLAS C. BURBULES is Grayce Wicall Gauthier Professor in the Department of Educational Policy Studies at the University of Illinois at Urbana-Champaign. He holds a Ph.D. in philosophy of education from Stanford University. Over the past ten years, he has also held visiting professorships in Argentina, Australia, Belgium, Brazil, and New Zealand. His research focuses on philosophy of education, technology and education, teaching and dialogue, and critical social and political theory. He has written several books, most recently, *Showing and Doing: Wittgenstein as a Pedagogical Philosopher,* coauthored with Michael Peters and Paul Smeyers (2008).

ORVILLE VERNON BURTON is director of the Institute for Computing in Humanities, Arts, and Social Science (I-CHASS) at the University of Illinois at Urbana-Champaign, where he is a University Distinguished Teacher/Scholar and professor of history, African American studies, and sociology. He is also associate director for Humanities and Social Sciences at the National Center for Supercomputing Applications, where he is a senior research scientist. Burton is the author of more than a hundred articles and the author or editor of fourteen books, including *The Age of Lincoln* (2007) and *In My Father's House Are Many Mansions: Family and Community in Edgefield, South Carolina* (1985), which is the subject of sessions at the Southern Historical Association and the Social Science History Association's annual meetings, and which was also nominated for the Pulitzer Prize. He is a recipient of the *Chicago Tribune*'s Heartland Literary Award for nonfiction. Recognized for his teaching, Burton was selected nationwide as the 1999 U.S. Research and Doctoral University Professor of the Year (presented by the Carnegie Foundation for the Advancement of Teaching and by the Council for Advancement and Support of Education). In 2004, he received the American Historical Association's Eugene Asher Distinguished Teaching Prize. Within the University of Illinois, he has won teaching awards at the department, school, college, and campus levels and received the 2006 Campus Award for Excellence in Public Engagement.

TIMOTHY CASH is a graduate student in educational psychology at the University of Illinois at Urbana-Champaign.

BILL COPE is a research professor in the Department of Educational Policy Studies at the University of Illinois at Urbana-Champaign. He is also a director of Common Ground Publishing, which develops innovative approaches to, and online software tools for, academic book and journal publishing. He is a former first assistant secretary in the Department of the Prime Minister and Cabinet and was director of the Office of Multicultural Affairs in the Australian government. His current research interests include theories and practices of pedagogy, cultural and linguistic diversity, and new technologies of representation and communication. He is a coauthor or editor, with Mary Kalantzis, of a number of books, including *The Powers of Literacy* (1993), *Productive Diversity* (1997), *A Place in the Sun: Re-creating the Australian Way of Life* (2000), and *Multilitera-*

cies: Literacy Learning and the Design of Social Futures (2000). Their most recent book is *New Learning: Elements of a Science of Education* (2008).

ALAN B. CRAIG has been with the National Center for Supercomputing Applications since early 1987. During his tenure there, he has been involved in numerous research and development efforts, including collaborative environments, distance education, multimodal interaction, scientific visualization, sonification, and virtual reality. In addition to papers and encyclopedia articles, Craig has coauthored the book *Understanding Virtual Reality* with William Sherman (2003) and is in the process, with William Sherman and Jeffrey Will, of publishing *Developing Virtual Reality Applications.* Craig earned his B.S., M.S., and Ph.D. at the University of Illinois at Urbana-Champaign.

ELIZABETH M. DELACRUZ is associate professor of art education at the University of Illinois at Urbana-Champaign, editor of *Visual Arts Research,* a Vice Chancellor's Teaching Scholar, research fellow at the UIUC Center on Democracy in a Multicultural Society, and former chair of art education at UIUC. She received her B.F.A. and M.A. in art education from UIUC, her Ed.S. in curriculum and instruction from the University of Florida, and a Ph.D. in art education from Florida State University. Delacruz has authored numerous scholarly works and is a frequently invited speaker for international audiences. Her university teaching has included undergraduate and graduate courses focusing on art education, elementary education, curriculum and instruction, technology, research methods, globalism and community, museum education, and service learning at the University of Illinois. Prior to coming to UIUC, she taught for several years in the public schools, teaching K–12 art, English, graphic design, and journalism to widely diverse student populations in rural and urban schools. Her current research, teaching, and public engagement are informed by her long-standing interest in ways that art teachers make a difference in the lives of children and families, and how schools and communities may be enriched, challenged, and improved through artistic practices and educational initiatives aimed toward social justice, sustainable development, and world peace.

STEVE DOWNEY is an assistant professor of instructional technology at the University of South Florida and a former research scientist at the National Center for Supercomputing Applications at the University of Illinois at Urbana-Champaign. His research interests center on development of pedagogical strategies for online learning and collaboration in virtual worlds and on cross-cultural influences on knowledge sharing and e-learning. Downey currently teaches graduate-level interactive media, video/graphics, and educational gaming courses at South Florida. While at Illinois, he taught graduate and undergraduate courses featuring instructional technologies (College of Education) and information technologies and knowledge management (Graduate School of Library and Information Science).

GUY GARNETT is an associate professor of composition-theory in the UIUC School of Music and director of the Cultural Computing Program at the Siebel Center for Computer Science. He has worked in computer music for twenty-seven years, producing works in a variety of media and developing technologies for audio and 3–D visualization. He has recently focused on developing technology for creating art in virtual 3–D worlds and for teaching students to create them.

STEVEN E. GUMP is Illinois distinguished fellow in the Department of Educational Organization and Leadership at the University of Illinois at Urbana-Champaign. He has written on a wide range of topics within the fields of education, international business communication, Japanese human resource management, and Japanese religion. He currently edits the *Southeast Review of Asian Studies.*

GAIL E. HAWISHER is professor of English and founding director of the Center for Writing Studies at the University of Illinois at Urbana-Champaign. Her work includes a series of publications that grow out of her interest in digital media for written and visual communication. With Cynthia Selfe, she continues to edit *Computers and Composition: An International Journal.*

CAROLINE HAYTHORNTHWAITE is a professor at the Graduate School of Library and Information Science at the University of Illinois at Urbana-Champaign. Her research examines how the Internet and computer media support and affect work, learning, and social interaction, with a focus on online social networks and participation and knowledge exchange in online learning communities. Her major publications include *The Internet in Everyday Life* (2002), edited with Barry Wellman; *Learning, Culture and Community in Online Education: Research and Practice* (2004), edited with Michelle M. Kazmer, a special issue of the *Journal of Computer-Mediated Communication* on computer-mediated collaborative practices and systems (2005), and *The SAGE Handbook of E-learning Research* (2007), edited with Richard Andrews.

CORY HOLDING is a Ph.D. candidate in the Center for Writing Studies and the Department of English at the University of Illinois at Urbana-Champaign. Her notable interests include creativity, creative writing and composition pedagogy, body rhetoric and affect theory, new media composition, and poetic and rhetorical modes of invention.

WENHAO DAVID HUANG is an assistant professor in the Department of Human Resource Education in the College of Education at the University of Illinois at Urbana-Champaign. His background comprises engineering, learning technology design, and business administration. He is interested in refining the e-game design process for the development of complex learning environments across disciplines.

ERIC JAKOBSSON is a professor in the Department of Molecular and Integrative Physiology and the National Center for Supercomputing Applications at the University of Illinois at Urbana-Champaign, and also has major commitments to the Center for Biophysics and Computational Biology and the Beckman Institute for Advanced Science and Technology on campus. He served from 2003 to 2005 as director of the Center for Bioinformatics and Computational Biology at the National Institute of General Medical Sciences and the chair of the Biomedical Information Science and Technology Initiative Consortium at the National Institutes of Health in Bethesda, Maryland. Jakobsson's research and academic interests are centered on computational studies of membrane structure and transport and on the use of computation in education. He is the director and principal investigator of the NIH National Center for the Design of Biomimetic Nanoconductors. Jakobsson is also a fellow of the American Physical Society in recognition of his work on ion and water permeation in channels.

TRISTAN E. JOHNSON is an assistant professor of instructional systems design and associate director of research at the Learning Systems Institute at Florida State University in Tallahassee. His research interests include assessment of team cognition, team-based learning, group learning processes measurements, and shared mental models measures.

MARY KALANTZIS is dean of the College of Education at the University of Illinois at Urbana-Champaign. Before that, she was dean of the Faculty of Education, Language and Community Services at RMIT University, Melbourne, Australia, and president of the Australian Council of Deans of Education. She has been a board member of Teaching Australia: The National Institute for Quality Teaching and School Leadership. With Bill Cope, she is coauthor or editor of a number of books, including *The Powers of Literacy* (1993), *Productive Diversity* (1997), *A Place in the Sun: Re-creating the Australian Way of Life* (2000), and *Multiliteracies: Literacy Learning and the Design of Social Futures* (2000). She is a member of Microsoft's Partners-in-Learning Board in Australia and is leader of a five-year project to evaluate the Partners-in-Learning program in Australia. Her current research includes four major projects examining pedagogies for e-learning.

SAMUEL KAMIN is an associate professor of computer science at the University of Illinois at Urbana-Champaign. He holds a Ph.D. degree in computer science from the State University of New York at Stony Brook. He was appointed director of undergraduate programs in computer science in 1999, and this position led to his interest in computer-based educational technologies. His original research areas were programming languages and formal methods of programming. These continue to resonate in his research in educational technology, where he is developing a system for end-user programming of educational applications for the tablet PC.

KARRIE G. KARAHALIOS is an assistant professor in computer science at the University of Illinois at Urbana-Champaign, where she heads the Social Spaces Group. Her work focuses on the interaction between people and the social cues they perceive in networked electronic spaces. Of particular interest are interfaces for public online and physical gathering spaces such as chat rooms, cafés, and parks. The goal is to create interfaces that enable users to perceive conversational patterns that are present, but not obvious, in traditional communication interfaces. Karahalios completed a S.B. in electrical engineering, an M.Eng. in electrical engineering and computer science, and an S.M. and Ph.D. in media arts and science at MIT.

JOYCELYN LANDRUM-BROWN is an assistant professor in psychology at the University of Illinois at Urbana-Champaign.

HANNAH LEE is a graduate student in English with a specialization in writing studies at the University of Illinois at Urbana-Champaign. She is interested in a range of topics within the field, from literacy studies, to discourse processes, to visual rhetoric and multimodal writing.

FAYE L. LESHT earned her Ph.D. in continuing higher education from the University of Illinois at Urbana-Champaign and her A.B. degree in psychology from Washington University in St. Louis. She serves as head of academic outreach in the Office of Continuing Education at UIUC. Her research interests include retention in online degree programs and academic leadership.

MARIA LOVETT is a visiting assistant professor in the College of Education and the Center for Urban Education and Innovation at Florida International University in Miami. She holds a Ph.D. in educational policy studies from the University of Illinois at Urbana-Champaign and a master's degree in media studies from The New School in New York. Lovett has worked professionally as a documentary filmmaker for more than fifteen years. Her work has been used in diverse settings as a tool for social activism. As an educator, she has taught youth media production and arts-based community action projects in more than half a dozen cities in the United States and in Montreal, Canada. At the University of Illinois, Lovett co-created the Writing with Video course. Supported by Art + Design and the Department of Writing Studies, this interdisciplinary cross-campus initiative uses video production as a useful form in critical communication and rhetoric. Her research continues to look for practical realizations of pedagogical theories committed to social change. Through a methodology she calls "video action pedagogy and research," she connects documentary production, visual ethnography, and critical pedagogical praxis to explore interdisciplinary ways of knowing and producing knowledge. Currently, she is implementing this methodology to investigate and represent the repercussions of Hurricane Katrina in New Orleans.

CHERYL McFADDEN is an associate professor in the Department of Educational Leadership at East Carolina University. She is a former school administrator and publishes in the area of online learning, program evaluation, and principal induction.

ROBERT E. McGRATH joined the National Center for Supercomputing Applications in 1994 and is now a senior software developer. He completed his Ph.D. in computer science at the University of Illinois at Urbana-Champaign. McGrath has published many reports and papers on distributed systems, scientific data, digital libraries, and advanced information technologies. At NCSA, he was a pioneer of World Wide Web and coauthored the book *Web Server Technology: The Authoritative Guide* (1996), with Nancy Yeager.

JAMES D. MYERS received his B.A. in physics from Cornell University and his Ph.D. in chemistry from the University of California at Berkeley. He is currently the associate director for cyberenvironments and technologies at the National Center for Supercomputing Applications at the University of Illinois at Urbana-Champaign. His prior professional experiences range from the development of a nationally recognized research program on collaborative computing systems and the design of scientific collaboratories for research and education, to the development of data acquisition and analysis software, as well as ultrafast laser systems, and the study of small-molecule photochemistry.

CHRISTA OLSON is a doctoral candidate researching the role of the arts in social movements in the Center for Writing Studies and the Department of English at the University of Illinois at Urbana-Champaign. Her interest in how communities mobilize images as cultural rhetoric has taken her to Ecuador, where she studies how representations of indigenous people have constituted and contested Ecuadorian national identity.

JAMES ONDERDONK is the associate director for education and outreach for the Institute for Computing in Humanities, Arts, and Social Science (I-CHASS) at the National Center for Supercomputing Applications and the head of Conferences and Institutes, a division of the Office of Continuing Education at the University of Illinois at Urbana-Champaign. He holds a Ph.D. from Old Dominion University and, prior to joining the University of Illinois, was responsible for distance education and degree-completion programs for U.S. Navy personnel stationed aboard ships and submarines of the Atlantic Fleet and in the United Kingdom.

MICHAEL A. PETERS is a professor of education at the University of Illinois at Urbana-Champaign. He has degrees in geography, philosophy, and education. He previously held a chair as research professor and professor of education at the University of Glasgow, as well as a personal chair at the University of Auckland; he also served as adjunct professor of communication studies at the Auckland University of Technology. He is the editor of three international journals: *Educational Philosophy and Theory, Policy Futures in Education,* and *E-learning.* He is also the author or editor of more than forty books, including most recently *Global Knowledge Cultures* (2007), *Knowledge Economy, Development and the Future of Higher Education* (2007), *Building Knowledge Cultures: Education in the Age of Knowledge Capitalism* (2006), and *Deconstructing Derrida: Tasks for the New Humanities* (2005). His current research interests concentrate on higher education and the knowledge economy, with a focus on scholarly communication and academic publishing.

EVANGELINE S. PIANFETTI is director of the Office of Educational Technology in the College of Education at the University of Illinois at Urbana-Champaign. She is also a visiting assistant professor in the Departments of Educational Psychology and Special Education. Pianfetti received her Ph.D. in educational psychology from the UIUC. Her research interests include new forms of literacies emerging from technological innovations, technology integration, and professional development in technology for P–12 and higher education faculty. She is the principal investigator on an Illinois Board of Higher Education/NCLB grant, "The TIMeS Project: A Technology-Intensive Mathematics and Science Model for Improving Instruction in High Needs Schools," which has been showcased twice at the Illinois State Capitol. Pianfetti is a Smithsonian Laureate for classroom innovation in technology and a Gold Award winner in the ThinkQuest for Tomorrow's Teachers competition for a technology-enriched curriculum she designed with teachers from Urbana Middle School in Urbana, Illinois.

PAUL PRIOR is an associate professor of English, director of freshman rhetoric, and associate director of the Center for Writing Studies at the University of Illinois at Urbana-Champaign. In a series of situated studies that draw on theoretical frameworks from cultural-historical activity theory and dialogic semiotics, he has explored connections among writing, reading, talking, learning, and disciplinarity.

FAZAL RIZVI is a professor in educational policy studies at the University of Illinois at Urbana-Champaign, where he directs the Global Studies in Education program. Previously, he held a number of senior academic and administrative positions in Australia, including pro vice chancellor (international) at RMIT University. He has published widely on globalization and educational policy, the cultural politics of education, and the internationalization of higher education. Between 1992 and 2000, he edited the journal *Discourse,* and he is a past-president of the Australian Association for Research in Education. His new book, *Globalizing Educational Policy,* will be published in 2009. He is currently researching the ways in which Indian higher education is responding to the pressures of globalization and the knowledge economy.

MEI-LI SHIH graduated from the University of Missouri in Columbia, where she received her bachelor's degree in teaching English as a second language in early childhood and elementary school. She earned her master's of education degree in educational technology from the University of Illinois at Urbana-Champaign. Her primary interest is improving students' learning with educational technologies.

JANINE SOLBERG earned her Ph.D. from the Center for Writing Studies and the Department of English at the University of Illinois at Urbana-Champaign and is currently an assistant professor of English at the University of Massachusetts, Amherst.

JOSEPH SQUIER is a professor and the associate director of the School of Art and Design at the University of Illinois at Urbana-Champaign, where he cofounded the New Media program. Squier earned an M.F.A. in studio art from the San Francisco Art Institute. Although trained as a painter and photographer, he has worked in the realm of electronic media for more than a decade. Squier has exhibited throughout North America, Europe, and Asia, and his work has been featured in more than a dozen books on electronic art.

KONA TAYLOR is a doctoral student in secondary and continuing education at the University of Illinois at Urbana-Champaign.

SHARON TETTEGAH is currently a faculty member at the University of Illinois at Urbana-Champaign in the Department of Curriculum and Instruction, Math, Science, and Technology Division. She is also part of the faculty in the Department of Educational Psychology, Cognitive Science in Teaching and Learning. Additionally, she is a faculty member at the Beckman Institute's Bio-Intelligence Group, Cognitive Neuroscience. Her Ph.D. is in educational psychology from the University of California, and her research focuses on the use of various technologies (e.g., social simulations, virtual environments) to measure empathy and empathic dispositions. Tettegah teaches courses on human development and learning with technologies, as well as the use of virtual environments for teaching and learning. Her research interests also include the use of Web-based animated narrative vignette technologies (simulations) as a methodology to understand cognitive and emotional responses of educators and other professionals in helping professions. She is the coeditor, with Richard Hunter, of *Technology and Education: Issues in Administration, Policy, and Applications in K12 Schools,* and she has coauthored, with Cynthia Colongne, *Identity, Learning and Support in Virtual Worlds* (forthcoming).

MICHAEL B. TWIDALE is an associate professor at the Graduate School of Library and Information Science at the University of Illinois at Urbana-Champaign. His research involves the intersections of human–computer interaction, computer-supported cooperative work, computer-supported collaborative learning, and increasingly ubiquitous computing. With a background in computer science, he draws on methods from education theory, ethnography, and library and information science to explore designing, learning, and use in context.

EDEE NORMAN WIZIECKI is coordinator of educational programs at the National Center for Supercomputing Applications at the University of Illinois at Urbana-Champaign.

HANNA ZHONG is a doctoral student in computer science at the University of Illinois at Urbana-Champaign.

Index

access grid. *See* grid computing
administration, e-learning, 189–93
Africa, sub-Saharan, education in, 109–18
African Virtual University, 110–14
AG Node (AGN), 160–63
Apache, x
art education, 131–38, 230–37
asynchronous learning, 5, 6, 15, 18, 42, 103, 131–32, 140, 212–13

Bardeen, John, x
Bauwens, Michel, 70
Benjamin, Harold, 21–23
Benkler, Yochai, 31, 35, 44, 68–69
biology, learning and teaching, 216–23
Biology Workbench, 220–28
Blue Waters, xi
broadband, 31, 50–51, 112
broadcasting, 6, 10, 49–54, 60, 68
BurdaStyle, 41–42

Castells, Manuel, 70, 110–11, 117
cell phones. *See* mobile phones
Center for Writing Studies, University of Illinois, 231
chemistry, learning and teaching, 124, 128, 216–25
Chit Chat Club, 173–87
clickers, 209
collaborative learning, 4, 9–11, 39, 102–6, 137–38; computer-supported, 29, 32–34, 64, 74–75, 79–81, 86–87, 120; cultures of, 127–28; theories of, 39
Collaboratory for Multi-scale Chemical Sciences (CMCS), 123–24
College of Education, University of Illinois, Urbana-Champaign, ix–x, 95
Commonwealth of Nations, 109–10
communities of practice, xi, 13, 35, 105
computing, learning and teaching, 210
Cooperative State Research, Education, and Extension Service (CSREES), 101
Creative Commons, 44, 51, 117
cyberenvironments, 119–29
cyberinfrastructure, 119–21, 129, 141

Dewey, John, 22–24, 79, 104, 203, 263
Diamond, Jared, 225
didactic teaching, 4, 8, 9–10, 116, 198
digital divide, 110–11
distributed cognition, 12–13, 31, 127, 137
diversity (learner), 11, 28, 44, 101, 126, 235, 250
Dreyfus, Hubert, 66–67

East St. Louis, Ill., 202–5
Environmental Cyberinfrastructure Demonstrator (ECID), 124–25
Eudora, x
expression wheel, 184–86

Facebook, 94
Flickr, 58
folksonomies, 7, 12, 31, 38, 58. *See also* taxonomies
Four Components Instructional Design Model (4C/ID-model), 151–52

games, 5, 27, 35, 78, 145–50, 208, 230. *See also* video games
Gee, James Paul, 10, 13, 14
Generation I, 93–95, 97–98
geospatial technologies, 9, 16, 27, 100–105
Google, 27, 33, 100
GPS. *See* geospatial technologies
grid computing, 42, 119, 121, 142, 156–70

handheld devices, ix, 16, 67, 101–2, 192, 232. *See also* mobile phones
higher education, 109–18, 146, 166, 190–92
history education, 197–203
HTML, 82, 232
humanities, learning and teaching, 199

immersive learning, 17, 27, 131–40
informal learning, 16, 18
information science program, Web-based, 42
instructional design, 145–54. *See also* pedagogy
Integrated Service Digital Network (ISDN), 158–59
interface (device), 4, 9, 73, 81, 85–87, 201; Access Grid, 159, 163, 165; Alzheimer's patients and, 59; Biology Workbench, 221; Chit Chat Club, 173–87; future of, 77; research on, 121, 131; variations in, 134, 141
Internet, 33, 66, 69; access to, 15, 95, 111–13, 129; body and, 66–67; disease and, 41; history of, 208, 218–19; intercultural communication and, 235; learning and, 31–32, 34, 132–33; news and, 50–51, 54, 56–57, 59
iPod, 10, 26, 78, 94

Jenkins, Henry, 14, 32, 34–36, 44, 54–55, 60

knowledge economy, 18, 69, 112, 144

laptop computers: classification of, 63; in classrooms, 39, 232, 243–44; learning and, 31; prevalence of, 3, 26; ubicomp and, 73–75. *See also* One Laptop Per Child
Lessig, Lawrence, 44, 65, 69
lifelong learning, 9, 18, 129, 138, 204, 247
literacy, 27, 41, 52, 57, 97, 128, 242–44, 254–55, 262–63

mashups, x, 123, 128
mass media, 49, 54–55
McChesney, Robert W., 49, 52, 60
metadata, 50, 58–59, 120
Microsoft, 85
mobile phones, 3, 63, 66; boundaries and, 43, 244; college students and, 26; GPS and, 9; landlines and, 7; as learning tools, 16, 31, 64, 87; mind and, 13; news and, 51; prevalence of, 78, 94, 134, 157, 244; text messaging and, 86; ubicomp and, 73. *See also* handheld devices
Mosaic, x
MP3 players, 62, 63, 232
multimedia, 25, 41, 119, 149, 157–59, 170, 200, 232–33, 245
Multimedia Environment for Remote Multiple Attendee Interactive Decision-making (MERMAID), 158
multimodality, 12, 14, 97, 103–4, 147, 149, 242, 255
Multipoint Control Units, 158
MySpace, 95, 243

National Center for Biotechnology Information, 220
National Center for Supercomputing Applications (NCSA), 120, 123, 124, 159, 162
networked intelligence, 17, 32
networks, networking, 32, 41, 56, 73, 156, 161, 200, 207, 211
Nintendo Wii, 145–46

One Laptop Per Child, 7
open content media, 50–55
open source, x, 42, 51, 52, 69–70, 117
over-the-shoulder learning (OTSL), 81–86

participatory culture, xi, 6, 31–37, 44, 49, 55
Paypal, x
pedagogy, 26, 38, 57; arts, 234–35; digital learning, 96–97, 115–17, 137–40; and games, 150–53; and informal learning, 9; new approaches, xi, 4, 7–8; writing, 243, 247–49
peer production, 31, 43, 62, 64, 69, 70

pen-enabled computers. *See* tablet computing
personal computer (PC), 73–75, 145, 206–8
personal digital assistants. *See* handheld devices
Personal Interface to the Access Grid (PIG), 163
PLATO, x, xii, 4–5, 144, 208–9
PlayStation, 145

RealOne player, 50
reciprocal teaching, xi, 237
RiverWeb, 200–205
Royal Melbourne Institute of Technology (RMIT), 113

Saul, John Ralston, 198–99
science, teaching and learning, 27–28, 95–97
Second Life, 131–41
Semantic Web, 120, 121, 197
SenseWeb, 157–58
Serious Games Initiative, 146
social networking, 13, 27, 37, 51, 124–25, 128, 208, 230, 243, 249
Sony PlayStation, 145
Spencer, Gwladys, 24–26
sub-Saharan Africa, education in, 109–18
synchronous learning, 5, 132, 140, 156–58, 208

tablet computing, 62, 73, 78, 173, 211–13
taxonomies, 12, 63. *See also* folksonomies
telesculpture, 174–80
television, 3, 6, 10–11, 18, 24, 51, 53, 68, 94

ubiquitous computing, ix, 3–4, 5–7, 15–16, 21, 29, 62, 72–78, 87, 173–74
Ubiquitous Learning Institute, ix
ubiquitous media, 49–60
University of Illinois at Urbana-Champaign, x–xi, 4, 24, 95, 112, 131, 163, 190, 208, 231, 243

Very Small Aperture Terminal (VSAT), 113
video games, 10, 94, 132, 134, 139–40. *See also* games
video production, 256–62
virtual worlds, 131–42, 187

Web-based Information Science Education (WISE) program, 42
Web 2.0, 31, 58, 63, 86, 192. *See also* World Wide Web
Wii, 145–46
Wikipedia: as collective intelligence, 58, 119, 197; contributions to, 6, 31, 35; as dialogue, 10; publishing and, 40; as source, 33, 63
wireless networks, 31, 64, 74, 210–11, 232
World Bank, 113
World of Warcraft (game), 132
World Wide Web, x, 34, 41–42, 64, 66. *See also* Web 2.0
writing, teaching and learning, 242–50, 254–58
Writing with Video (course), 243–50, 255

youth learning, 102–6
YouTube, x, 6, 10, 27, 51, 55, 57, 123, 243, 248

The University of Illinois Press
is a founding member of the
Association of American University Presses.

Composed in 10/12.75 Adobe Minion Pro
with Frutiger display
by Jim Proefrock
at the University of Illinois Press
Manufactured by Cushing-Malloy, Inc.

University of Illinois Press
1325 South Oak Street
Champaign, IL 61820-6903
www.press.uillinois.edu